Tony H

PLAYS TWO

Tony Harrison was born in Leeds in 1937. His volumes
of poetry include *The Loiners* (winner of the Geoffrey
Faber Memorial Prize), *Continuous*, *v.* (broadcast
on Channel 4 in 1987, winning the Royal Television
Society Award), *The Gaze of the Gorgon* (winner of
the Whitbread Prize for Poetry) and *Laureate's Block*.
Recognised as Britain's leading theatre and film poet,
Tony Harrison has written extensively for the National
Theatre, the New York Metropolitan Opera, the BBC,
Channel 4, and for unique ancient spaces in Greece and
Austria. His film *Black Daisies for the Bride* won the
Prix Italia in 1994; this and his volume of film/poems
The Shadow of Hiroshima and other film/poems and his
feature film *Prometheus* are published by Faber and
Faber.

by the same author

poetry
THE LOINERS
PALLADAS: POEMS
FROM THE SCHOOL OF ELOQUENCE
CONTINUOUS
V.
SELECTED POEMS
A COLD COMING
LAUREATE'S BLOCK

plays
THE TRACKERS OF OXYRHYNCHUS
SQUARE ROUNDS
TONY HARRISON: PLAYS ONE
(*The Mysteries*)
TONY HARRISON: PLAYS THREE
(*Poetry or Bust, The Kaisers of Carnuntum,*
*The Labourers of Herakle*s)
TONY HARRISON: PLAYS FOUR
(*The Oresteia, The Common Chorus Parts I & II*)

film/poems
BLACK DAISIES FOR THE BRIDE
THE SHADOW OF HIROSHIMA AND OTHER FILM/POEMS
(*A Maybe Day in Kazakhstan, The Gaze of the Gorgon,*
The Blasphemer's Banquet, Loving Memory)
PROMETHEUS

TONY HARRISON

Plays Two

The Misanthrope

Phaedra Britannica

The Prince's Play

Introduced by
the author

This collection first published in 2002
by Faber and Faber Limited
3 Queen Square London WC1N 3AU
Published in the United States by Faber and Faber Inc.
an affiliate of Farrar, Straus and Giroux LLC, New York

Typeset by Country Setting, Kingsdown, Kent CT14 8ES
Printed in England by Mackays of Chatham plc, Chatham, Kent

The Misanthrope and *Phaedra Britannica*
first published in 1981 by Rex Collings Ltd
published in 1985 in *Dramatic Verse 1973–1985* by Bloodaxe Books
published in 1986 in *Theatre Works 1973–1985* by Penguin Books
© Tony Harrison, 1981, 1985

The Prince's Play first published in 1996
by Faber and Faber Limited © Tony Harrison, 1996
For music to *The Prince's Play* please apply direct to the composer,
Richard Blackford, 44 Parliament Hill, London NW3 2TN,
or e-mail: richard@blackford.co.uk

Introductions © Tony Harrison, 2002

A CIP record for this book is available from the British Library

0-571-21041-4

2 4 6 8 10 9 7 5 3 1

Contents

THE MISANTHROPE

Le Misanthrope
by Molière
in an English version
by Tony Harrison

Introduction

JANE EYRE'S SISTER

This version of *Le Misanthrope* commissioned by the
National Theatre for production in 1973, the tercentenary
of Molière's death, sets the play in 1966, exactly three
hundred years after its first performance. One of the
focuses for mediating the transition was the famous series
of articles that André Ribaud contributed to the French
satirical paper, *Le Canard Enchaîné,* under the title of *La
Cour,* with Moisan's brilliant drawings, interpreting the
régime of General de Gaulle as if he were Louis XIV. The
articles were continued under M. Pompidou as *La Régence.*
There are some obvious advantages to such a transposition: characters can still on occasions refer to 'the Court',
but it is intended in the sense of M. Ribaud: the subversive
pamphlet, foisted on Alceste in the same way as one was
foisted on Molière by enemies angered by *Tartuffe,* can be
readily accepted in a period during which, from 1959
to 1966, no fewer than three hundred convictions were
made under a dusty old law which made it a crime to
insult the Head of State; above all it has the advantage of
anchoring in a more accessible society some of the more
far-reaching and complex implications of Alceste's dilemma, personal, social, ethical, political. Once the transition
had been made other adjustments had to follow. The
sonnet I first wrote for Oronte has now been replaced
by something closer to my own experience of today's poetaster. To adapt what John Dryden, one of my masters and
mentors in the art of the couplet, said of his great translation of Virgil's *Aeneid,* 'I hope the additions will seem
not stuck into Molière, but growing out of him': no more
intrusive, that is, than the sackbut, psaltery, and dulcimer

3

the Jacobean translators of the Bible introduced into the court of Nebuchadnezzar, or the Perigord pies and Tokay that the anonymous translator of 1819 introduces into his version of *Le Misanthrope*. That same version seems to base its Clitandre on Lord Byron. I have used contemporary, but less talented models. The version itself is my form of exegesis.

I was 'educated' to produce jog-trot versions of the classics. Apart from a weekly chunk of Johnson, Pitt the Younger and Lord Macaulay to be done into Ciceronian Latin, we had to turn once living authors into a form of English never spoken by men or women, as if to compensate our poor tongue for the misfortune of not being a dead language. I remember once making a policeman in a Plautus play say something like '*Move along there*', only to have it scored through and '*Vacate the thoroughfare*' put in its place. This tradition lingers in the verse versions of the nineteenth and twentieth centuries. This is a typical piece of ripe Virgilian translation:

> Penthesilea furent, the bands leading
> Of lune-shield Amazons, mid thousands burns,
> Beneath exserted mamma golden zone
> Girds warrior, and, a maid dares cope with men.

That would have earned some marginal VGs from my mentors. With the help of Gavin Douglas, John Dryden, Ezra Pound, and Edward Powys Mathers I managed to escape from all this into what I hope is a more creative relationship with foreign tongues. So my translation, when I do it now, is a *Jack and the Beanstalk* act, braving the somnolent ogre of a British classical education to grab the golden harp.

The problems of the academic coming to grips with a classic of foreign literature, in this case some three centuries old, puts me in mind of Francis Galton, the cousin of Charles Darwin, on his travels in Damaraland, southern Africa in 1851, who wishing to measure the phenomenon of steatopygia in what he called 'a Venus of Hottentots', but restrained by Victorian *pudeur,* took a series of observations with his sextant, and having obtained the base and angles, proceeded to work out the lady's intriguing 'endowments' by trigonometry and logarithms. The poet, and the man of the theatre, have to be bolder and more intimate.

The salient feature of Molière's verse is its vigour and energy, rather than any metaphorical density or exuberant invention, and it is this which gives his verse plays their characteristic dramatic pace. In *Le Misanthrope* the effect of the rhyming couplet is like that of a time-bomb ticking away behind the desperation of Alceste, and Célimène's fear of loneliness. The relentless rhythm helps to create the tensions and panics of high comedy, and that *rire dans l'âme* that Donneau de Visé experienced on the first night of the play in 1666. The explosion never comes. But the silence, when the ticking stops, is almost as deafening. There is an almost Chekhovian tension between farce and anguish. To create this vertiginous effect verse (and *rhymed* verse) is indispensable. Neither blank verse nor prose will do. I have made use of a couplet similar to the one I used in *The Loiners,* running the lines over, breaking up sentences, sometimes using the odd half-rhyme to subdue the chime, playing off the generally colloquial tone and syntax against the formal structure, letting the occasional couplet leap out as an epigram in moments of devastation or wit. My floating *'s* is a way of linking the couplet at the joint and speeding up the pace by making the speaker deliver it as almost one line not two. And so on. I have made use of the occasional Drydenian triplet, and, once in Act Three, of something I call a 'switchback' rhyme, a device I derive from the works of George Formby, e.g. in *Mr Wu*:

Once he sat down – those hot irons he didn't spot 'em.
He gave a yell – and cried 'Oh my – I've gone and
    scorched my . . . singlet!'

or

    Oh, Mister Wu at sea he wobbles like a jelly,
    but he's got lots of pluck although he's got a yellow . . .
       jumper!

I have also tried both before and during rehearsals to orches-
trate certain coughs, kisses, sighs and hesitation mechan-
isms into the iambic line. These are sometimes indicated
by (/) in the text.

    An American scholar (forgetting Sarah Bernhardt) said
of rhymed translation that it was 'like a woman undertak-
ing to act Hamlet'. A similar, though much more appro-
priate summary of the kinship between my version and the
original was given by my six-year-old son, Max. 'I know
that Molière,' he said, with true Yorkshire chauvinism,
though he was born in Africa, 'she's Jane Eyre's sister.'

MOLIÈRE NATIONALISED

I

Even the *Pictorial Record of the National Theatre 1963–71*
on sale at the Old Vic bookstall was discouraging. 'Molière,'
it says curtly of the National's production of *Tartuffe* in
1968, 'rarely works in English and the National failed to
find the key.' I began to feel that I had involved myself in
a masochistic enterprise. What the key to Molière in
English was I had no clear idea but I had vague notions of
what it wasn't. The trouble with many versions of verse
plays done by poets is that publication tends to be primary
and performance secondary. It has obvious effects on the
resulting text. Despite the growth of public poetry read-
ings in the last ten years and the obvious feedback of oral
performance into some of the poetry now being written in
Britain or the USA, the poet is still very much bound to the

private pleasure of the solitary literate. This doesn't help much when it comes to writing for the theatre. I had to re-examine a great many rhetorical presuppositions. Above all, it seemed to me that, if Molière was to work in English, the verse, while retaining his sort of formality, should be as speakable as the most colloquial prose. The negative idea of rhyme as an obstacle one tried to sur-mount as best one could, I discarded and tried to think of it in positive terms as a way of continuously throwing the action forward, accelerating the pace of the play when necessary, and controlling the flow in a way that prose could never do. The playing time of a verse version tends to be shorter than an equivalent version in prose, and this is a considerable advantage. From the very earliest drafts of my *Misanthrope* I resolved that publication would be as secondary to my purpose as providing a printed score for the concert-goer would be for the composer.

When I first met the director John Dexter in September 1971, he had asked me for a version for seventeenth-century costume, accurate, speakable, no anachronisms, no jarring slang, but in 'modernish' colloquial English. An almost impossibly paradoxical request, I thought at the time. My earliest drafts tried to create the illusion of the colloquial by syntactical means rather than by lexical. Deprived of a really up-to-date lexicon and with a barrier across my choice of image at 1666, the date of the play's first perfor-mance, the energy of the spoken lines had to come largely from the syntactical contractions and elisions of modern speech. Some of these problems tied up with those I was try-ing to cope with in my own poems. I have always listened closely to speech and noted down the devices of relaxed in-formal styles. I took long walks and spoke the drafts aloud to myself, going over and over the lines to make them as naturally speakable as I could, and at the same time as form-ally impeccable as possible. I counted lines like the follow-ing as an early success with the diction I was aiming for:

> But what I'd like to know 's what freak of luck's
> helped to put Clitandre in your good books?

> *Mais au moins dites-moi, Madame, par quel sort*
> *Votre Clitandre a l'honneur de vous plaire si fort.*
>
> *vv.* 475–6

Or this kind of exchange between Alceste and Célimène:

> CÉLIMÈNE I can't not see him. He'd be most upset.
> ALCESTE I've never known you 'not see' people yet.

The elision of *is*, as in the first example, in positions natural to English speech, though uncommon in representations of that speech in English verse, was one of the first devices I hit upon to create the illusion of the colloquial and to capture some of the pace of the original, a recording of which I played continuously as I worked, as a way of keeping my mind on performance rather than on the page. Here is an example of the same elision used in a position which enables the speaker to run the couplet together:

> and what I mean to do
> 's find out what her love is: false or true.

The same device can be extended over three lines without violating natural English usage:

> what use would all our virtues be, whose point,
> when all the world seems really out of joint,
> 's to bear with others' contumely and spite,
> without annoyance, even though we're right.

Sometimes my contractions can look, as the 'Commentary' column of the *TLS* (16 March 1973) put it, 'messy on the page', quoting as an example Célimène's line:

> Surely I'd've thought it wouldn't've mattered . . .

but adding that 'English isn't well equipped to point out its vernacular elisions.' I have, for a long time, felt that it ought to be better equipped. One has great need of notations as these things must be scored for the actor in a form as metrically tight as the heroic couplet. The work wasn't written for the page but to be spoken. I wanted the illusion of real people talking and arguing, in a context where we have come to expect declamation and verse arias. The rigorous form of the verse, though, is necessary to create the detachment from reality so essential to the workings of comedy. I worked in this way from the beginning of November 1971 to the end of January 1972, more or less all day every day. As well as the problem of idiomatic speech rhythms which had to be free from slang, I tried to vary the rhythm of the couplet, which is capable of a great deal more variety than it is often given credit for, so that I could give elements of a characteristic rhythm to each actor – the rather rocking rhythm of Philinte, both conciliatory and somewhat complacent; the barbed wit of Célimène, where the end-stopped couplet of Pope was effective; the sly insinuating rhythm of Arsinoé; the staccato oiliness of Oronte; and leaving a much wider scale of variations for Alceste: implacability, satirical outrage, baffled love. Another problem, and one which is perennial in translating from French poetry, is the greater degree of physical concretisation characteristic of the genius of English poetry. I did feel the need to anchor sentiments and statements much more closely to the specific, but I had been very careful, at this stage, to research my concretisations so that they remained in period and I introduced nothing into the text after 1666. John Dexter's reaction to the first draft was that it was very speakable; at the same time it was so free of vocabulary exclusively modern that Sir Laurence Olivier picked out only two words, *manic* and *randy*, and the phrase *so what?* as being too modern to be spoken in period costume. I revised the text only a little between January and August and then only in a direction away from anything I thought a mere gesture to the dubious permanence of the printed page. In early August I had a letter from John Dexter saying that he had decided to produce the play in 'modernish dress'. We met for a discussion and I felt somewhat worried that his decision to transfer the setting had rather marooned my text in the seventeenth century. There were so many references to things specifically of the period: clothes, customs, institutions, the King and the Court with all its etiquette and protocol.

II

The problems of translating a classic of the stage seem to me inextricable from the problems of production. The problems with a version of *Le Misanthrope* are vastly different from those of producing an English play of the seventeenth century in modern dress. There the text is fixed. With a translation the text need not be fixed, and, when the collaboration was as close and open as ours was, the words could anchor the production in its chosen time as much as the clothes and the setting. It seems to me now, after the experience of creating a version of the *Lysistrata* for Nigerian actors (unplayable outside West Africa) and of *Le Misanthrope* for the National, that the best way of creating a fresh text of a classic is to tie it to a specific production rather than aim, from the study, at a general all-purpose repertory version. This undoubtedly gives a limited lifetime to the version, but this is no bad thing, as I believe that a 'classic' needs to be retranslated continuously. It seems to me that one could do worse than treat a translation as one does décor or production as endlessly renewable. Indeed one could say that one of the marks of a literary classic is its capacity for change and adaptation. I have been very impressed by (and all translators could

learn from) the probably obscure but indefatigable labours
of John Ogilby (1600–1676) who did two *entirely different*
translations within a short space of time of a poem as vast
as Virgil's *Aeneid,* nearly 10,000 lines, five times as long
as *Le Misanthrope.* His first version was in 1649 and his
second in 1654. What happened to change not only his
but the whole period's focus on the poem were the mom-
entous events leading up to the execution of Charles I
in 1649. Ogilby's second version is a far more explicitly
Royalist version than the first. History had shocked him
into a fresh appraisal of a complex poem, capable of many
interpretations though some of them mutually exclusive.
Here, for example, is a piece of Virgil's Latin about the
activities of the subversive Fury Alecto:

> tu potes unanimos armare in proelia fratres
> atque odiis versare domos, tu verbera tectis
> funerasque inferre faces, tibi nomina mille,
> mille nocendi artes, fecundum concute pectus,
> disice compositam pacem, sere crimina belli;
> arma velit poscatque simul rapiatque iuventus.
>
> *Aeneid* VII, 335–40

Here is Ogilby's version of 1649:

> Thou loving brothers canst provoke to War,
> Houses destroy with hate, both sword and flames
> Bring to their roofs; thou hast a thousand names,
> As many nocent arts; then quickly shake
> Thy pregnant breasts, and peace confirmed, break;
> Lay grounds for cruel war, make with thy charms
> Their wilde youth rage, require, and take up arms.

Five eventful years later the same translator sees the same
passage through the disturbances of his own times:

> Unanimous Brothers thou canst arm to fight,
> And *settled Courts* destroy with deadly spight;

Storm *Palaces* with Steel, and Pitchy Flames,
Thou hast a thousand wicked Arts: and Names,
The Bosom disembogue, with Mischief full,
And Articles concluding Peace annull.
Then raise a War, and with bewitching Charms
Make *the mad People* rage to take up Arms.

The implications of those changes are obvious. Civil War
has become a vision of revolution. Dryden's version of
1697 is informed with the same Hobbesian fears. Momen-
tous events, and even minor, less spectacular shifts in our
mores and environment, give us new attentions and demands on the long-surviving classic, whose very survival
is dependent on its being, in the widest possible sense,
retranslated. History gave Simone Weil her sudden, illumi-
nating insight into the *Iliad* as 'the poem of force', and
made Shakespeare a 'contemporary' in Eastern Europe. If
we were to expand a usual organic metaphor for a work
of art, we could say that, like the rose, for example, in a
state of nature, a work is constantly throwing up new
growths. Into these new growths it gradually directs its
sap, and the older growths become starved out. The
activity of pruning, in our case the historical consciousness at work in the mind of the director or translator of
the classic, is to hasten the rejection of the old wood and
to encourage the instincts for producing new growths
especially (the gardening manuals tell us) *from the base* of
the plant. And pruning of this kind is a regular, recurrent
task. In the oral cultures of Africa when words or phrases
no longer signify, thrill, or seem relevant to the hearers of
a recitation in a particular society, they tend to become
changed. There is in this sort of culture a homeostatic process at work which we in our museum culture must often
envy, that which the anthropologists call 'structural amnesia', a form of constant, often barely conscious, pruning
that keeps a work continuously alive. In our conditions of

literacy and individualism this 'structural amnesia' is frustrated by a concern for the text which is almost fetishistic. We update Shakespeare; we clothe him in modern dress; we give his words new emphases, but those words are fixed. It is precisely because of this rigidity in the text that we have come to expect fluidity in the changing focuses of production. The American linguist Charles Hockett has drawn some rather disturbing implications from the objective comparison of oral and literate cultures and he says:

> In an illiterate society the precise shape of a poem may be gradually modified, a word replaced here, a rhythm or rhyme brought up to date there, in such a way as to keep pace with the changing language. On this score the introduction of writing has some implications which might be called unfortunate. Once a poem is written down it is fixed; it has lost its ability to grow with the language. Sooner or later, the poem is left behind.

We then, even in our own language, have to translate. The implications for an essentially oral art like the theatre are even more interesting. It is in theatrical production and translation that we of a late literate culture can in some measure reassert our lost instincts for 'structural amnesia'. The original is fluid, the translation a static moment in that fluidity. Translations are not built to survive though their original survives through translation's many flowerings and decays. The illusion of pedantry is that a text is fixed. It cannot be fixed once and for all. The translation is fixed but reinvigorates its original by its decay. It was probably on these lines that Walter Benjamin was thinking when he said in his *The Task of the Translator* that 'the life of an original reaches its ever-recurring, latest and most complete unfolding in translation'. It was with thoughts such as these in the back of my mind that I took away my version of *Le Misanthrope* to revise. Between then and

22 February 1973 when the play opened I must have re-written over half the play, though the basic *stylistic* choices had already been made.

III

The first things to be updated were the clothes. The *grands canons*, *vaste rhingrave* and *perruque blonde* of the foppish Clitandre became in Alceste's mockery to Célimène:

> What makes *him* captivate the social scene?
> Second-skin gauchos in crêpe-de-chine?
> Those golden blow-wave curls (that aren't his own)?
> Those knickerbockers, or obsequious tone?
> Or is it his giggle and his shrill falsett-
> o hoity-toity voice makes him your pet?

Clitandre's 'knickerbockers' came in only very late after I had seen what Tanya Moisiewitsch had given him to wear in the last act. Clitandre's *ongle long*, the long fingernail of seventeenth-century fashion, I found hard to contextualise, as I only knew of Brazil where the fashion persists into our own day. Finally I made Clitandre an habitué of Angelina's tea-shop on the Rue de Rivoli:

> What amazing talents does the 'thing' possess,
> what sublimity of virtue? Let me guess.
> I'm at a loss. No, let me see. *I know!*
> It's his little finger like a *croissant*, so,
> crooked at *Angelina's* where he sips his tea
> among the titled queens of 'gay' Paree!

I had one couplet in the first draft which went:

> proof of all the mean and dirty tricks
> of Mankind circa 1666.

I changed this to 1966, thinking, I suppose, to execute a circle of three hundred years for the Molière tercentenary. A fetishistic gesture, perhaps, and at this stage little more than that. Then I was reminded of André Ribaud's series of articles in *Le Canard Enchaîné,* which adopted the style of Saint-Simon's *Mémoires* and under the title of *La Cour* satirised the autocratic regime of de Gaulle as if he were Louis XIV, under whose reign, of course, *Le Misanthrope* was first performed. The pieces were re-issued in a paperback collection by Juillard in 1972. The series continued under M. Pompidou as *La Régence.* The point is that these articles in *Le Canard Enchaîné* appeared regularly over a long period and terms such as *le roi* and *la cour* in M. Ribaud's sense were as current as, say, 'Grocer' was with us. Now the phrase 'circa 1966' seemed exactly right and *La Cour* gave me cues for the rewriting of all the many references to 'the Court' and 'the king' etc. As I rewrote in this way some of the implications of *Le Misanthrope*, so often concealed under the frills of the traditional courtier, became much clearer to me. I let two references to 'the Court' stand but put them in the inverted commas of *Le Canard Enchaîné.* Some became 'the Elysée', and others more knowingly became 'over there' and the king a whispered confidential 'HE'. One, if not the sole. cause of the guarded, wary *politesse* of court society was precisely its autocratic nature. 'La Cour,' wrote Saint-Simon, *'fut autre manège de la politique du despotisme.'* Perhaps, I thought, by concentrating less on the *forms* of this *politesse* and more on its *meaning* I would be able to clarify a little the discrepancy between Alceste's violent attacks on the *symptoms* of social corruption and his complete lack of an objective *diagnosis.* The outer Court of real power is reflected in the brilliant mirror of the 'court' of Célimène's *salon.* It seems more than a linguistic accident that makes many commentators refer to Célimène's *salon* as a 'court'. Lucien Gossman brings out some of the inferences:

The court of Célimène with its urbanity, wit and formal civility masking subterranean rivalries and resentments calls to mind a passage in Saint-Simon's *Mémoires* which describes another and more celebrated court:

Les fêtes fréquentes les promenades particulières à Versailles, les voyages furent des moyens que le Roi saisit pour distinguer et pour mortifier en nommant les personnes qui a chaque fois en devaient être, et pour tenir chacun assidu et attentif à lui plaire. Il sentait qu'il n'avait pas a beaucoup pres assez de grâces à repandre pour faire un effet continuel. Il en substitu donc aux véritables d'idéales, par la jalousie, les petits préférences qui se trouvaient tous les jours, et pour ainsi dire à tous moments, par son art. Les espérances que ses petites préférences et ces distinctions faisaient naître, et la consideration qui s'en tirat, personne ne fut plus ingénieux que lui a inventer sans cesse ces sortes de choses . . .

While it would be ludicrous to suggest that Molière deliberately dressed Louis XIV up as Célimène it is worth noting that some acute observers discovered in the supreme social reality of Molière's own time the same structure of relations as that which binds Célimène and her world together in the supreme comedy of that same time.

It seems very worth noting, though the last thing I wanted to suggest was that Diana Rigg was Charles de Gaulle in drag. The *roi soleil* shines on some and leaves others in outer darkness. It was written of de Gaulle quite recently that 'he was so narcissistically self-absorbed in being the Idea of France on the international plane that a great many Frenchmen came to feel half-consciously that they were only anonymous fodder for his representational ego'. The sense of intrigue is strong in the play, outside and inside, even in the minor off-stage characters, impaled only on the spike of Célimène's wit in the portrait scene, Timante 'the cloak-and-dagger-ite', and the resentments of Adraste 'the utter megalomaniac'. There is an off-stage autocratic power 'over there' and once the rehearsals got on to the set this became literally so, for the Elysée Palace was through the window and over the way. This power continually enters into the conversation of the *salon*, in its consciousness of being 'in', its knowingness. Later the power irrupts into the room in the threat of arrest for a subversive pamphlet. Both Oronte and Arsinoé are tempters in that they offer Alceste 'influence', they will 'oil the wheels' or obtain a 'place' or a 'sinecure', if only he will admire a piddling poem or show some sexual interest. Acaste and Clitandre come to Célimène's 'party' directly from the Elysée. There is a constant feeling of the nearness of political power. There is also something in the restless gaiety of such a *salon* that conceals defeat and desperation. It seems to be a recurrent phenomenon in all periods of impending change. One recalls Gérard de Nerval's comment on a similar brilliance of his own set in *Sylvie*:

> . . . *où toute mélancolie cédait devant la verve intarissable . . . tel qu'il s'en est trouvé dans les époques de rénovations ou de décadence, et dont les discussions se haussaient à ce point, que les plus timides d'entre nous allaient voir parfois aux fenêtres si les Huns, les Turcomans ou les Cosaques n'arrivaient pas enfin pour couper court à ces arguments . . .*

It is difficult with this reading of the background of the play to assent to the Romantic interpretations of it, though they have helped to focus on the obvious *subjective* anguish of Alceste. The play is not a tragedy, not even the *tragédie bourgeoise* that Brunetière called it, and certainly it is utterly absurd to call it 'an uncompromising left-wing play' as one critic did. It is too complex a play to be claimed by either left or right. Alceste is not a political radical, and far from being a proto-Marxist, and certainly, as he wavers between the *salon* of a coquette and a country estate, no activist. One has to clear *désert* of its Romantic accretions and go to Madame de Sévigné and the Furetière dictionary of 1690 for the meaning, country estate. Alceste's *désert* is rather like an inverted image of the Moscow of the *Three Sisters of* Chekhov. I have already said how the modern background helps to show the absence of real objective social analysis in Alceste's outbursts, though it by no means should exclude his subjective pain and anguish, which make him a both comic and moving figure. Others have been less lenient with Alceste. Mauriac said of him that 'in a world where injustice is rife, he is up in arms against trivialities'. Against this judgement Martin Turnell in *The Classical Moment* asks us to set Stendhal's view of Alceste:

> His mania for hurling himself against whatever appears odious, his gift for close and accurate reasoning and his extreme probity would soon have led him into politics or, what would have been much worse, to an objectionable and seditious philosophy. Célimène's *salon* would at once have been compromised and soon become a desert. And what would a coquette find to do in a deserted *salon*?

One must also remember how horrified he is to have a subversive pamphlet foisted on to him by his enemies, in the way that Molière himself had by *dévots* angered by *Tartuffe*. It seems to me that the production at the National took cognisance of both these extremes of opinion, and while recognising Alceste's *potential* for political thought, is faithful to Molière in leaving in ambiguity any fulfilment of that potential. If the play is set 'circa 1966' the spectator worried by these issues can always ask himself the question, 'What would the position of this Alceste be in *les événements* of May 1968?' The transposition, in my view, helps to make the background more important, though none the less *background* to the central human relationship, than the stereotypes of period costume perhaps allow.

Erich Auerbach's brilliant study of the meaning *of La Cour et La Ville* in the seventeenth century shows that real power has by-passed such people as Acaste and his whole class, 'meaningless, without economic or political or any other organic foundation'. Alceste is only partially or potentially liberated from this milieu. With Gossman I find something almost Chekhovian in *Le Misanthrope*. 'Chekhov,' he writes, 'joins hands over the centuries with his great predecessor, for Molière's *Misanthrope* is the first profound statement in modern terms of the world's silent indifference to those who no longer have any significant place in it or relation to it.'

IV

We began rehearsals in late December 1972 with a text that was for me still only partially anchored in the recent past. I felt that I had by no means solved all the problems of the transposition, but we had decided to leave the text as it stood as a 'springboard' into the play, and we hoped that I would be able to do what rewriting seemed necessary in a concentrated way after hearing the actors' reactions and earliest interpretations. The best way to illustrate what happened during rehearsals and how much the text owes to the close collaboration of director, actors and poet, is to take a few examples. I had earlier objected to John Dexter that since we were now in the sixties of this century a poetaster like Oronte was unlikely to produce a sonnet. Others agreed, and Kenneth Tynan felt that a parody of a modern style would be better. The more I heard the sonnet in rehearsals the more convinced I became that it wasn't right. I had originally given Oronte a sonnet in octosyllabics as in Molière:

> Hope can ease the lover's pain,
> make anguish easier to bear,
> but, Phyllis, that's a doubtful gain
> if all that follows hope 's despair.
>
> Great kindness to me once you showed.
> You should have been I think less kind.
> Why so much so soon bestowed
> if hope was all you had in mind?
>
> With all eternity to wait
> a lover's zeal turns desperate
> and looks for hope in last extremes!
>
> Lovely Phyllis, I'm past care
> but lovers like me all despair
> if offered only hope and dreams.

I planted deliberate excrescences for Alceste to pick up in his outburst when it finally comes, making the criticism a little more specific than in the original:

> You followed unnatural models when you wrote;
> your style's stiff and awkward. Let me quote:
> 'last extremes' tautologous, the rest, hot air;
> it goes in circles: *bear/care*, *despair/despair*,
> *wait/desperate*, all pretty desperate rhymes.
> It's repetitive: hope you use five times.

When the sonnet went, that went too. I had earlier re-written all the entrances in the first three acts to adapt to John Dexter's idea of running those acts together with a party going on downstairs as a means of overcoming the perennial problem of 'visiting' in seventeenth-century plays. This also led to the brilliant juxtaposition of Lully's music to the same music transposed into a modem pop idiom by

Marc Wilkinson. We had still not solved the problem of an equivalent for the Marshalsea of France, an office of the seventeenth century created to arbitrate in quarrels between gentlemen after the abolition of duelling. It is an obscure enough office to warrant a note in all editions and translations. The dramatic point lies in the discrepancy between the machinery brought to bear and the triviality of the quarrel between Alceste and Oronte over the trifling poem in question. I made the Marshalsea the *Académie Française* at John Dexter's suggestion. Kenneth Tynan had suggested that Oronte should threaten to have Alceste blackballed from *Le Jockey Club,* which though socially plausible, hadn't, we decided, the right imposing sound for an English audience unacquainted with French high life. But I had tried a version with *Le Jockey Club.* I imagined Oronte coming over to Célimène's party, a little drunk and over-fed, from Maxim's where the Club Committee, say, had been dining, with his poem, clearly intended for Célimène, doodled on the Maxim's menu which he turned this way and that as he reconstructed the jottings as he recited. I tried to retain the theme of the original sonnet, with its contrast between a lover's hope and despair, while trying to draw the metaphors from the new context. It went something like:

That kiss was my *apéritif,*
that cuddle the *hors d'oeuvres.*
Now I'm wanting the roast beef
that's something you won't serve.

Passion's a sort of super chef
and you his *spécialité.*
Fulfilment the head waiter's deaf
and never looks my way.

And so alone at Love's *Maxim's*
I gnaw the empty air.

Here's my plate of hopeless dreams,
my drained glass of despair.

Neither Alec McCowen nor Diana Rigg, whose insights
into comedy were a constant inspiration for me to produce
them better lines, thought the new Oronte poem appro-
priate. I could see that they were right and I rejected it
there and then. Diana Rigg went to her dressing-room and
brought back a 'little magazine' of poetry, and said that
she thought Oronte was more likely to write something
like the poems in it. We all read them aloud and decided
she was right. Memories of editing little magazines came
back to me, and that evening after rehearsals, prompted
by the magazine Diana Rigg had given me 'for inspiration', I wrote Oronte's poem as it now stands, again
preserving the theme if nothing else:

Hope was assuaging:
its glimmer
cheered my gloomy pilgrimage
to the gold shrine of your love . . .

a mirage of water pool and palms
to a nomad lost in the Sahara . . .

but in the end it only makes thirst worse.

Darling, if this hot trek
to some phantasmal Mecca
of love's consummation
is some sort of Herculean Labour
then I've fallen by the wayside.

A deeper, darker otherwhere
is unfulfilment . . .

we who have bathed in the lustrous light
of your charisma
now languish in miasmal black despair

and all we hopeless lovers share
the nightmare of the bathosphere.

Alceste's outburst, to correspond to Oronte's new literary
excrescences, I felt had to be somewhat ruder than before:

> Jesus wept!
> It's bloody rubbish, rhythmically inept,
> vacuous verbiage, wind, gas, guff.
> All lovestruck amateurs churn out that stuff.
> It's formless, slack, a nauseating sprawl,
> and riddled with stale clichés; that's not all.
> 'Thirst worse' cacophonous, and those 'ek eks'
> sound like a bullfrog in the throes of sex.

The bullfrog, of course, came partly from Aristophanes
and partly from the grotesque appearance of the huffing,
much padded Gawn Grainger as Oronte.

Another passage that was rewritten in rehearsal was
Eliante's speech beginning:

> *L'amour pour l'ordinaire, est peu fait à ces lois.*
> *Et l'on voit les amants vanter toujours leur choix*
>
> vv. 711–12

Many editors, I think wrongly, find the dramatic justifi-
cation of this speech a little doubtful, and try to explain its
presence by saying that Molière was using up an old
version of Lucretius' *De rerum Natura* (IV. 1160–69) that
he had written in his youth. The piece has a relevance I
haven't the space to dwell on, but one cannot escape the
feeling that the lines have the air of a prepared set piece,
as though Eliante were only able to be witty through the
proxy of quotation as opposed to Célimène's spontaneous
crackle. I decided to take those critics head-on and allow
Eliante to call her speech 'not inapposite' to the situation.
I also went back to the Latin of Lucretius for the examples
of love's euphemisms and made Eliante introduce her speech

with the admission that what was to follow was a quotation from a well-known source:

> How does that bit in old Lucretius go,
> that bit on blinkered lovers? O, you know . . .

I could give many examples of lines, phrases, whole couplets, words, which I revised in collaboration with the actors, when they were reaching for something better, or funnier, or simply dramatically more effective. Often I went away and produced a set of possible alternatives for one couplet and the actor in question and John Dexter and maybe others involved in the scene would test them and vote on which was best. The last alteration to be made was in the same Eliante speech. It was something I had felt to be wrong but, I suppose, had hoped that at this late stage no one would notice. I had all along tried to maintain the illusion of 'Frenchness' by making use of French words, not necessarily in the original, which were common currency in English, often as rhyme words to stress their presence, phrases like: *au fait*, *bons mots*, *mon cher*, *entrée*, *ordinaire*, *enchanté*. But in Eliante's speech I had

> The 'svelte gazelle' 's the girl all skin and bone.
> 'Majestic, regal' means, say, fifteen stone.

Sir Laurence Olivier noticed it at the first dress rehearsal and said it jarred, so two days before the opening the lines became:

> The loved one's figure's like Venus de Milo's
> even the girl who weighs a hundred kilos.

[1973–4]

This version of Molière's *Le Misanthrope* was first produced by the National Theatre Company at the Old Vic on 22 February 1973 with the following cast:

Alceste Alec McCowen
Célimène Diana Rigg
Arsinoé Gillian Barge
Acaste Nicholas Clay
Clitandre Jeremy Clyde
Oronte Gawn Grainger
Dubois James Hayes
Philinte Alan MacNaughtan
Eliante Jeanne Watts
Secretary of the Academy Clive Merrison
Basque Paul Curran

Production John Dexter
*Scenery and Costume*s Tanya Moiseiwitsch
Lighting Andy Phillips
Music Marc Wilkinson
Stage Manager Diana Boddington
Deputy Stage Manager Tony Walters
Assistant Stage Managers
   Elizabeth Markham, Phil Robins
Assistant to Producer Harry Lomax

Act One

Alceste sits alone in darkness, listening to the music of Lully. Philinte enters from the party in progress downstairs, switches on the light, sees Alceste, and turns off the hi-fi.

PHILINTE

Now what is it? What's wrong?

ALCESTE

O go away!

PHILINTE

But what is it? What's wrong?

ALCESTE

Please go away!

PHILINTE

Alceste, please tell me what's got into you . . .

ALCESTE

I said leave me alone. You spoil the view.

PHILINTE

Don't start shouting and, please, hear people out.

ALCESTE

No, why should I? And, if I like, I'll shout.

PHILINTE

But why this typical 'splenetic fit'?
Though I'm your friend, I don't think friends permit . . .

ALCESTE

Me, your friend? You can cross me off your list.
After what I've just clapped eyes on I insist
our friendship's finished. 'Friends' (so-called) who'll sell
their friendship everywhere can go to Hell.

PHILINTE

Now that's not fair, Alceste. It's most unjust.

ALCESTE

You should be mortified with self disgust.
There's no excuse for it. That sort of trick
revolts all decent men, and makes me sick.
Downstairs just now, what did I see you do?
You hoist your glass and hail, not hail, *halloo*
some person from a distance, and then zoom
into warm embraces from across the room,
drench the man with kisses, smile and swear
your lasting friendship, shout *mon cher, mon cher*
so many times you sounded quite inspired,
then when you sidled back and I inquired:
Who's that, the long-lost friend you rushed to hug?
all you do's look sheepish, and then shrug.
No sooner is his back turned than you start
picking him to pieces, pulling him apart,
all that 'friendship' faded from your heart.
It's foul and ignominious to betray
your own sincerity in this cheap way.
If, God forbid, it'd been me to blame,
I'd hang myself tomorrow out of shame.

PHILINTE

O surely not! I think I'll just remit
your sentence this time, and not swing for it.

ALCESTE

Don't think you'll soften me with that sweet smile.
Your humour's like your actions: infantile!

PHILINTE

But seriously, what would you have me do?

ALCESTE

Adopt behaviour both sincere and true.
Act like a decent man, and let words fall
only from the heart, or not at all.

PHILINTE

But if a man shows friendship when you've met,
you should pay back the compliments you get,
and try as best you can to match his tone
and balance his good manners with your own.

ALCESTE

Disgusting! Every modish socialite
bends over backwards to appear polite.
There's nothing I loathe more than empty grins
and cringing grimaces and wagging chins,
politeness-mongers, charmers with two faces,
dabblers in nonsensical fine phrases,
outvying one another in their little game
of praise-me-I'll-praise-you. It's all the same
if you're idiot or hero. What's the good
of friendship and respect if it's bestowed
on any nincompoop and simpleton
your praiser-to-the-skies next happens on?
No! No! Not one right-thinking man, not one
'd want such ten-a-penny honours done.
Glittering praise can lose its brilliance
when we see it shared with half of France.
Esteem's based on a scale, it's not much worse
praising nothing than the universe.
You'll be no friend of mine if you comply
with these false manners of society.
From the bottom of my heart I must reject
that sort of indiscriminate respect.

If someone honours me I want it known
that it's an honour for myself alone.
Flinging love all over's *not* my line.
The 'buddy' of Mankind's no *friend* of mine.

PHILINTE

But in society (if we belong that is)
we must conform to its civilities.

ALCESTE

No, we must be merciless in our tirade
against this pseudo-civil masquerade.
Let real feelings shine out through our speech,
a deep sincerity where guile can't reach,
no pretty compliments, but true regard,
open, not hidden in some slick charade.

PHILINTE

But there're times when speaking out one's mind
'd be ridiculous or plain unkind.
With all due deference to your strict code
there are occasions when restraint is good.
All kinds of social chaos would ensue
if everybody spoke his mind like you.
Supposing there's a man we can't abide,
do we say so, or keep our hate inside?

ALCESTE

Say so, say so!

PHILINTE

                    I see; and would you tell
Emilie (poor superannuated *belle*),
she's past all beauty, and a perfect scream
under the make-up and foundation cream?

ALCESTE

Yes.

PHILINTE

And Dorilas how much he bores us all
with how-I-won-back-France for Charles de Gaulle,
the Maquis mastermind who saved the war?
Would you say that to him?

ALCESTE

I would, and more!

PHILINTE

You're making fun of me.

ALCESTE

I don't make fun.
In things like this I won't spare anyone.
The City, Politics, the Arts (so called!)
I've seen them all, Philinte, and I'm appalled.
Black rage comes over me, it makes me rave
seeing the dreadful way most men behave.
There's not a walk of life where you don't meet
flattery, injustice, selfishness, deceit.
I'm utterly exasperated and my mind
's made up, I'm finished, finished with mankind!

PHILINTE

Your dark philosophy's too bleak by half.
Your moods of black despair just make me laugh.
I think by now I know you pretty well . . .
we're very like Ariste and Sganarelle,
the brothers in that thing by Molière,
you know, *The School of Husbands*, that one where . . .

ALCESTE

For God's sake, spare us *Molière* quotations!

PHILINTE

But, please, no more hell-fire denunciations!
The world's not going to change because of you.
You're fond of frankness . . . do you know it's true

that people snigger at this quirk of yours?
Everywhere you go, society guffaws.
Your fulminations on the age's lies
just make you seem comic in most men's eyes.

ALCESTE

So much the better! Comic in their sight?
That only goes to prove that my way's right.
Mankind's so low and loathsome in *my* eyes,
I'd start to panic if it thought me wise.

PHILINTE

I think you'd write off all humanity!

ALCESTE

Because I hate them, all of them, that's why.

PHILINTE

We're living in bad times I know, that's true,
but even so there *must* be just a few . . .

ALCESTE

A few? Not one! Not one a man can trust.
The whole lot fill me with complete disgust.
Some because they're vicious, all the rest
because they nod at vice and aren't depressed
or full of righteous anger at the thought
of wickedness at large, as good men ought.
It's taking tolerance to wild extremes
to tolerate that swine and his low schemes,
that awful, foul, objectionable swine –
the one who's tried to grab this land of mine,
whose trumped-up action's hauled me into court.
Cultivating monsters of that sort!
There's plainly a villain under that veneer.
The truth of what he is is all too clear.
Those sheepish humble looks, that sickly grin
take only those who've never met him in.

The guttersnipe! There's no one who can't guess
the tricks he's stooped to for his quick success.
The niche he's carved himself, in padded plush
makes talent vomit and real virtue blush.
Call him a bastard and everyone hoorays
but he's still the blue-eyed boy of smart *soirées*.
That grinning hypocrite, that nepotist's
on all society reception lists.
Despite his obvious and blatant flaws
his smirk's his Sesame through *salon* doors.
In rat-race intrigue he's a class apart
straight to the post before his betters start.
When I see vice given its head I feel
the pity of it pierce me like cold steel.
In these moods what I want's some wild retreat
where humanity and I need never meet.

PHILINTE
A little understanding's what's required.
Humanity leaves much to be desired
I know that very well, but let's not rant
about its vices. Let's be tolerant.
Moderation's where true wisdom lies.
What we should be is *reasonably* wise.
You're living in the past. Diogenes
isn't quite the type for times like these.
All your harping on that ancient theme
strikes the modern age as too extreme.
Compromise; accommodate; don't force
your principles to run too stiff a course.
It's sheer, outrageous folly to pretend
you'll change things or imagine you'll amend
mankind's perversity one little jot.
You think your anger's wisdom, but it's not.
Like you I see a hundred things a day
that could be better, but I don't inveigh

against them angrily, and unlike you,
I've learnt to be tolerant of what men do,
I take them as they come, put up with them.
'Bile' 's no more philosophical than 'phlegm'.
In social intercourse the golden rule
's not curse, like you, but, like me 'keep one's cool'.

ALCESTE

So, whatever vast disaster or mishap
you're philosophical and never flap?
If you were in my shoes and someone planned
to gain possession of your precious land;
betrayed you, slandered you, what then? What then?
Would you still show 'tolerance' for men?
Maligned, betrayed, and robbed! You'd be a fool
to watch all that occur and 'keep your cool'.

PHILINTE

But when I see self-interest, graft, deceit,
when I see men swindle, steal, lie, cheat,
I feel about as much sense of dismay
as if I'd seen some beast devour its prey,
or if I'd watched, say, monkeys in the zoo
doing what monkeys are supposed to do.
All your diatribes are off the track.
It's basic human nature you attack.
That's your humanity. There's no escape.
These are the antics of the 'naked ape'.

ALCESTE

So, I'm to see myself knocked down, laid low,
and torn to pieces, robbed and never . . . O
it's pointless talking and I'll say no more.

PHILINTE

Calm down, Alceste. And turn your mind to law.
Your 'hypocrite', remember, and his suit.

ALCESTE

But there's absolutely nothing to dispute.

PHILINTE

But you've selected your solicitors?

ALCESTE

Yes, reason and the justice of my cause.

PHILINTE

And won't you pay the judge the usual visit?

ALCESTE

No! I see, my case is doubtful is it?

PHILINTE

Of course not, no, but if the man's in league
with others, then there's bound to be intrigue.

ALCESTE

There's right and wrong. There's no two ways about it.

PHILINTE

I wouldn't be too sure. I rather doubt it.

ALCESTE

I won't budge an inch.

PHILINTE

              He will though; he'll plot
your overthrow.

ALCESTE

And if he does, so what?

PHILINTE

You'll find out you were wrong.

ALCESTE

              Let's see then, eh?

PHILINTE

But . . .

ALCESTE

I'll gladly see the verdict go his way.

PHILINTE

You'll what! . . .

ALCESTE

My adversary's success
will only go to show man's wickedness.
To prove men low enough to prostitute
fair play, before the world, I'll lose my suit.

PHILINTE

What a man!

ALCESTE

That satisfaction'll be worth
every penny, though it costs the earth.

PHILINTE

Alceste, people'll laugh and call you mad
to hear you talk like that.

ALCESTE

That's just too bad.

PHILINTE

Has the widow you're besotted by eschewed
frivolity for your stern rectitude,
this dug-out of ideals? Does Célimène
share your strenuous moral regimen?
I'm flabbergasted that, for one whose face
seems to be turned against the human race,
in spite of everything you *say* you hate,
one member of it still can fascinate,
and even more astonished by the one
you've lavished this strange adoration on.

Eliante, whose sincerity commands respect,
who thinks of who most kindly, you reject.
One most respectable Arsinoé,
has feelings for you that are thrown away.
And you love Célimène, whose acid skits
make her the reigning queen of bitchy wits
a Jezebel, whose whole style typifies
those 'dreadful modern ways', that you despise.
Faults that in others you ruthlessly attack
in lovely Célimène don't seem so black.
Does beauty cancel them? Or don't you mind?
If you can't *see* her faults you must be blind.

ALCESTE

Not blind! No, absolutely wide awake!
No standards lowered for the widow's sake.
Although I love her I'm the first to seize
on all her obvious infirmities.
But not withstanding those, in spite of all,
La Belle Dame sans Merci has me in thrall.
The rest is modishness, that's something I,
through my deep love for her, can purify.

PHILINTE

That's no mean feat if you're successful. If!
And you're convinced she loves you?

ALCESTE

                                                        Positive!
I couldn't love her if she weren't sincere.

PHILINTE

Then if her love for you's so very clear,
why do your rivals cause you such distress?

ALCESTE

True love desires uniquely to possess
its object, not go shares with other men.
That's what I've come to say to Célimène.

37

PHILINTE

If I were you her cousin Eliante
'd be the sort of lover that I'd want;
she thinks a lot of you, that's very clear.
She's tender, frank, dependable, sincere.
Sincere, Alceste, which means she's so much more
the sort of person you've a weak spot for.

ALCESTE

That's true, and reason tells me so each day.
But love won't function in a rational way.

PHILINTE

I'm rather worried though that your affair 's . . .

*Enter Oronte, glass in hand, from the party
downstairs.*

ORONTE

Lovely party! Marvellous do downstairs!

To Alceste.

Heard you were up here, though, and thought what luck
to catch Alceste alone . . . I've read your book.
I know your essays backwards, read the lot!
We two should get acquainted better, what?
You really are a most distinguished man.
I love your work. Consider me your 'fan'.
Your talents draw my homage and applause.
I would so love to be a friend of yours.
Friendship with someone of my stamp and sort
's not to be sneezed at, really, I'd've thought.
Excuse me, (*cough*) it's you I've been addressing,

Alceste looks surprised.

I'm sorry I can see that I'm distressing . . .

38

ALCESTE

No, no, not in the least. It's just I'm dazed
to find myself so eloquently praised.

ORONTE

It should be no surprise to hear your name
made much of; why, the whole world does the same!

ALCESTE

Monsieur!

ORONTE

Your reputation's nation-wide.
Not only I, all France is starry-eyed.

ALCESTE

Monsieur!

ORONTE

In my humble view, for what it's worth,
there's nobody quite like you on God's earth.

ALCESTE

Monsieur!

ORONTE

Let lightning flash and strike me dead
if there's the slightest lie in all I've said.
To show you let me demonstrate, like this,
and seal all I've been saying with this kiss.
Your hand, then, on our friendship, yours and mine!

ALCESTE

Monsieur!

ORONTE

Not interested? Do you decline?

ALCESTE

The honour that you do me's far too great.
Friendships develop at a slower rate.

It's the very name of friendship you profane
if you repeat the word like a refrain.
It's judgement, choice, consideration pave
the way to friendship and we can't behave
as if we're bosom friends until we've found
we actually share some common ground.
Our characters may prove so different.
We'd soon regret our rushed vows and repent.

ORONTE

Excellently put! Your insight and good sense
just make my hero-worship more intense.
If time will make us friends I'll gladly wait,
but, in the meantime, please don't hesitate,
if there's anything at all that I can do,
Elyséewise, a place, an interview,
just say the word. Most people are aware
just what my standing is with those 'up there'.
There can't be many men much more *au fait*
with all that happens at the Elysée.
I'm 'in' with those that matter, even HE
treats me like his own; yes, honestly!
So count on me to help you 'oil the wheels'.
Now, since you're an author, and a man who feels,
to inaugurate our friendship I'll recite
a little poem I've felt moved to write.
I'd welcome your reactions and some hint
on whether it seems good enough to print.
Perhaps you could suggest (I know it's cheek)
which editors you know are *sympathique*.

ALCESTE

I'm afraid I'm not well suited to the task.

ORONTE

O, not well suited? Why's that may I ask?

40

ALCESTE

Frankness is my *forte*. I'm afraid you'd find
I'm uncomfortably prone to speak my mind.

ORONTE

Frankness! Just what I ask. No, I insist.
I'm not just looking for a eulogist.
I've come expecting you to be quite straight.
I'll feel resentful if you hesitate.
I'm not afraid of, I demand sincerity.

ALCESTE

Since you insist, monsieur, then yes, I'll try.

ORONTE

HOPE . . . it's about a girl, a little thing
who's rather kept me dangling on a string.
HOPE . . . just my inmost feelings, nothing planned.
It's just as it came out you understand.

ALCESTE

Proceed!

ORONTE

            HOPE . . . what I'd really like to know 's
if the intensity of feeling shows
and if I've got the rhythm right, or wrong.

ALCESTE

Read it and we'll see.

ORONTE

                    Didn't take me long.
Not fifteen minutes. Came to me in bed.

ALCESTE

Time's immaterial. Please go ahead.

ORONTE

HOPE . . . that's the title, HOPE. Before I read . . .

ALCESTE

I think we've got the picture. Please proceed!

ORONTE
(*reads*)

Hope was assuaging:
its glimmer
cheered my gloomy pilgrimage
to the gold shrine of your love . . .

a mirage of water pool and palms
to a nomad lost in the Sahara . . .

but in the end it only makes thirst worse.

PHILINTE

That's rather touching. Yes. I like that bit.

ALCESTE
(*aside*)

How can you like that stuff, you hypocrite?

ORONTE
(*reads*)

Darling, if this hot trek
to some phantasmal Mecca
of love's consummation
is some sort of Herculean labour
then I've fallen by the wayside.

PHILINTE

Intriguing, yes, I like your turn of phrase.

ALCESTE
(*aside*)

Flatterer! It's rubbish, not worth any praise.

ORONTE
(*reads*)

'A deeper, darker otherwhere
is unfulfilment . . .

we who have bathed in the lustrous light
of your charisma
now languish in miasmal black despair

and all we hopeless lovers share
the nightmare of the bathosphere.

PHILINTE

That 'dying fall!' It closes beautifully!

ALCESTE
(*aside*)

I wish *he'd* fall and break his neck and die
and cart his doggerel with him off to Hell.

PHILINTE

I've never before heard verses . . . shaped . . . so well.

ALCESTE
(*aside*)

Good God!

ORONTE
(*to Philinte*)
It's just your kindness, I'm afraid.

PHILINTE

No, no!

ALCESTE
(*aside*)
What is it then you . . . renegade!

ORONTE
(*to Alceste*)
What do you think? And don't forget your pact.
Your frank opinion, mind. I don't want tact.

ALCESTE

It's very delicate. I think we'd all admit
a need for flattery, at least a bit,

43

when it's a question of our taste at stake.
We must be careful just what line we take.
I'll tell you something, though. One day I'd read
a certain someone's verses and I said,
'A man in your position *has* to know
exactly to what lengths he ought to go
and keep his itch to scribble well in hand.
Poetry's a pastime, understand;
one shouldn't go too far and let the thing
get out of hand and think of publishing.
The man who can't say no and who persists
ends up a sitting duck for satirists.'

ORONTE
And just what is it that you're hinting at?
That I waste my time?

ALCESTE
                    No, I don't say that.
What I told him was . . . I said, 'Now, look,
nothing's more humdrum than a boring book.
It's the one thing people can't forgive.
They'll always latch on to the negative.
No matter what good qualities you've got,
people'll judge you by your weakest spot.'

ORONTE
It *is* my poem that you're getting at!

ALCESTE
I wouldn't say that. No! I don't say that.
I reminded him of men in our own times
who'd come to grief through turning out bad rhymes.

ORONTE
Do *I* write badly? Am I one of those men?

ALCESTE
I don't say that. This is what I hinted then.

44

'Why write at all, unless the urge is bad,
and if so, keep it to yourself, don't add
more slim volumes to the mounds of verse.
Writing's mad, but publishing's far worse.
The only poets the public can forgive
're those poor so-and-sos who write to live.
Take my advice, resist the itch, resist
the urge to star on some poor poetry list,
to end up laughing stock and *salon* martyr,
all for some private press's *imprimatur*.'
That's the advice I tried to get across.

ORONTE
I take your point, but still I'm at a loss
to know what's in my poem . . .

ALCESTE
                    Jesus wept!
It's bloody rubbish, rhythmically inept,
vacuous verbiage, wind, gas, guff.
All lovestruck amateurs churn out that stuff.
It's formless, slack, a nauseating sprawl,
and riddled with stale clichés; that's not all.
'Thirst worse' cacophonous, and those '*ek eks*'
sound like a bullfrog in the throes of sex.
Ah! terrible stuff gets written nowadays.
Our ancestors, though crude in many ways,
had better taste, and, honestly, I'd trade
all modern verse for this old serenade!

> If Good King Harry said to me
> *You may possess my gay Paree*
> *if you will send your love away*,
> then this is what I'd say:
> *Good King Harry, Sire, thankee*
> *for offering me your gay Paree,*
> *I'd liefer keep my love by far,*
> *yea, Sire, my love, tra-la!*

45

The rhyming's awkward, and the style's *passé*.
but far better than the rubbish of today,
that pretentious gibberish you all admire.
Here speaks the true voice of desire:

> If Good King Harry said to me
> *You may possess my gay Paree,*
> *if you will send your love away*
> then this is what I'd say:
> *Good King Harry, Sire, thankee*
> *for offering me your gay Paree.*
> *I'd liefer keep my love by far,*
> *yea, Sire, my love, tra-la!*

There speaks the voice of true authentic passion

> *Oronte and Philinte laugh.*

Mock on, mock on. In spite of current fashion
I much prefer it to the flowery haze
and gaudy glitter all the critics praise.

ORONTE
And I maintain my poem's rather good.

ALCESTE
I suppose there's every reason why you should.
You must excuse me if I can't agree.

ORONTE
That many others do 's enough for me.

ALCESTE
Yes, they can do what I can't, that's pretend.

ORONTE
Ah, so you're 'an intellectual', my friend?

ALCESTE
You'd say so, if I praised your verse, no doubt.

ORONTE

Your praise is something I can do without.

ALCESTE

You'll have to, I'm afraid.

ORONTE

     I'd like to read
a poem of your own dashed off at speed.

ALCESTE

Mine might be just as bad as yours, God knows,
but I wouldn't shove the thing beneath your nose!

ORONTE

Such arrogance! I don't know how you dare . . .

ALCESTE

O, go and find your flattery elsewhere!

ORONTE

Now, little man, just watch your manners, please.

ALCESTE

Don't take that tone with me, you . . . Hercules!

PHILINTE

Gentlemen, enough. I beg you, please, no more.

ORONTE

Apologise for that behaviour, *or* . . .!

ALCESTE

You'll bring your famous 'influence' to bear?

ORONTE

And all I have to do is cross that square.

*Exit Oronte. Philinte watches him go down the stairs
and then pours two drinks. He begins to follow
Alceste with them.*

47

PHILINTE

You see what your 'sincerity' can do?
There's bound to be bad blood between you two.
All the man wanted was a little pat.

ALCESTE

Don't talk to me.

PHILINTE

But I . . .

ALCESTE

Not after that!

PHILINTE

It's too . . .

ALCESTE

Leave me alone.

PHILINTE

If I . . .

ALCESTE

No more, I say.

PHILINTE

But what . . .

ALCESTE

No more.

PHILINTE

But . . .

ALCESTE

Still?

PHILINTE

Is that the way . . .?

ALCESTE

O, stop following me about, you pest.

PHILINTE

I'd better keep my eye on you, Alceste.

Philinte notices Célimène enter from downstairs. He gives the two glasses of champagne to Célimène. Exit Philinte. Célimène approaches the abstracted Alceste, and clinks the glasses together. As Alceste speaks Célimène drains first one glass, then the other.

ALCESTE

I'll come straight to the point if you don't mind.
There're things in your behaviour that I find
quite reprehensible. In fact I'm so annoyed
I honestly can't see how we'll avoid
the inevitable break. I can't pretend –
sooner or later this thing's bound to end.
And if I swore my patience was unending
reality'd soon prove I *was* pretending.

CELIMENE

So that's why you stormed off? I see. I see.
Another moral lecture. (*Sigh.*) Poor me!

ALCESTE

It's not a moral lecture.

Pause.

Célimène
you're rather too hospitable to men.
Far too many swarm here round your door.
I'm sorry, I can't stand it any more.

CELIMENE

Am I to blame if men can't keep away?
I'm not the one who's leading them astray.
They're sweet. They visit. What do you suggest?
A mounted sentry, or an entrance test?

ALCESTE

No, not a sentry, but you might . . . well . . . mm

temper the welcome you extend to them.
I know that there's your beauty, and there's you,
and that's one single entity, not two,
your beauty's something that you can't conceal,
a woman can't sequester sex-appeal –
one glance though from those eyes brings men to heel.
Then small attentions here, a favour there
keep all your hopefuls from complete despair.
The hopes you dangle out before them all
just help to keep them at your beck and call.
If, once or twice perhaps, you could say NO,
they'd take the hint all right, and they'd soon go.
But what I'd like to know 's what freak of luck's
helped to put Clitandre in your good books?
What amazing talents does the 'thing' possess,
what sublimity of virtue? Let me guess.
I'm at a loss. Now let me see. *I know!*
It's his little finger like a *croissant*, so,
crooked at *Angelina's* where he sips his tea
among the titled queens of 'gay' Paree!
What makes *him* captivate the social scene?
Second-skin gauchos in crêpe-de-chine?
Those golden blow-wave curls (that aren't his own)?
Those knickerbockers, or obsequious tone?
Or is it his giggle and his shrill falsett-
o hoity-toity voice makes him your pet?

CELIMENE
You mustn't go on like this. It isn't fair.
Just why I lead him on you're well aware.
You know he's said he'd put in a good word
to get my lawsuit favourably heard.

ALCESTE
Lose your lawsuit and have no cause to pander
to odious little pipsqueaks like Clitandre.

CELIMENE

It grows and grows this jealousy of yours!

ALCESTE

Those you let court you grow, so there's good cause.

CELIMENE

Surely I'd've thought it wouldn't've mattered
to see my friendliness so widely scattered?
You'd really have much more to shout about
if there were only one I'd singled out.

ALCESTE

You blame me for my jealousy, but what,
I ask you, sets *me* above that other lot?

CELIMENE

The joy of knowing that my love's for you.

ALCESTE

Yes, yes, but how can I be sure that's true?

CELIMENE

The simple fact I've told you that it's so
should be enough, and all you need to know.

ALCESTE

But how can I be certain that you're not
saying the same thing to that other lot?

CELIMENE

A pretty compliment that is, a fine way
for a lover to be talking, I must say.
To kill all your mad jealousies stone dead
I take back everything that I just said.
Now you won't need to worry any more.
Satisfied?

ALCESTE

God, what do I love you for?

If I could only wriggle off the hook,
I'd give thanks to the Lord and bless my luck.
I've done everything I can to break this gaol
and gain my freedom but to no avail.
My efforts just don't get me anywhere.
My love for you's a cross I've got to bear.

CELIMENE

It's certainly unique, I must admit.

ALCESTE

Nothing in the world compares with it.
Imagination just can't plumb my heart.
The love I bear for you's a thing apart.

CELIMENE

It's the novel way you show it though, Alceste.
All you seem to love for 's to protest.
You can't tell crankiness and love apart.
It's bloody-mindedness that fires your heart.

ALCESTE

Then give my 'bloody-mindedness' some peace.
This wilful vacillation's got to cease.
Look, Célimène, there's just the two of us.
Let's use these precious moments to discuss . . .

Enter Basque.

BASQUE

The marquis's downstairs, madame.

CELIMENE

                              Which one?

BASQUE

                                        Acaste.

CELIMENE

Then show the marquis up, please . . .

ALCESTE
                              Damn and blast!

Exit Basque.

Can I never have two words with you alone
and must you be 'at home' to everyone?

CELIMENE
I can't not see him. He'd be most upset.

ALCESTE
I've never known you 'not see' people yet.

CELIMENE
But he wouldn't come to see me any more
if he thought I thought he was a bore.

ALCESTE
Would that matter so much, Célimène?

CELIMENE
Alceste, we've *got* to cultivate such men.
They're influential people with a say
in big decisions at the Elysée.
Their tongues do nothing much by way of good
but their sharp edges can and do draw blood.
Whoever else you may have on your side
falling foul of that set 's suicide.

ALCESTE
What you mean is, given half the chance,
you'd be at home to all the men in France,
though all the arguments of reason show . . .

Enter Basque.

BASQUE
The *other* marquis, ma'am.

ALCESTE
(*making as if to leave*)
Clitandre! O, no!

CELIMENE
And where're you going to?

ALCESTE
I'm off.

CELIMENE
No stay!

ALCESTE
Why?

CELIMENE
Please!

ALCESTE
No!

CELIMENE
For me?

ALCESTE
No, I'm away!
Unless you're really spoiling for a battle
you'd want to spare me all their tittle-tattle.

CELIMENE
Please stay. I want you to.

ALCESTE
I couldn't, no.

CELIMENE
O please do what you like, and, go, please, go!

Alceste sits. Enter Eliante and Philinte.

ELIANTE

They're coming up the stairs, the two marquis.
Were you aware?

CELIMENE
(*nodding, and to Basque*)
Champagne and glasses, please.

To Alceste.

Not gone yet?

ALCESTE
No, not yet. I'm here to see
you finally decide on them or me.

CELIMENE

Ssssshh!

ALCESTE
Make up your mind. This very minute!

CELIMENE

Such madness!

ALCESTE
Yes, but there's some method in it.

CELIMENE

Are you demanding I . . .

ALCESTE
decide.

CELIMENE
Decide?

ALCESTE

Decide. My patience has been more than tried.

Enter Clitandre and Acaste.

CLITANDRE
(still laughing and removing tie)
We've been at a lateish evening 'over there'.
Hilarious, (*kiss-kiss*) the whole affair!
I was absolutely helpless. Who'd've thought
Elysée functions could provide such sport?
That old buffoon Cléonte convulsed 'the Court'
until the table heaved with stifled laughs
at his gauche manners and his social gaffes.
Couldn't someone let him know that's *not* the way
he'll get 'preferment' at the Elysée?

CELIMENE
That wine-stained tie he wears, those baggy breeches
have everyone he meets at once in stitches.
He never learns. He just gets more bizarre,
adding new *faux pas* to his repertoire.

ACASTE
Talking of weird people, my head's sore
after a session with the world's worst bore,
blabbermouth Damon – on the street, my cab
waiting at the kerbside; blab, blab, blab!

CELIMENE
When Damon's logorrhoea's in full spate
he's like an LP played at 78,
and all that comes across when Damon speaks
is squeaking gibberish and high-pitched shrieks.

Clitandre utters a high-pitched shriek.

ELIANTE
(to Philinte)
What did I tell you? They're off to a good start,
pulling their friends' characters apart.

ACASTE
And what about Timante? He's rather odd.

CELIMENE

Our cloak-and-dagger-ite! A grudging nod
in passing's all you get from that tin god,
as though he'd got such urgent things to do
he hadn't a second he could spare for you.
It's all an act. If he's got news, it's *pssts*
and sideways glances like stage anarchists.
He'll halt a conversation in mid-word
to whisper something hush-hush, and absurd.
He looks around him, beckons you away,
leans closer, cups his hands, and breathes: *Nice day!*

ACASTE

And Géralde?

CELIMENE

   Him? O, I've never been so bored!
He'll only deign to mention a milord.
Rank's his mania. His conversation runs
on nothing else but horses, hounds and guns.
The Almanach de Gotha, A to Z,
he's learnt by heart and carries in his head.
If anyone's got blood tinged slightly blue
Géralde knows his first name and calls him *tu*.

CLITANDRE

He and Bélise are on good terms, I hear.

CELIMENE

Poor silly creature, and so dull. My dear,
I suffer martyrdoms when she comes round.
Getting conversations off the ground
with her 's like slavery; one sweats and strains
for subjects, honestly one racks one's brains
but she's so unforthcoming, so half-dead,
chat plummets to silence like a lump of lead.
A little warmer? Turned out nice again!
Chilly, don't you think? It looks like rain!

gambits to break the ice with anyone
but not Bélise; one sentence and she's done.
It's bad enough her visiting at all,
but dragged out half the day, intolerable.
Look at the clock, yawn, play the busy host,
she no more budges than a wooden post.

ACASTE

Adraste?

CELIMENE

An utter megalomaniac!
His conversation's just one long attack.
The 'foul Establishment' 's his constant theme
because it doesn't share his self-esteem.
How could the latest Government 've passed
him over, him, the great-I-am, Acaste?
The 'old-boy network', 'the incestuous set'
stops him starring in the Cabinet.
Something Machiavellian and underhand
prevents *his* being a power in the land.

CLITANDRE

You've heard the trend? These days the rendezvous
for people who are 'in' 's *chez* you-know-who.

CELIMENE

But they only go to Cléon's for the food.

ELIANTE

Cléon's cuisine though 's not to be pooh-poohed.

CELIMENE

The dinner turns to sawdust on one's lips
when Cléon's served with everything, like chips.
He tells a boring story and you'd swear
the Château Mouton Rothschild's *ordinaire*.

PHILINTE

His uncle Damis though 's well spoken of.

CELIMENE

Yes, we're friends.

PHILINTE

He's sound and sensible enough.

CELIMENE

Yeees! But exasperating nonetheless.
Those superior displays of cleverness!
He's like some sort of robot, stiff and slow,
and programmed only to repeat *bon mots*!
Since he's turned his mind to being a 'wit',
he's got 'good taste' and nothing pleases it.
He's supercilious about new plays.
The critic is the man who won't show praise;
only idiots laugh, and fools applaud;
the clever thing to be 's blasé and bored.
His weekly condescending book review
's never about the books but his IQ.
Ordinary smalltalk too he quibbles at.
He's far too exalted for that sort of chat.

ACASTE

Yes, dammit, yes, that's Damis to a tee.

CLITANDRE

You're marvellous. I love your mimicry.

ALCESTE

Go on, go on, and give the knife more twists.
You socialites are such brave satirists
behind men's backs. If one showed up, you'd rush
to greet the man effusively and crush
him to your bosom in a false embrace
and only say *enchanté* to his face.

CLITANDRE

Why pick on us, Alceste? You should address
your disapproval to our kind hostess.

ALCESTE

No, dammit, no! It's you two that I blame.
Your fawning makes her slander men's good name.
The lady's gifted with malicious wit,
but it's your flattery that fosters it.
Once she finds there's no one to applaud
her badinage she'll soon enough get bored.
Most infringement of the moral code 's
the fault of sycophants and fawning toads.

PHILINTE

Why take up their cause? You yourself condemn
the frailties we criticise in them.

CELIMENE

His whole life-style depends on saying no.
Alceste, agree? He'd never stoop so low.
No! Mustn't he go on proving he was born
under the stars of dissidence and scorn?
He's not one of us, no, not Alceste;
not wanting to seem so makes him protest.
He's contradictory in every way;
when all the rest are AYES, he's always NAY,
so contradictory he's even peeved
once his own ideas 've been believed.
When someone else has held them he's been known
to demolish opinions that *were* his own.

Laughter.

ALCESTE

They're on your side. You're safe. Go on, enjoy
the public torture of your whipping boy!

PHILINTE

But isn't she half-right? It is your way
to contradict whatever people say.
No matter what *their* feelings, pro or con,
it's always the opposition that you're on.

ALCESTE

Because they're always so far off the track,
I always have good grounds for my attack.
They sometimes flatter and they sometimes sneer,
either shameless and corrupt, or cavalier.

CELIMENE

But . . .

ALCESTE

But nothing, though it's the end of me,
I've got to say I hate your repartee.
These people only wrong you when they fawn
on flaws like yours which secretly they scorn.

CLITANDRE

Speaking for myself, I really wouldn't know.
I've always found her perfectly just so.

ACASTE

The most charming lady that I've ever met.
I haven't noticed any defects yet!

ALCESTE

I've noticed plenty, *and* I'm not afraid
of saying so. I call a spade a spade.
If loving someone deeply means you creep,
if love means criticism's put to sleep,
keep it. That may be love for such as you;
it's not the sort of love that I call true.
I'd banish those wet lovers who kow-towed
to every half-baked thought I spoke aloud,
who laughed at my bad jokes, who cheered my views,
who treated last year's gossip as hot news,
'worshipped the very ground on which I trod'
and grovelled to my whims, as if I'm God.

CELIMENE

And if you had your way, my dear Alceste,

we'd say our keenest critics loved us best.
Sweet-talk's finished, kindness is no use.
The surest sign of love is foul abuse.

ELIANTE

How does that bit in old Lucretius go,
that bit on blinkered lovers? O, you know;
it's something like: 'whatever's negative 's
soon metamorphosed by new adjectives:
the girl whose face is pinched and deathly white
's not plain anaemic, she's "Pre-Raphaelite".
The loved one's figure's like Venus de Milo's –
even the girl who weighs a hundred kilos!
"Earth Mother" 's how some doting lover dubs
his monstrous mistress with enormous bubs.
"A touch of tarbrush?" No, that's healthy tan.
The one called "Junoesque" 's more like a man.
The slut's "Bohemian", the dwarf's virtue
's *multum in parvo* like a good haiku.
There's "self-respect" for arrogant conceit.
The windbag's extrovert, the dumb's "discreet";
stupidity's "good nature", slyness "wit",'
et cetera . . . it's not inapposite!

ALCESTE

But *I* . . .

CELIMENE

I think we've heard enough from you.
Come to the balcony and see my view.

To Acaste and Clitandre.

Going already, gentlemen?

ACASTE

No!

CLITANDRE

No!

ALCESTE
(*to Célimène*)

You seem to be worrying in case they go.

To Acaste and Clitandre.

Go when you like. But let me make this clear.
When you decide to go, I'll still be here.

ACASTE

Unless our hostess thinks I'm in the way.
I'm absolutely free.

CLITANDRE
And *I* can stay.

CELIMENE

Is this your notion of a joke, Alceste?

ALCESTE

I want to see whose presence suits you best.

Enter Basque.

BASQUE
(*to Alceste*)

Sir, there's a man downstairs 'd like a word.
Says it's important. Not to be deferred!

ALCESTE

There's nothing I'm aware of that can't wait.

BASQUE

Something about a 'feud' to arbitrate.
Perhaps I should say, sir, the person *says*
he's official, sir. *Académie Française.*
I'd say myself he's *bona fide*, sir:
the car's a black one with a tricolour.

Enter Official of the Académie Française.

ALCESTE
They tell me that you're from the *Académ*—

OFFICIAL
—*ie française,* indeed, sir, yes.

ALCESTE
                            Well, here I am.

OFFICIAL
It's just a word or two, sir, in your ear.

ALCESTE
Then out with it, dear fellow, loud and clear.

OFFICIAL
The *Académie française,* whose members are . . .

ALCESTE
At midnight?

OFFICIAL
            . . . taking their brandy and cigar
at *Maxim's,* sir, wondered if you've time to spare.
There's a little matter that they'd like to air.

ALCESTE
So late?

OFFICIAL
        If you don't mind.

ALCESTE
                        What can they want?

PHILINTE
It's that ridiculous business with Oronte.

CELIMENE
(*to Philinte*)
What's this?

64

PHILINTE

      O, he was his usual self about
a poem of Oronte's and they fell out.
The sort of private row they like to handle.
They don't like media creating scandal.
They simply want to stop it getting worse.

ALCESTE

No compromise. I refuse to praise his verse!

PHILINTE

Alceste! It is the Academicians though!
I'll come with you. Come on. We'd better go.

ALCESTE

If they suppose they're going to persuade . . .
to . . . somehow . . . change my mind, then I'm afraid,
with all due deference to those gentlemen,
the *Académie française* can think again.
Admire his poem? No, I'm adamant.
His verse is vile. I can't and won't recant.

PHILINTE

But couldn't you try to be a little . . .

ALCESTE

                        No!
It's dreadful and I'll go on saying so.

PHILINTE

You ought to be a little more accommodating.
Let's go. We mustn't keep the members waiting.

ALCESTE

I'll go but nothing will induce me to . . .

PHILINTE

We must go *now*, Alceste. But couldn't you . . . ?

ALCESTE

Listen, only a Special Powers Act
passed by the Elysée 'd make me retract,
but, otherwise, whatever Paris thinks,
I'll go on saying that his poem stinks.
The author of that poem should've been
beheaded for it on the Guillotine.

Laughter.

Dammit, I wasn't aware my words could cause
such wild amusement and inane guffaws.

CELIMENE

Go, at once.

ALCESTE

Yes, but I'll be back again
to finish off *our* business, Célimène.

*Exit Alceste. Clitandre and Acaste continue laughing
for some moments.*

CLITANDRE

Mon cher marquis, you positively beam
with untroubled *joie de vivre*, and self-esteem.
But, frankly, do you really have good cause
for this wide-eyed complacency of yours?

ACASTE

Well, all things considered, I fail to see
the slightest cause at all for misery.
I'm young and healthy, rich, my blood's as blue
as any in all France can lay claim to.
Connections help, and when your family tree 's
as illustrious as mine it guarantees
an open *entrée* into most careers:
the Diplomatic Corps, the Grenadiers,
and, if I fancied, my family could fix

66

some cushy sinecure in politics.
My nonchalant panache, my poise, my flair
shine both in *salons* and the open air:
I've ridden, skied, played polo, fenced
better than any I've been matched against.
I've a lot of talents! And as for wit,
though I say so myself, I've heaps of it.
Impromptu apophthegms and suave *bon goût*
got me my column in the right review.
First-night audiences at all new plays
hold back their condemnation or their praise
until they've read 'Acaste's piece', *then* they know
just what the reactions are they ought to show.
I'm the arbiter. If I'm bored, they're bored,
and if I write SEE THIS the sheep applaud.
Assured and polished and a handsome creature
(my teeth, I think my most outstanding feature)
my sportsman's figure and my splendid gear
easily made me *Best Dressed Man* last year.
Where women are concerned I get my way.
I'm *persona grata* at the Elysée.
Comb Europe if you like. You'd be hard put
to find anyone at all so fortunate.
Honestly I couldn't, even if I tried
feel any other way but satisfied.

CLITANDRE

The whole world's at your feet. I wonder you
waste time here as often as you do.

ACASTE

I wouldn't dream of coming to pay court
in vain; I'm afraid I'm not that sort.
I leave all that for chappies less endowed –
'to burn for beauties pitiless and proud',
to languish at their feet, and to submit
to haughty treatment. I'll have none of it.

Your half-baked lovers in the end resort
to sighs and blubbing when they're paying court,
and hope to gain, by laying siege with tears,
what merit couldn't in a thousand years.
But pukka men like me, sir, don't fork out
their love on credit and then go without.
All women have their value, men as well
fetch market prices when they want to sell.
If a woman wants to boast she's made a kill
and bagged my heart, all right! She'll foot the bill.
One has to strike a bargain, and to make
the scale weigh even, give and *take*.

CLITANDRE

You think you stand a chance the way things go?

ACASTE

I've pretty good reasons for believing so.

CLITANDRE

I wouldn't be too sure. You've got it wrong.
It's just been wishful thinking all along.

ACASTE

That's right, wrong all along, Clitandre.
And to think it's only now the truth has dawned.

CLITANDRE

You're sure?

ACASTE

No, I've been wrong!

CLITANDRE

But can you prove . . .

ACASTE

Wrong, all along!

CLITANDRE

Has she confessed her love?

68

ACASTE

No, she treats me badly . . .

CLITANDRE

No, really, please!

ACASTE

Cold shoulder only.

CLITANDRE

Acaste, please don't tease.
What signs *has* she given? Or are there none?

ACASTE

None. I'm rejected. You're the lucky one.
She really hates me. Yes, my only hope
's oblivion; poison or a length of rope.

CLITANDRE

O balls! This quarrelling's no earthly use.
What I suggest we need 's to make a truce.
Then if, for example, I get some sure sign
that Célimène's decided she'll be mine,
or you, I suppose, that she'll be yours,
the one not chosen graciously withdraws,
and lets the favourite take a few lengths lead.

ACASTE

Absolutely! A bargain! Yes, agreed!
But sshhh . . .

Enter Célimène.

CELIMENE

Still here?

CLITANDRE

Love roots us to the spot.

ACASTE

Was that a car I heard downstairs, or not?

CELIMENE

Yes, guess who's turned up now? Arsinoé!
I had been hoping that she'd stay away.
The darling's downstairs now with Eliante.
What's on her mind this time? What can she want?

ACASTE

Prim and proper isn't she, Arsinoé?
Prudish and puritan, or so they say.

CELIMENE

It's all hypocrisy. I'm not impressed.
At heart she's just as randy as the rest.
All that disdainful holier-than-thou
hides nothing more holy than a sacred cow.
She *longs* to get her hooks into a man,
but, however hard she tries, she never can.
The sight of others' lovers makes her green
with jealousy and so '*the world's obscene*',
she says, '*the age is blind*' (that's to herself)
because she knows that she's left on the shelf.
Her role as puritan's transparent cover
for her frustrated life without a lover.
She brands all beauty sinful. She's afraid
it puts her feeble 'charms' into the shade.
She'd like a lover, that's what she'd like best,
even (can you imagine it?) Alceste!
If Alceste's nice to me, she's got the nerve
to think I'm trespassing on *her* preserve.
She's so envious, poor dear, she takes delight
in doing me down to others out of spite.
Prim and proper is she. O that's rich.
She's stupid, rude . . . in fact a perfect . . . Dar–

Enter Arsinoé.

–ling! I was worried for you. Here you are!
Nice to see you, Arsinoé, my dear!

70

ARSINOE

It's something that I think you ought to hear.

CELIMENE

It's good you've come.

Exeunt Acaste and Clitandre laughing.

ARSINOE

It's just as well they've gone.

CELIMENE

A drink?

ARSINOE

No, thank you! I've no need of one.
I've always thought true friendship shows up best
and puts sincerity to the surest test
in matters of most importance, such as things
touching on a friend's good name, which brings
me here in haste and genuine concern
to do you and your honour a good turn.
Yesterday I called on people known
for their principles and high moral tone
whose conversation soon came round to you;
your conduct and the scandals that ensue
were not thought proper I'm afraid to say:
the crowds that flock here almost every day
and you encourage, your flirtatiousness,
the goings-on, found censure in excess
of what was just. Of course, you'll be aware
whose side I was on in this affair!
I did everything I could to justify
your good intentions and sincerity,
but, as you well know, even for a friend,
there are some things one simply can't defend,
and even I, reluctantly, confessed
your style of living wasn't of the best.

People imagine things (you know how it is).
They see so many 'improprieties'.
One does hear rumours, dear, but if you chose,
an effort at reform could soon scotch those.
Not that I believe you've gone too far,
God forbid! Well, you know what people are!
They think the slightest rumour's proof of blame.
One must be good in deed as well as name.
I know you'll take this warning as well meant,
a token only of my good intent.
Think about the things I recommend.
Believe me, I speak only as a friend.

CELIMENE

Honestly, I'm grateful for your kind concern,
so grateful, let me straightaway return
the favour done me, and, since you've been so nice,
let me offer *you* some good advice.
I'm very grateful, not at all upset.
Honestly, you've put me in your debt.
The friendship that you proved when you related
all this gossip, now must be reciprocated.
In distinguished company the other day
a discussion started on the proper way
for people to live lives of rectitude.
Your name came up at once: '*That prude,*'
said one, '*she's over-zealous, far too keen
to be the sort of model that I mean.*'
'*Pious fraud,*' said one, another '*Pseud!*'
plus something unrepeatable and pretty lewd.
Nobody found it in him to excuse
the pompous shambles of your moral views,
that coy blush, that clearly put-on pout
whenever a few bad words get flung about,
that prissy, patently transparent *moue*
even if the air's turned slightly blue,

72

that scornful high-horse manner you employ
in all your dealings with the hoi polloi.
Your bitter killjoy sermons that resent
everything that's pure and innocent.
One who professes such concern for God
doesn't go to Mass dressed *à la mode*!
(Their words, not mine) and one who seems so pure
shouldn't spend so much on *haute couture*.
And someone who devotes herself to prayer
reads a Bible, not *Elle* and *Marie Claire*.
She looks like Lady Pious when she prays
but not to the maids she beats and underpays.
She'd daub a fig leaf on a Rubens nude
but with a naked *man* she's not a prude.
I sprang to your defence as best I could,
naturally, but I couldn't do much good.
Denounced their talk as scandal, but no use,
just one good word against so much abuse.
They all ganged up against me. In the end
they came to this conclusion, my dear friend:
best leave the sins of others well alone
until you've made some headway with your own.
Only a long self-searching can equip
someone to be the age's scourge and whip.
And even then reform's best left to them
ordained by God almighty to condemn.
'I know *you'll* take this warning as well meant,
a token only of my good intent.
Think about the things I recommend.
Believe me I speak only as a friend.

ARSINOE

One lays oneself wide open when one tries,
however constructively, to criticise,
but if this is the reaction that I get,
I can see how deeply that you've been upset.

73

CELIMENE

No, not at all. It might be a good thing
if everyone took up this 'counselling'.
Frankness may well open people's eyes
to those parts of themselves they fantasise,
their self-deceptions and their vanities.
We ought to make these little talks routine,
a, say, weekly survey of the social scene.
The latest tittle-tattle, all the chat,
the two of us swap gossip, tit for tat?

ARSINOE

Not much gossip about you comes to my ears.
I'm the usual target for their sneers.

CELIMENE

We celebrate, we praise; we scorn, we scold,
and all depending if we're young or old.
When young, we love, then later we abide
by decorum and act all dignified.
And dignity, I gather, 's no bad ploy
when you've got no more youth left to enjoy.
I've heard it helps a woman sublimate
her inability to snare a mate,
and earns her pure frustration a good name.
When I'm your age I may well do the same
and cultivate your scorn of 'turpitude'.
But twenty's far too soon to be a prude.

ARSINOE

A trivial advantage! No cause to shout
and nothing to get so uppity about.
What difference there is gives you no cause
to brag so rudely of this 'youth' of yours.
But why this tizzy? I'm really at a loss
to know why you flare up and get so cross.

CELIMENE

And I, my dear, have no idea why
you should criticise me in society.
It's not my fault, that I should bear the brunt
of all your spinsterish impoverishment.
There's nothing I can do to change the fact
that lovers want me or my looks attract.
I sympathise. But, look, Arsinoé,
the field's wide open. No one's in your way.

ARSINOE

As if one cared about your lovers. Pooh!
I don't care what great packs sniff after you.
As if your lovers could make me upset.
Lovers aren't so difficult to get.
If a woman seeks attention, and success,
one knows the price she pays, O, dear me, yes.
Is men's 'pure love' entirely what it seems?
Is it your 'character' that fills their dreams?
I doubt it very much. We're all aware
just what you're getting up to everywhere.
There're many women I know well endowed
with all a man could wish, but there's no crowd
of lovers yapping all hours at *their* door.
So what, we ask ourselves, are men here for?
The conclusion that we come to straightaway 's:
Those conquests? Elementary! *She pays.*
It's not for your sweet smile that men come here.
Your little victories must cost you dear.
Don't flaunt your petty triumphs out of spite,
or think your looks give you some sort of right
to sneer at others. God, if anyone
were envious of the victories you've won,
she could, by flinging caution to the wind
like you, get lovers, if she had the mind.

CELIMENE

Then do! Then do! Ha! Ha! I do believe
you've got some secret weapon up your . . . sleeve.

ARSINOE

I think we'd better leave things as they are,
or one of us I'm sure 'll go too far.
Believe me, if I hadn't had to wait,
I'd've gone much sooner, but my driver's late.

CELIMENE

You know you're welcome, dear Arsinoé.
Please don't imagine you must dash away.
And, O how very timely, that Alceste's
come back again. I *must* attend my guests.
I'm sure you won't feel sorry if I go.

Enter Alceste.

I must see what they're doing down below.
Alceste, dear, entertain Arsinoé,
then she won't think me rude if I don't stay.

Exit Célimène.

ARSINOE

So! We're left together for a little chat!
You know, I don't at all object to that.
She couldn't've done better if she'd tried.
I'm overjoyed our visits coincide.
You must realise, Alceste, a woman finds
a lot to love and honour in fine minds.
When I contemplate your gifts, I must confess
I feel immense concern for your success.
But you're neglected and the powers-that-be
've passed you over, I think, shamefully.

ALCESTE

I don't see why the State should condescend
to honour me. What for? I can't pretend

76

I've rendered any service; so why fret?
There's nothing that I've done they *can* forget.

ARSINOE

Not everybody honoured by the State
's done something stirring to commemorate.
Know-how counts, the right time and right place.
That your talents 're passed over 's a disgrace.

ALCESTE

My talents! Nothing there to shout about.
I'm very sure that France gets by without.
You can't expect the Powers-that-be to ferret
men's buried talents out and dig for merit.

ARSINOE

Real talent doesn't need it. It's with good cause
that certain people set high store by yours.
Yesterday I heard your praises sung
in two high circles of the topmost rung.

ALCESTE

There's so much sheer confusion nowadays,
everybody gets fair shares of praise.
It makes the greatest honours seem quite petty
when they're flung about like cheap confetti.
Anyone at all! the lowest of the low
get picture-profiles in *Le Figaro*.

ARSINOE

If only politics attracted you,
then your great talents 'd receive their due.
The slightest glimmerings of interest!
Just say the word and I could do the rest.
I've got good friends who'd easily ensure
you got promotion or a sinecure.

ALCESTE

And what would I do, ME, among such sham?

I shun such places. It's the way I am.
Politics! I'm afraid I'm just not suited.
My lungs can't breathe an air that's so polluted.
I just don't have the qualities of guile
to cut a figure there or 'make my pile'.
The thing I'm best at 's saying what I mean
not double-talk and -think, and saccharine.
The man who can't tell lies won't last two ticks
in the suave chicanery of politics.
I'm well aware that people who aren't 'in'
don't get their ribbons and their bits of tin.
What sort of title could 'the Court' confer
on perfect candour? Mm? *Légion d'honneur?*
But there are advantages – one needn't grovel
or praise the Minister's most recent novel
or be some *grande dame*'s lapdog, or applaud
the so-called humour of some other fraud.

ARSINOE

Well, if you wish, let's leave the matter there.
What worries me far more though 's your affair.
Quite frankly and sincerely I'd prefer
your heart bestowed on anyone but *her*.
You deserve far better, someone far above
the creature you've entrusted with your love.

ALCESTE

Think of what you're saying. You pretend
to be the woman that you slander 's friend . . .

ARSINOE

I know, but I feel affronted, hurt, and sad,
to see the sufferings your poor heart 's had.
I feel for you, my friend, but I'm afraid
I have to tell you that your trust's betrayed.

ALCESTE

Thank you! I appreciate your kind concern.
It's things like that a lover wants to learn!

ARSINOE

My friend she may be, but I've got to say
a fine man like yourself 's just thrown away
on one like Célimène whose love's all show.

ALCESTE

You may be right. I really wouldn't know
what goes on in people's hearts. But it's unkind
to put suspicious thoughts into my mind.

ARSINOE

Of course, if you're quite happy to remain
deceived, there's nothing simpler. I'll refrain.

ALCESTE

No, but innuendoes I can do without.
There's nothing more tormenting than half-doubt.
And I'd be far more grateful if you tried
to tell me facts that could be verified.

ARSINOE

Very well, that's good enough for me!
I'll give you evidence that you can *see*.
Come with me to my house and there I'll give,
once and for all, I hope, proof positive
of the infidelities of Célimène.
Then, if you ever feel like love again,
if may be that Arsinoé can find
some far gentler way of being kind.

Exeunt Alceste and Arsinoé.

Act Two

Enter Eliante and Philinte.

PHILINTE

Never in my life, never have I met
a man so stubborn and so obstinate.
We thought we'd have all night to stand about
before this weird affair got sorted out.
Academicians can't have ever heard
another case so trivial and absurd;
tried everything they knew to budge Alceste,
but, at each attempt to shift him, he'd protest:
No, gentlemen, he says, *No, absolutely not!*
I won't take back a thing. No, not one jot.
What is it that he wants my praises for?
Recommendation for the Prix Goncourt?
It's no dishonour that he can't write well.
One can be bad and still respectable.
A man of great distinction in his way,
brave and brilliant, but not *Corneille!*
His style of living's lavish, and, of course,
he looks magnificent astride a horse;
he's marvellous in many, many ways –
I'll praise his grand munificence, I'll praise
his expert fencing and his spry 'gavotte'
but his poetry, no, absolutely not.
That sort of doggerel, slapdash and slipshod
's best read aloud – before a firing squad!
After fresh persuasions and more parley
the members brought him to a grudged finale,

and almost had to go down on their knees!
This was his concession: *I'm hard to please.
I'm sorry I'm so grudging with my praise.*
(Collapse of stout Académie Française!)
Believe me (to Oronte) *how very sad
it makes me here to say your poem's bad!*
On that the two shook hands. M. Malraux
seemed heartily relieved to see him go.

ELIANTE

He is a *bit* obsessive, I suppose,
but my admiration for him grows and grows.
It's heroic, even noble, how he clings
to his proud motto: *Frankness in all things.*
These days that sort of virtue's very rare.
There should be people like him everywhere.

PHILINTE

The more I know of him the more bizarre
it seems to me his slavish passions are.
Given the kind of star Alceste's born under,
the fact he loves at all 's an earthly wonder.
I'm utterly amazed, but far, far more
that it's your cousin he's a weak spot for.

ELIANTE

Clearly a case of 'Unlike poles attract'.
They haven't much in common, that's a fact.

PHILINTE

From what you've seen, do you believe she cares?

ELIANTE

It's so difficult to say in these affairs.
How *can* one tell, Philinte? I think you'd find
she was confused as well in her own mind.

Sometimes she loves and doesn't quite know why.
Sometimes she swears she does, but it's a lie.

PHILINTE

I rather think our friend 's in for far more
from your dear cousin than he's bargained for.
If I were him I'd turn my thoughts elsewhere
and put my feelings in *your* tender care.

ELIANTE

I can't disguise I care and wouldn't try.
It's things like this demand sincerity.
Although it's not to me his feelings turn
his welfare and not mine's my one concern.
For his sake I'd be only too delighted
if, in the end, our two friends *were* united,
but if it comes about (and it might well,
love always being unpredictable)
things don't work out exactly as he's planned
and Célimène gives someone else her hand,
then I'll be waiting to accept Alceste
and not be bothered that I'm second best.

PHILINTE

And how could I object when I approve
the focus of your interests and love?
Alceste can bear me out on how I've tried
to speak on your behalf and take your side.
But if and when they marry, *if* and *when*
Alceste at last succeeds with Célimène,
and you must put your feelings on the shelf,
I'll gladly, gladly offer you myself.
I'd feel most honoured, absolutely blessed
to offer you my love as second best.

ELIANTE

Ah, Philinte, you're making fun of me!

PHILINTE

No, I'm sincere. I mean it. Seriously.
If this were the occasion, Eliante, I'd lay
my heart wide open; and so I will; one day.

Enter Alceste in a towering fury.

ALCESTE
(*to Eliante*)

Help me punish her! This is the last straw.
My constancy can't stand it any more.

ELIANTE

But what is it?

ALCESTE

I just don't want to live.
I'll kill myself. There's no alternative.
The world could hurtle back to Nothingness
and I'd be stoical. But this! But this!
It's all . . . my love's . . . I can't speak even . . . I . . .

ELIANTE

Now come, Alceste. You must calm down. Please try.

ALCESTE

God in Heaven. How can one reconcile.
something so beautiful and yet so vile.

ELIANTE

But what's happened?

ALCESTE

Over! Done! Who'd've believed . . . ?
She . . . it's Célimène . . . she's . . . *I've been deceived!*

ELIANTE

Are you sure?

PHILINTE

Jealousy creates all kinds
of fantastic monsters in suspicious minds.

ALCESTE

Go away, you! The letter I've got here
in her own writing makes it all too clear.
A letter to . . . Oronte! This envelope
contains her blackened name, my blasted hope.
Oronte! Of all the men *the* unlikeliest!
He wasn't even *on* my rivals' list.

PHILINTE

Letters can be deceptive and the harm
one imagines done a false alarm.

ALCESTE

I've told you once before. Leave me alone.
Bother yourself with problems of your own.

ELIANTE

Now, now, you must keep calm and this disgrace . . .

ALCESTE

. . . is something only you can help me face.
It's to you now that I turn to set me free
from this bitter, all-consuming agony.
Avenge me on your cousin, who betrays
a tenderness kept burning all these days.
Avenge me, Eliante. I'm torn apart.

ELIANTE

Avenge you? How can I?

ALCESTE

                Accept my heart.
Take it, instead of the one who tortures me.
Yes, take it, please. It's simple, don't you see?
By offering you my tenderest emotion,
my care, attention and profound devotion,
by laying all my feelings at your feet,
I can get my own back on her foul deceit.

ELIANTE

As sorry as I am to see you suffer
and not ungrateful for the love you offer,
I can't help wondering when you decide
that everything's been over-magnified
and you've found out you've made too big a fuss,
what happens to your vengeance? And to us?
Lovers' quarrels see-saw, we all know,
backwards and forwards, up/down, to and fro,
bad reports believed, then unbelieved,
sentenced one minute, and the next reprieved.
Even when it's clear, the case quite watertight,
guilt soon becomes innocence, wrong right.
All lovers' tiffs blow over pretty soon,
hated this morning, loved this afternoon.

ALCESTE

No! The knife's been twisted too far in.
I'm absolutely through with Célimène!
Ab-so-lute-ly! No question of retreat.
I'd rather die than grovel at her feet.
Is that her now? It is. I feel my hate
go fizzing up its fuse to detonate!
I'll spring the charge on her. She'll be nonplussed.
Then when I've ground her down into the dust,
I'll bring to you a heart made whole again
and free of the treacherous charms of Célimène.

Enter Célimène.

God, help me master my emotion!

CELIMENE

Ah!

To Alceste.

Now, Alceste, what's all this new commotion?

85

What on earth's the meaning of those sighs,
those terrible black looks, those blazing eyes?

ALCESTE

Of all foul things on Earth I know of few
whose damnable evil 's a patch on you.
If Heaven or Hell, or both combined
spawned worse demons, they'd be hard to find.

CELIMENE

Charming! Thank you! Now that's what I call love.

ALCESTE

It's no laughing matter. I've got proof
of your deceptions. Incontestable! Now
you should blush, not laugh, if you know how.
All my premonitions have proved right.
It wasn't for nothing that my love took fright.
You see. You see. Suspicion's a good scout.
I followed in its trail and found you out.
In spite of your deceit my guiding star
's led me to discover what you are.
Love's something no one has much power over.
Its growth's spontaneous in every lover.
Force is quite useless. Hearts can't be coerced
except if they consent to submit first,
and if, at the very outset, Célimène,
you'd rejected my advances, there and then,
I'd've only had my luck not you to blame,
but to have been encouraged and had the flame
fanned into hopeful fire so shamelessly
's unforgiveable; sheer downright treachery!
And I've got every reason to complain
and every reason now to give full rein
to anger, yes, after such hard blows,
watch out, Célimène, be on your toes,
I'm not responsible for what I do.
My anger's on the prowl because of you.

CELIMENE

Such wild behaviour!

To Philinte.

Too much wine downstairs?

ALCESTE

No, too much Célimène and her affairs.
The baited barb of beauty. Gobble that,
you're hooked, you're skinned, you're sizzling in the fat.

Pause.

Looks are so deceptive. I thought you *must*
've meant sincerity and truth and trust.

CELIMENE

What is it then that's given you offence?

ALCESTE

How very clever! You! all innocence!
Very well then. Straight down to the cause.
Look at this.

Produces letter.

This writing? Is it yours?
Of course! This letter damns you right enough.
There's no plea possible against such proof.

CELIMENE

And is it *this*, that all your upset 's for?

ALCESTE

Look at it, Célimène, and blush some more.

CELIMENE

Why should I blush?

ALCESTE

Brazen as well as sly!
There's no signature and so you'll lie.

CELIMENE

Why should I disown it when it's mine?

ALCESTE

Read it! You're condemned by every line.
Look, and deny you're guilty if you can.

CELIMENE

Really, you're a foolish, foolish man.

ALCESTE

No shrugging off this letter, I'm afraid,
and is it any wonder I'm dismayed
that it's Oronte's love that you really want?

CELIMENE

Who told you that this letter 's to Oronte?

ALCESTE

Those who gave me it. Perhaps there's some mistake?
And if there is, what difference does it make?
Am I less injured, you less stained with shame?

CELIMENE

But if it's to a woman, where's the blame?
Can you interpret *that* as an affront?

ALCESTE

Ah, very clever! Absolutely brilliant!
So that's the way you'll throw me off the scent?
Oh, of course, that finishes the argument.
How dare you try on such deceitful tricks?
Or do you take us all for lunatics?
So now let's see what deviousness you try
to give support to such a blatant lie.
A woman! How can you possibly pretend
this note's intended for a woman friend?
Please explain, to clear yourself, just what
does this mean here . . .

CELIMENE

        I certainly will not!
Your behaviour really puts me in a fury.
What right have you to play at judge and jury?
How dare you say such things? It's a disgrace
to fling such accusations in my face.

ALCESTE

Now let's not lose our tempers or complain.
This expression here now. Please explain . . .

CELIMENE

No! No! I'll do nothing of the kind.
I don't care any more what's on your mind.

ALCESTE

Please explain what proves this letter to be meant
for a woman friend, then I'll relent.

CELIMENE

No, I'd rather you believed it's to Oronte.
It's *his* attentions that I really want.
His conversation, his 'person' pleases me.
So say anything you like and I'll agree.
Carry on your quarrel as you think best,
but don't, don't pester *me* again, Alceste.

ALCESTE

God, could anything more cruel be invented,
and was ever any heart so much tormented?
I come to complain how cruelly I'm used
and in the end it's me who stands accused!
The woman does her damnedest to provoke
my jealousy then treats it as a joke,
lets me believe the worst, then crows, and cackles,
and I can't hack away these dreadful shackles,
the heavy ball and chain, the dangling noose,
I see them very well but can't break loose.

O what I need to steel me 's cold disdain
to scorn ingratitude and sneer at pain.

To Célimène.

You're diabolical! You take a man's weak spots
and tie the poor fool up in subtle knots.
Please clear yourself, it's more than I can bear
to leave the question hanging in the air.
Please don't make me think you love another man.
Show me this note's innocent, if you can.
Try to *pretend* you're faithful. Please, please, try.
And I'll try to pretend it's not a lie.

CELIMENE

Jealousy 's turned your brain, my poor friend.
You don't deserve my love. Pretend? Pretend?
Why should I lower myself to be untrue
I'd like to be informed? To humour you?
Well, really! And if I had another *beau*,
wouldn't I be sincere and tell you so?
Are all my frank assurances in vain
against those fantasies you entertain?
Should they matter? You've had my guarantee.
Even to half-believe them insults me.
A woman who confesses love like this
breaks through great barriers of prejudice.
The so-called 'honour of the sex' prevents
a frank expression of her sentiments.
If a woman's overcome that sense of shame
and the man's not satisfied, then *he's* to blame.
After all the woman's had to struggle through
surely the man could be assured it's true.
Ah! Your suspicions make me angry. You're . . .
you're absolutely not worth caring for.
It's too absurd. I'm really not quite sane
to go on being kind when you complain.

I should find someone else instead of you.
Then all your allegations *would* come true.

ALCESTE

Ah, it never fails to take me by surprise,
my feebleness. Your sweet talk may be lies,
but I must learn to swallow it all whole.
I'm at your faithless mercy, heart and soul.
I'll hang on till the bitter end and see
just how far you'll go with perfidy.

CELIMENE

No, you don't love me as you really ought.

ALCESTE

My love goes far beyond the common sort.
So keen was I to show it that I wished
you were unlovable, impoverished,
a pauper and a beggar and low-born,
an object of derision and of scorn
and with one act of sudden transformation
my love could raise you from your lowly station,
in one fell swoop make up for that poor start,
by making a public offer of my heart,
so that the world could see and know and say:
He made her everything she is today.

CELIMENE

O such benevolence deserves a plaque!
Whatever could I do to pay you back . . .
O here's Dubois. About to emigrate!

Enter Dubois laden with luggage.

ALCESTE

What's this?

DUBOIS

Allow me, sir, to explicate.

ALCESTE

Please do.

DUBOIS

It's something most bizarre. Mysterious.

ALCESTE

But what?

DUBOIS

Yes, very strange, and *could* be serious.

ALCESTE

But how?

DUBOIS

Have I your leave to . . .

ALCESTE

speak, or shout

for all I care, but, quickly, spit it out.

DUBOIS

In front of . . .

ALCESTE

all the world if needs be, man.

For God's sake tell me, clearly, *if* you can.

And *now*.

DUBOIS

The time, sir, 's come to expedite,

to put it rather crudely, sir, our flight.

ALCESTE

Our what?

DUBOIS

Our flight, sir, flight. We must proceed

with all due caution, but at double speed.

ALCESTE

What for, man?

DUBOIS

Sir, once more let me stress
we must leave Paris by the next express.

ALCESTE

Leave Paris, why?

DUBOIS

No time at all to lose.
No time for long farewells or fond adieus.

ALCESTE

What does this mean?

DUBOIS

It means (to specify,
to be absolutely blunt) it means . . . Goodbye!

ALCESTE

I'm warning you, Dubois . . . Dubois, look here.
Start again, at once, and make things clear.

DUBOIS

A person, sir; black looks, black coat, black hat,
appeared, sir, in the kitchen, just like that,
deposited a paper, and then went –
a very legal-looking document.
It looks to me a little like a writ
with stamps and signatures all over it,
some sort of summons, surely, but I'm blessed
if I could make it out, Monsieur Alceste.

ALCESTE

And why, please, does this paper that you say
the man delivered mean our getaway?

DUBOIS

Then after, sir, about an hour or so,
another person called, and *him* you know,
he calls quite often on you, seemed distressed

to find you out tonight, Monsieur Alceste.
Yes, most disturbed, but knowing he could send
dependable Dubois to help his friend,
he urged me, very gravely, to convey,
without procrastination or delay,
this urgent message to my master, sir . . .
his name was . . . just a minute . . . mm . . . mm . . . er . . .

ALCESTE
O never mind his name. What did he say?

DUBOIS
One of your friends, he was, sir, anyway.
He said, and I repeat, sir: *Tell Alceste
he must leave Paris and escape arrest.*

ALCESTE
Escape arrest, and was that all he said?

DUBOIS
Except it would be better if you fled.
He dashed a quick note off for me to bring.
He said the note would tell you everything.

ALCESTE
Give it to me then.

CELIMENE
What's all this about?

ALCESTE
I'm not quite sure. I'm *trying* to find out.

To Dubois.

You, you great idiot, not found it yet?

DUBOIS
(*after a long search*)
I must have left it somewhere . . . I forget . . .

ALCESTE

I don't know what . . .

CELIMENE

Alceste! You ought to sort
this nonsense out at once, you really ought!

ALCESTE

No matter what I do, it seems that fate
's imposed its veto on our *tête-à-tête*.
I've still got many things to say to you.
When I come back, please, one more interview?

Act Three

On stage, Alceste and Philinte.

ALCESTE
No, my mind's made up I've got to go.

PHILINTE
Must you? Really? However hard the blow.

ALCESTE
Coax and wheedle to your heart's content.
My mind's made up, and what I said I meant.
This age is fastened in corruption's claws.
I'm opting out of this foul world of yours.
This world where wrong seems right, and right seems
   wrong
can count me out of it. I don't belong.
After what's happened in my lawsuit, how . . .
how can I possibly remain here now?
Everything that renders life worthwhile,
everything that counters lies and guile –
Justice, Honour, Goodness, Truth and Law
should've crushed that swine, or else what's Justice for?
All the papers said my cause was just
and I'm the one who's trampled in the dust.
Thanks to black perjury that ruthless sinner
whose past's notorious comes off the winner.
Truth drops a curtsey to the man's deceit,
and Justice flops, and crawls to kiss his feet!
He'd get away with anything; he'd quote
some legal precedent, then cut my throat.
His hypocritical grimace never fails –
one quick smirk at the jury tips the scales.

To crown it all the Court gives him a writ.
Harried and hounded by that hypocrite!
Not satisfied with that. Not satisfied,
there's yet another trick the devil's tried.
A pamphlet's just been published, and suppressed.
All booksellers that stock it risk arrest.
This obscene libel seeks to implicate
some of the closest to the Head of State.
Although he hasn't mentioned me by name,
he's dropped hints to the Press that I'm to blame.
And, look at this, this headline here, just look!
SEARCH FOR AUTHOR OF SUBVERSIVE BOOK:
EXPERT OPINION ANALYSES STYLE!
And a picture of Oronte (just *see* that smile!).
Which author does 'expert' Oronte suggest:
'There's only one it could be, that's Alceste.'
Oronte! Someone I tried my very best
to be quite fair with, yes, Oronte, the pest,
coming with his verses for a 'fair' critique,
and when I *am* fair, and, in all conscience, seek
to do justice to the truth and him as well,
he helps to brand me as a criminal.
All this irreconcilable bad blood
and all because his poem was no good!
And if that's human nature God forbid!
If that's what men are like then I'm well rid.
This is the sort of good faith, self-respect,
concern for truth, and justice I expect.
Their persecution 's more than I can face.
Now I'm quitting this benighted place,
this terrible jungle where men eat men.
Traitors! You'll never see my face again.

PHILINTE

I'm pretty sure the problem's not as great
as you make out. If I were you I'd wait.

Whatever charges they've trumped up, Alceste,
you've managed so far to avoid arrest.
Lies can boomerang and choke the liar.
All these tales and scandals could backfire.

ALCESTE

He doesn't mind. He thrives on his disgrace.
His crimes seem licensed. Far from losing face
his stock 's sky-high; he's lionised in town,
and all because he's made me look a clown.

PHILINTE

Up till now most people have ignored
the malicious gossip that he's spread abroad,
and so I wouldn't worry any more
if I were you; at least not on that score.
As for your lawsuit, where you rightly feel
hard done by, you could easily appeal.

ALCESTE

No second hearings! I accept the first.
The last thing that I'd want is it reversed.
Let it stand. Then posterity 'll know
how far corruption and abuse can go,
proof of all the mean and dirty tricks
of Mankind circa 1966.
If it costs 20,000 francs, I'll pay;
I'll pay, and earn the right to have my say,
denounce the age and hate man and dissever
myself from all his wickedness for ever.

PHILINTE

But after all . . .

ALCESTE

       But after all! What, what
do you propose to say about all that
that's not superfluous? You wouldn't dare
try to excuse this sickening affair.

PHILINTE

No! No! Everything you say. Agreed! Agreed!
The world *is* governed by intrigue and greed.
Cunning and fraudulence *do* come off best,
men *ought* to be different, yes, Alceste,
but does man's lack of justice give you cause
to flee society with all its flaws?
It's through these very flaws we exercise
the discipline of our philosophies.
It's virtue's noblest enterprise, the aim
of everything we do in virtue's name.
Supposing probity *were* general,
hearts were open, just and tractable,
what use would all our virtues be, whose point,
when all the world seems really out of joint,
's to bear with others' contumely and spite
without annoyance, even though we're right.
Virtue in a heart can counteract . . .

ALCESTE

Quite a performance that, yes, quite an act!
You've always got so many things to say.
Philinte, your fine talk's simply thrown away.
What reason tells me I already know:
it's for my good entirely if I go.
I can't control my tongue. It won't obey.
I'm not responsible for what I say.
Look at all the trouble I've incurred!
Trouble seems to stalk my every word.
Now, leave me to wait here. And no more fuss!
I've a little proposition to discuss
with Célimène and what I mean to do
's find out what her love is: false or true.

PHILINTE

Let's go up to Eliante. We could wait there.

ALCESTE

I've too much on my mind I must prepare.
You go. I'm better left to nurse this mood
of black resentment here in solitude.
This gloomy little comer suits me best.

Sits.

The perfect setting! O I'm so depressed.

PHILINTE

You'll find yourself bad company in that state.
I'll fetch down Eliante to help you wait.

Exit Philinte. Enter Célimène and Oronte.

ORONTE

I need some proof. It goes against the books
to keep a lover years on tenterhooks.
If you welcome my attentions, as you say,
please stop wavering and name the day.
Some little gesture that would help to prove
that you reciprocate my ardent love.
And all I ask 's Alceste's head on a plate.
Banish him today and don't prevaricate.
Please say to him . . . today . . . please . . . Célimène,
say: *Never show your face round here again!*

CELIMENE

What's happened between you two, I'd like to know?
You thought him marvellous not long ago.

ORONTE

The whys and wherefores just don't signify.
More to the point though 's where your feelings lie.
Keep one of us and set the other free.
You really have to choose: Alceste or me.

ALCESTE

(*emerging from his corner*)

Choose, yes, choose. Your friend here's justified
in his demands which I endorse. Decide!
His impatience is my own, his anguish mine.
I too insist on having some sure sign.
Things can't go on like this indefinitely.
The time has come to choose: Oronte or me!

ORONTE

I've no desire to prejudice your chances
by indiscreet, importunate advances.

ALCESTE

Jealousy or not, I certainly don't want
to share her heart with you, Monsieur Oronte.

ORONTE

And if she chooses your love and not mine . . .

ALCESTE

If it's to *you* her sympathies incline . . .

ORONTE

I'll give up all those hopes I had before . . .

ALCESTE

I swear I'll never see her any more.

ORONTE

Now, you can speak. No need to hum and hah.

ALCESTE

Don't be afraid to tell us how things are.

ORONTE

Only decide which one 's the one for you.

ALCESTE

To clinch the matter, choose between us two.

Pause.

ORONTE

It can't be difficult to pick one out!

ALCESTE

Can you hesitate at all, or be in doubt?

CELIMENE

This isn't the time and place and that's a fact.
O such demands. Please, gentlemen, some tact!
It's not that I've got anything to hide,
my heart's not wavering from side to side,
but what I *do* find difficult to do
's announce my choice in front of both of you.
I think that anything at all unpleasant
shouldn't be spoken with another present.
It's possible to hint one's attitude
without going to extremes and being rude.
I think that gentle clues are quite enough
to let a lover know he's lost his love.

ORONTE

No, not at all. It's frankness that we want.
I've no objections.

ALCESTE

And *I'm* adamant.
I insist. Choose now between our loves.
I surely don't need handling with kid gloves.
You try to keep the whole world on a string.
It's got to end at once, this wavering.
No more half-hints, no titillating clues,
We want it cut and dried: accept/refuse.
Silence itself 's a sort of answer though.
I take it silence means quite simply: NO!

ORONTE

I'm grateful that you've been so down-to-earth.
I second what you say for all I'm worth.

CELIMENE

I'm really quite fed up of this affair.
Demanding this and that! It isn't fair.
Haven't I told you why I hesitate?
Here's Eliante. Ask her. She'll arbitrate.

Enter Eliante and Philinte.

Eliante! Look, I'm the victim of a plot.
They cooked it up together, like as not.
They both go on and on to make me choose,
which one of them I'll have, and which refuse.
They want me to announce it just like that,
one to be chosen, one to be squashed flat.
Please tell them, Eliante, it's just not done.

ELIANTE

If you want allies, sorry, *I'm* not one.
I belong to the opposition. I'm inclined
to side with people who can speak their mind.

ORONTE
(*to Célimène*)

It's pointless your protesting I'm afraid.

ALCESTE

You can't depend on Eliante for aid.

ORONTE

Please speak, and put an end to our suspense.

ALCESTE

Or don't. It doesn't make much difference.

ORONTE

One little word; then let the curtain fall.

ALCESTE

I'll understand if you don't speak at all.

Enter Arsinoé, Acaste, Clitandre.

ACASTE
(*to Célimène*)

Have you got two minutes you can spare for us?
We've got a 'little something' to discuss.

CLITANDRE
(*to Alceste and Oronte*)

A good thing you're here too. The reason why
you'll discover to your horror by and by.

ARSINOE

Forgive me for intruding once again,
but they requested it, these gentlemen,
who turned up at my house in such a state
of agitation to insinuate
such dreadful things against you, dear, that . . . well . . .
they seemed quite utterly incredible.
Of course I couldn't believe that it was you,
knowing how kind you are; and thoughtful too.
I said: *No, it can't be!* The case they made
did seem rather damning, I'm afraid.
Forgetting, then, our little *contretemps*
for 'auld lang syne', my dear, I've come along
with these two gentlemen to hear you clear
yourself at once from this new slander . . . dear.

ACASTE

Yes, let's all be calm and civilised and see
Just how you bluff this out and wriggle free.
This is a letter to Clitandre from you.

CLITANDRE

And this is to Acaste, this *billet doux*.

ACASTE

We won't need any expert to decipher
this all too well-known hand we've all an eye for.
I've had, and so, I know, have all of you,

sizeable amounts of *billet doux*,
so proof's superfluous. This little note
's a fine example, gentlemen, I quote:

Reads.

'My dear Clitandre,
What a strange man you are to moan when I'm in high
spirits and to complain that I'm never so lively as when
I'm not with you. Nothing could be further from the
truth. And if you don't come very soon to beg my
pardon for this insult, I'll never forgive you as long as
I live. That great hulk of a viscount.' (*he ought to have
been here!*) '. . . That great hulk of a Viscount, you
complain of first, isn't my type at all. Ever since I
watched him spitting for at least three quarters of an
hour into a well to make circles in the water, I've not
much cared for him. As for the little marquis,' (*that's me,
gentlemen, though I shouldn't boast*) '. . . As for the little
marquis, who held my hand so interminably yesterday,
he's of no account at all, absolutely insignificant, a
tailor's dummy, that's all the little marquis is. As for that
character in green velvet,' (*your turn, Alceste*) '. . . As
for that character in green velvet well, he's occasionally
amusing with his blunt irascibility and forthright ways,
but there are a million other times when I find him the
world's worst bore. As for the would-be poet,' (*your bit
this*) '. . . as for the would-be poet, who fancies himself
one of the intelligentsia, and tries desperately to pass
himself off as an author, in spite of what everybody tells
him, I can't even be bothered listening any more, and his
prose is about as tedious as his verse. So try to believe
me when I say I don't enjoy myself, quite as much as
you imagine, and that I miss you more than I'd ever
like to say at all those "entertainments" I'm forced to go
to, and that there's nothing quite like the company of
one who loves to add real zest to life.'

CLITANDRE

And now for me!

Reads.

'My dear Acaste,
Your little hanger-on Clitandre, who plays the
languishing lover all the time, is the very last man on
earth I could feel real friendship for. He must be out of
his mind if he's convinced himself that I feel anything
at all for him; and you must be out of yours to believe
that I don't love you. Be reasonable and take a leaf out
of his book, and come and see me as often as you can.
That would be some compensation for my having to
be pestered by Clitandre.'

This does your character enormous credit.
You really are a . . . No, I haven't said it!
We're going now and everywhere we call
we'll show this likeness of you, warts and all.

Exit Clitandre.

ACASTE

I could say much. It's not worth the attempt.
You're quite beneath all anger and contempt.
Your 'little marquis' certainly won't cry:
He's got far better fish than you to fry

Exit Acaste.

ORONTE

So after all those letters that you wrote
you turn on me like this and cut my throat!
You little gadabout, you seem to swear
undying, false devotion everywhere.
I've been a fool, but now the truth has dawned.
I'm grateful for the favour. I've been warned.
I've got my heart back and I'm glad to get it.
My only satisfaction's *you'll* regret it.

To Alceste.

I'm thankful I've escaped this creature's claws.
I won't stand in your way. She's yours; all yours.

Exit Oronte.

ARSINOE
O never have I felt so much disgust.
I'm shocked, I must speak out. I really must.
This fine and worthy man, Monsieur Alceste
(I'm not so much concerned about the rest)
who worshipped you (to everyone's surprise)
Alceste, who thought the sun shone from your eyes,
Alceste . . .

ALCESTE
       I'll handle this if you don't mind.
Please don't waste your time in being kind.
Crusading for my cause in this keen way
's not something I'd feel able to repay.
If, to avenge myself on Célimène,
you think that I'll choose you, please think again.

ARSINOE
What gave you the idea that I did?
As if I'd try to snare you! God forbid!
Such vanity! There's something monstrous in it,
if you can think such things a single minute.
This madam's surplus stock 's a merchandise
I'd be an idiot to overprize.
Come down off your high horse before you fall.
My class of person 's not your type at all!
Dance attendance on that creature there.
You and that woman make a perfect pair!

Exit Arsinoé.

ALCESTE

I've waited in the wings all this long time
patiently watching this strange pantomime.
Have I proved my powers of self-control
and may I now . . .

CELIMENE

unburden your whole soul.
Yes, go on. I deserve all your complaint.
You're free to criticise without restraint.
I'm wrong and I admit it. Enough, enough,
no more pretending, no more lies and bluff.
I could despise the anger of the rest,
but you I know I've wronged, my poor Alceste.
Your resentment's justified. I realise
how culpable I must seem in your eyes.
All the evidence you've been given leads
to conclusive proof of my misdeeds.
There's every reason why you should detest
me utterly. You have my leave, Alceste.

ALCESTE

Ah, you traitor, I only wish I could.
If tenderness were crushable, I would.
I want, I want to let myself give way
to hate, but my heart just won't obey.

To Eliante and Philinte.

Just how degrading can a passion get?
Now watch me grovel. You've seen nothing yet.
There's more to come. Just stay and watch the show.
You'll see my weakness reach an all-time low.
Never call men wise. Look how they behave.
There's no perfection this side of the grave.

To Célimène.

You've no idea what 'being faithful' means . . .

But I'm willing to forget these painful scenes,
concoct excuses for your crimes and say
the vicious times and youth led you astray,
provided that, on your part, you consent
to share my self-inflicted banishment,
away in the country, where I want to find
a life-long haven and avoid mankind.
In this way only, in the public eye,
can you do penance for the injury
those letters caused, and only if you do,
can I pick up the threads of loving you.

CELIMENE

Renounce the world before I'm old and grey?
Go to your wilderness and pine away?

ALCESTE

But if your love were anything like mine,
you'd forget the outside world and never pine.

CELIMENE

I'm only twenty! I'd be terrified!
Just you and me, and all that countryside!
I'm not sufficiently high-minded to agree
to such a fate. It's simply just not me!
But if my hand's enough and you're content
to marry and stay in Paris, I consent,
and marriage . . .

ALCESTE

    No, now I hate you, loathe, abhor.
This beats anything you've done before.
If you can't think of me as your whole life
as I would you, you'll never be my wife.
This last humiliation's set me free
from love's degrading tyranny.

 To Eliante.

To me you're beautiful, your virtue's clear,
and you're the only one who seems sincere.
I started to admire you long ago
and hope you'll let me go on doing so,
but, please, with all my troubles, understand
if now I hesitate to seek your hand.
I feel unworthy of it. It seems that Fate
didn't intend me for the married state.
Cast off by one not fit to lace your shoes,
my love's beneath your notice. You'd refuse.

ELIANTE

Don't blame yourself, my friend. I understand.
I'm sure there'll be no problem with my hand.
I think a little pressure might persuade
your good friend here to volunteer his aid.

PHILINTE

This makes my deepest wishes all come true.
I'd shirk no sacrifice in serving you.

ALCESTE

I hope you'll always feel so, and both win
a joy and happiness that's genuine.
For me, betrayed on *all* sides and laid low
by heaped injustices, it's time to go,
and leave man floundering in this foul morass
where vice goes swaggering as bold as brass,
and go on looking for a safe retreat
where honesty can stand on its own feet.

Exit Alceste.

PHILINTE

Let's go after him, and see if we can't find
some way (*any* way!) to change his mind.

*Exeunt Philinte and Eliante together. Célimène
remains seated, alone.*

PHAEDRA BRITANNICA

after Racine's
Phèdre

Introduction

Prétends-tu m'éblouir des Fables de la Grèce? ...
Quoiqu'au-dessus de nous ils sont ce que nous sommes,
Et comme nous enfin Héros sont des Hommes.
Pradon: Phèdre et Hippolyte (1677)

I

Racine took two years to write *Phèdre,* and I took two years to adapt it for the English stage. My methods, such as they are, a mixture of what Dryden called metaphrase and paraphrase, are no more original than Johnson's *Vanity of Human Wishes* or than Racine's who made his play out of the Greek of Euripides and the Latin of Seneca, as well as earlier dramatic versions of the myth in his own tongue. In a pre-Romantic age I would feel little need for self-justification, nor feel I need be defensive about the poet's role as adapter. Nothing better could be said on that issue than what was written by Lion Feuchtwanger in his poem 'Adaptations' (1924) composed after collaborating with Brecht on their version of *Edward II* after Marlowe:

> I, for instance, sometimes write
> Adaptations. Or some people prefer the phrase
> 'Based on', and this is how it is: I use
> Old material to make a new play, then
> Put under the title
> The name of the dead writer who is extremely
> Famous and quite unknown, and before
> The name of the dead writer I put the little word 'After'.
> Then one group will write that I am

Very respectful and others that I am nothing of the
  sort and all
The dead writer's failures
Will be ascribed
To me and all my successes
To the dead writer who is extremely
Famous and quite unknown, and of whom
Nobody knows whether he himself
Was the writer or maybe the
Adaptor.

Critics of *Phaedra Britannica* have provided a spectrum
of opinion as wide and as contradictory as that in the
Feuchtwanger poem, from the English critic (to whom
Racine was, no doubt, 'quite unknown') who accused me
of taking a 'crowbar' to the original, to the French critic
Jean-Jacques Gautier writing in *Le Figaro* and finding that
in my version '*la noblesse linéaire, la flamme, la grandeur
de l'ouvrage original est préservée*'.

II

When a play becomes a 'vehicle' only, the greater part of
it has died. If we go to see *Phèdre,* wrote Roland Barthes,
it's on account of a particular great actress, a certain number of felicitous lines, some famous *tirades* set against a
background of obscurity and boredom. We tolerate the
rest. Barthes was writing after the production by Jean
Vilar at the TNP in 1957 with Maria Casarès, and his
reluctant conclusion was prominently displayed in the
programme of a production I saw in Paris in 1974 at the
Théâtre Essaion: '*Je ne sais pas s'il est possible de jouer
Racine aujourd'hui. Peut-être sur scène ce théâtre est-il
aux trois-quart mort.*' Similarly Jean-Louis Barrault in his
Mise en scène de Phèdre (1946) writes that audiences went

to see Sarah Bernhardt as Phèdre, but they didn't go to see the *pièce*. They didn't even go to see the divine Sarah in the *entire* role, but the two scenes in which she excelled, the declaration of Act II and the despair of Act IV. '*Phèdre n'est pas un concerto pour femme,*' Barrault warns us, '*mais une symphonie pour orchestre d'acteurs.*' The solution to the problem offered by Barrault could well apply to the revival of any classic play that has become simply a one-role play by coming adrift from its social origins: '*Phèdre femme doit de nouveau s'incorporer dans Phèdre tragédie.*' A play is 'about' everyone who sets foot on the stage, principals and mutes alike. The way to re-energise *Phèdre*, setting aside for the moment the well-nigh insuperable problems of doing that for an English audience, is to rediscover a *social* structure which makes the tensions and polarities of the play significant again. To make the roles, neglected for the sake of the 'vehicle' role, meaningful again. To grasp the *play* entire. It is only when the characters around her are duly reinstated that the central figure can be seen in her true light. One can begin by going back to the title displayed on the original edition of Racine's text in 1677: *Phèdre et Hippolyte.* In order to correct the theatrical imbalance and sharpen the focus, one needs such, perhaps overloaded, assertions as Leo Spitzer's that Thésée is the most important person in the play. He is after all left alive with the awareness of the consequence of his actions, and the knowledge of the deaths of his wife and son. He has the last word.

III

There is a mode of literary criticism, built upon the ruins of neoclassicism, and deriving from a period which was beginning to value intensity of experience at the expense of structure, a mode of criticism that extracts the principle

'beauties' of a work, Arnoldian 'touchstones', as though
the essence of poetry resided in a few reverberant lines,
and long works like Homer's were nothing more than a
handful of titillating monosticha, rooted out of grey un-
appealing tracts by Romantic truffle-hounds. It's an attitude represented at its extreme by Poe's opinion that 'there
is no such thing as a long poem'. It made assayer Matthew
Arnold call Dryden and Pope 'classics of our *prose*'. Racine
has suffered similarly in France. Henri de Montherlant
thought that there were only twenty-seven lines of 'poetry'
in the whole *oeuvre* of Racine, some 20,000 lines. Jean
Dutourd thought that Racine's Alexandrines were ninety-
nine per cent rhetoric and one per cent 'poetry'. One line
which has consistently seemed to glitter from all this dross
is one which Flaubert thought the most beautiful line in
the whole of French literature, and which Proust valued
for its *beauté dénuée de sens*. It's a line which, typically,
can only be understood, like most of Arnold's rhapsodical
nuggets, by referring it back to the total context from
which it was prised, by reconstructing the strata from
which it was hastily lifted. One has to assume the responsibility of the archaeologist among so many opportunist
treasure-seekers. The line in question is the famous one
spoken by Hippolyte describing Phèdre as

La fille de Minos et de Pasiphaé.

Admittedly it is a crucial line. A line full of mythical rever-
berations. For those who know the myth. And it's not
enough to refer the *reader*, as most French editions do, to
the *tableau généologique* or the *index mythologique*. For
one thing we are preparing a piece for the stage and not
the study. Tableaux and indices are not theatrical, at least
in a would-be Racinian recreation. The line is the key to
the inner struggle of Phèdre, to her essential torment. For
those who are at home in the obscure genealogies of
Crete! As an eighteenth-century commentator puts it, this

line 'semble préparer le spectateur à ce caractère mélangé
de vices et de remords que le poète donne a Phèdre'. The
key word in this is mélangé. Many simply stress that the
line signals the bad heredity of Phèdre, as if it were simply
a case of the mother, Pasiphaë, though R. C. Knight ten-
tatively suggests that 'Minos may perhaps stand for moral
conscience'. Both elements of Phèdre's parentage are of
equal importance. The problem about expanding the line,
and absorbing into it the facts given in study texts by
genealogies impossible to project theatrically, is that the
line occurs in a context of nervous reticence. It is an old
story for Hippolyte and Théramène. Théramène cuts off
Hippolyte with an abrupt 'J'entends'. The line foreshadows
the causes of Phèdre's shame and her need to break
through the barriers of shame; it articulates her tension,
without Hippolyte having to transgress his own sense of
propriety by being specific. It is an 'enough said' situation.
The polarities represented by Minos and Pasiphaë are
those which maintain the tension of the whole play and
not simply the character of Phèdre. Minos and Pasiphaë,
an emblematical marriage, are the opposite poles of the
human consciousness. Minos (whose function we cannot
ignore and who is given a disastrously misleading emphasis
in Robert Lowell's epithet 'homicidal') is one of the three
judge figures in Greek mythology. He is the judge who
punishes crime, as opposed to Aeacus, who represents
division of property, and Rhadamanthus, the rewarder of
virtue. Interiorised psychologically, as he is in Phèdre, he
is that part of our selves which is judgement, prescription,
that part that creates moral codes, imposes laws, fixes
limits, the 'frontiers' of experience, defines the acceptable,
and punishes transgression. Pasiphaë is the transgressor of
the codes created by Minos, that part of our selves that
hungers for every experience, burns to go beyond the frontiers of current acceptability, specifically, in her case,
to gratify her sexuality with a bull, incur the guilt of

forbidden bestiality. She is what Henri de Montherlant made of her in his play *Pasiphaé* (1928), the woman who wants to transcend morality, accept *every* part of her nature, however 'animal' or 'bestial' it has been branded by the law-makers, to assert that nothing is unhealthy or forbidden. She rejects the codes of her husband Minos. The Minos/Pasiphaë duality is yet another statement of 'civilisation and its discontents'. In that sense we are all children of Minos and Pasiphaë. The wedlock of Minos and Pasiphaë is a dynamic power struggle for the upper hand fraught with matrimonial tension, uneasy even in brief armistice. The struggle lives on in their daughter Phèdre with the father Minos continually more assertive. I have isolated the function of Minos, and made him simply 'the judge', who represents internally the moral conscience, and is, in the exterior political world, a representative of 'the rule of reason', like the ambiguously placed Governor himself, only utterly unimpeachable:

> a judge so unimpeachable and just
> to have a wife destroyed by bestial lust!

That may well seem a far cry from the cherished

> *La fille de Minos et de Pasiphaé*

and it is not intended as its formal equivalent. I have had to redistribute the energies of that renowned line over my whole version, surrender the more obvious nugget for a concession to work the whole seam more painstakingly.

The problem, then, of Phèdre, as of us all, is that she contains within herself both Minos *and* Pasiphaë. That is the essence of the genealogy. She condemns the mother/female/accepter/'transgressor' in herself with the voice of the father/the male voice of punishment/repression/rigid social code. That is the psychological dynamic of the character. As with the outer political dynamic I have sought to create an equivalent, but redistributed, nexus of imagery for the internal tensions. The 'bestiality' of Pasiphaë is seen as part of the threat of the alien, of that personified, often apostrophised INDIA upon which the exiled British projected all that was forbidden in their own culture. The temple sculpture and painting of India depicts, in a spirit of acceptance, what one particular picture reproduced in the National Theatre programme for *Phaedra Britannica* called 'the love of all creatures'. It is a painting from Rajasthan of circa 1780 showing not only pairs of animals copulating but women in joyful congress with a variety of beasts. One could well apply to it the long passage of the power of Venus from Seneca's *Phaedra*:

> The dolphin of the raging sea doth love:
> the elephants by Cupid's blaze do burn:
> Dame Nature all doth challenge as her own,
> And nothing is that can escape her laws.

That in the translation of John Studley, 1581, the first English version of Seneca's play. But the Indian picture goes just a little further, extends the frontiers of Venus into bestiality. This is quite beyond the limits of acceptability for the British in India, totally alien, though no doubt present in the dark recesses of the imagination. To Western eyes India seemed actually to celebrate a world where everything was sexually possible. The Western reaction was both fascinated (Pasiphaë) and repressive (Minos). It is the voice of Minos we hear speaking through Lieutenant General Sir George MacMunn:

> In the description of the astounding indecency which to Western eyes the temples of Conjeveram, of Jaganath and the Black Pagoda offer, mention has been made of the bestiality recorded: the mingling of humans and animals in intimate embrace . . . The ancient religions did permit such terrible abominations and India has always apparently been more openly acquainted with such matters than the rest of the world.

When the guilt of Pasiphaë, which, it should be noted, is never specifically referred to in Racine, although it is, characteristically, in Seneca, is mentioned in my version it is intended with reference to what is depicted in the temples listed by Sir George MacMunn:

> Mother! Driven by the dark gods' spite
> beyond the frontiers of appetite!
> a *judge's* wife! Obscene! Such bestialities
> Hindoos might sculpture on a temple frieze.

And the monster which kills Thomas Theophilus (Hippolyte) and seems to represent the suppressed passions of all the principle characters is described by Burleigh as being

> like one of those concoctions that one sees
> in dark recesses on a temple frieze.

But on the faces of the women in the painting from Rajasthan, women being joyfully pleasured by everything from a peacock to an elephant, we have the spirit of Pasiphaë seeking the total joy that seems to lie beyond all remorse and moral codes. One senses the Yeatsian cry:

> When such as I cast out remorse
> So great a sweetness flows into the breast
> We must laugh and we must sing,
> We are blest by everything
> Everything we look upon is blest.

The nearest my Memsahib ever gets to understanding such a mood is, ironically, in her envy of the young lovers she imagines untrammelled by the agonies that destroy her:

> To follow one's feelings through nature's course
> without recriminations and remorse,
> not to feel criminal, and meet as though
> the sun shone on one's love and watched it grow!
> Ah! Every day they must wake up and see
> vistas with no black clouds, and feel so free!

The tensions of the Minos/Pasiphaë polarity are maintained too in my images of the hunter, the Victorian type,
projecting his inner repressed desires on to the fauna of
India, amassing tigerpelts, covering his walls with animal
heads, collecting obsessive proof that he is in control of
his own animal nature, that he is the fit representative of
'the rule of reason'. The Governor himself is renowned as
a great hunter, naturally, often scorning the rifle with its
distant rationally controlled despatch for closer gladia-
torial combat with a bayonet. The images of the hunt are
maintained, in one degree or another, in all the versions of
the story: Euripides, Seneca. Racine. At the beginning of
the Euripides play Aphrodite (Venus) herself complains of
Hippolytus that he denies her not cnly by ignoring women
but also by driving wild animals off the face of the earth.
Venus, the principle of generation, replenishes the stocks
exhausted by the hunter. The nurse in Seneca tells the
destructively chaste young man as much, imagining the
world as an unpopulated desert without the influence of
the love goddess:

> Excedat, agedum, rebus humanis Venus,
> Quae supplet ac restituit exhaustum genus;
> Orbis iacebit squallido turpis situ;
> Vacuum sine ullis classibus stabit mare;
> Alesque coelo deerit, et silvis fera . . .   469–73

The first speech of the Seneca play is one in praise of the
excitement of hunting and a list of quarry. Ironically one
of the beasts listed – 'latis feri cornibus uri', probably some
sort of buffalo – is described in an edition of 1902 as 'ex-
tinct' owing to the untiring perseverance of the hunter!
There is another element to the obsessive animal-slaying.
What is part of human nature, but not acknowledged, tends
to be labelled 'animal'. Even in today's papers behaviour
which does not even transcend the limits of acceptability
as much as Pasiphaë's is labelled by the Minos voice of

judgement from the British bench as 'animal' or 'bestial'. We are very nervous of our status on what used to be called 'the scale of Creation'. And this is the point of the animal abuse with which the Memsahib finally rejects her 'lower' self in the shape of her ayah, or with which the Governor denounces Thomas Theophilus, when he tries to reimpose *within* his household the rigid limits he himself has clearly gone beyond outside the home.

The Governor's own position on this shifting scale of transgression and animality, with Minos at one end and Pasiphaë at the other, is decidedly ambiguous. The Governor both accepts and represses, he is both law and transgression. He is in many ways the classic male hypocrite. He avidly seeks experience outside the limits of his own code, or the code his society ostensibly subscribes to, but to do so he finds it necessary, as many Victorians did, to adopt 'native costume'. Sir Richard Burton is only one of the most well known of models for such behaviour. In some ways the Governor carries the whole burden of the male Victorian dilemma. I wanted to state the conflict at a social and political level as well as at the psychological, as it is in Racine in slightly different form. Another redistribution. I took the clues for this from what the Victorian imagination found not only in its Indian experience, but also in its assessment of the Theseus legend itself. All ages have used the long surviving classical heroes like Odysseus, Aeneas, Theseus to realise their own natures and preoccupations. W. B. Stanford's *The Ulysses Theme* has charted the fortunes of Odysseus from Homer to Joyce, and Anne C. Ward's *The Quest for Theseus* (Pall Mall Press, London, 1970) has done more or less the same for the hero of our present play. To the Victorians who often cast themselves into the roles of classical heroes reborn, Theseus was a type of Victorian. John Ruskin in Letter XXII dated 1872 of *Fors Clavigera* sees in Theseus:

The great settler or law-giver of the Athenian state; but he is so eminently as the Peace-Maker, causing men to live in fellowship who before lived separate, and making roads passable that had been infested with robbers and wild beasts. He is that exterminator of every bestial and savage element.

With this as a guide one may specify merely from those combats with monsters, grotesques, giants and brigands that Racine uses:

> Les monstres étouffés et les brigands punis,
> Procuste, Cercyon, et Scirron et Sinnis,
> Et les os dispersés du giant d'Epidaure,
> Et la Crète fumant du sang du Minotaure.

The accounts of early 'law-giving', the establishment of 'the rule of law' in British India, read like a British version of the same kind of heroic, semi-mythical exploit. And not simply the obvious sources like Sleeman's account of the suppression of Thuggee, legendary brigands and murderers worthy of any Theseus, but others mentioned always in mythologising tones by, for example, James Douglas in his *Bombay and Western India* (1893): 'England is the St George that has slain the great dragon of infanticide which among the Jhadejas ravaged Kach and Kathiawar.' 'Jauhar, that Cyclopean monster of self-immolation', 'the Hashashin' (from whom we derive our word assassin), 'Dacoits', 'Aghori Cannibals', 'the anthropophagous Mardicura'. Douglas is also typical when he dramatises in a mythological almost hagiographical way the tiger-slaughter of, for example, Sir James Outram, who in ten years was present at the deaths of 191 tigers, 15 leopards, 25 bears and 12 buffaloes. He doesn't mention what Aphrodite thought of Sir James Outram but he hails him as 'another St Paul, [who] had been a day and a night in the deep and fought with wild beasts'. 'The wild beasts and wilder men' of accounts like Douglas's of the establishing of 'the rule of law' in British India represent the same stage of civilisation of the Greeks before Theseus, and the Victorians saw their own confrontation in his. So the Governor in *Phaedra Britannica* is, as John Ruskin wrote, 'that exterminator of every bestial or savage element', but, at the same time, he is also, as someone called Sir Richard Burton, 'an authority on all that relates to the bestial element in man'. This authority is acquired, of course, as the Governor, who represents 'the rule of reason' and suppresses alien bestiality, while, at the same time, as his other ('lower') self he explores his own animality in his forays 'in native costume'. It is with these two contrasting elements in his father that Thomas Theophilus has to struggle. In an article in *MacMillan's Magazine* for August 1889 Walter Pater adds an important qualification to a summary of the character of Theseus that, in other respects, is similar to Ruskin's. His Theseus:

> figures, passably, as a kind of mythic shorthand for civilisation, making roads and the like, facilitating travel, suppressing various forms of violence, *but many innocent things as well.*

As law-giver, then, Theseus/Thésée/the Governor shares an element of repression with the father of Phaedra/Phèdre/the Memsahib. But only part. The other side of his nature, the seeker of new experiences, especially sexual, often 'in disguise' precisely because he cannot relate the two halves of his nature, goes hand in hand with the hunter of beasts and the suppressor of bestial custom. That which he is most fascinated by he represses most ruthlessly. He is a kind of mythic shorthand, if you like, for civilisation *and* its discontents.

The Khan who imprisons the Governor in my version of 'a season spent in Hell' lies, on this scale of transgression, somewhere between the Governor and Pasiphaë. There is even a slight note of envy perhaps in these lines of the Governor's:

My captor was a beast, obscene, perverse,
given to practices I won't rehearse,
to crude carnalities that overrode
every natural law and human code.
He'd draw the line at nothing. No taboo
would stop him doing what he wanted to.

The Governor has gone beyond 'the frontier' both geographically and psychologically. Some of the vocabulary of territory from our Anglo-Indian experience marks the boundaries very well. 'The frontiers of appetite . . . of virtue . . . of blood.' The Governor has gone beyond 'the frontier', beyond the Indus, known everywhere as 'the forbidden river'. H. Bosworth Smith in his *Life of Lord Lawrence* speaks of the Khyber Pass as 'the forbidden precincts over whose gloomy portals might well have been inscribed the words of Dante':

All hope abandon, ye who enter here.

So the hellish overtones, the Stygian symbolism, were created for me by those with some historical experience of the Anglo-Indian period I chose for my setting. Whatever the Governor has experienced, and he is, possibly through fear or shame, vaguely unspecific, he has finally seen the limits of the acceptable. His version of hell is being subjected to another's unlimited will, and suffering in the way that many victims of his casual sexual whims might well have suffered. His experience is a vision of the monstrous, the non-human other, beyond all human access and control, even for a 'law-giver', something more terrible than mere animal or beast, something that cannot finally be suppressed or mounted on a Residency wall, nor even physically embraced. This monster defeats both Minos and Pasiphaë. A monster to whom victims must be fed.

('Is there not a home among us that has not paid blood tribute to that relentless monster?' writes an Anglo-Indian lady, meaning India.) The Governor's vision is probably a glimpse of the monster that finally destroys his son. Whatever the experience he has had of Hell it is one which makes him long for the circumscribed, apparently ordered world of his marriage and home. But the boundaries of that he finds are now shaken, the barriers in need of reconstruction, the edges blurred between inner and outer, Hell and earth . . .

A season spent in Hell, I've no desire
for whiffs of brimstone from the household fire.

IV

Neoclassical plays are about sex and politics. From as early as classical times there has been a healthily vulgar if slightly overdone satiric scorn for Phaedra's problems. The taboo of incest between stepmother and stepson seems irrelevant in societies with different kinship restraints. It is easy for us to feel self-satisfied at what we think of as our own permissiveness and to sneer at sexual problems which were at the time agonisingly real. If literature is what Ezra Pound said it was, 'news that stays news', then dramatic agony should stay agony, but this is difficult when the tensions involved have come adrift from their social origins. To Ovid, the Roman poet of sexual opportunism, Phaedra's passion was not only not incestuous, Hippolytus had to be chivvied by her beyond *his* consciousness of taboo:

Nec, quia privigno videar coitura noverca
   Terruerint animos nomina vana tuos
Ista vetus pietas, aevo moritura futuro,
Rustica Saturno regno tenente fuit.
                    'Phaedra Hippolito' – *Heroides* III

And this in the translation of poet/dramatist Thomas Otway who also did a version of Racine's *Bérénice* into heroic couplets:

> How can'st thou reverence thy Father's Bed,
> From which himself so Abjectly is fled?
> The thought affrights not me, but me enflames;
> Mother and Son are notions, very Names
> Of Worn out Piety, in Fashion Then
> When old dull Saturn rul'd the Race of men.
> But braver Jove taught pleasure was no sin,
> And with his sister did himself begin.

These attitudes to a 'Worn out Piety', repeated often enough throughout the ages, are mild enough compared with a version of the story published only five years after Racine's play in Alexander Radcliffe's *Terrestrial Hymns and Carnal Ejaculations* (1682). This is a Phaedra Britannica, isolated in 'a Farm-House in Putney in Surrey', who has no feelings of restraint whatsoever, either Euripidean Greek or neo-classical French:

> When Young, I cou'd have cur'd these am'rous stings
> With Carrots, Radishes, or such like things;
> Now there's no pleasure in such Earthly cures,
> I must have things apply'd as warm as yours.
> Where lies the blame, art thou not strong, and young?
> Who would not gather fruit that is well hung?

In this case Pasiphaë has triumphed over Minos, and re-working the passage already quoted from Ovid and Otway, Radcliffe has:

> Wee'd no such opportunity before:
> Your Father is at London with his Whore.
> Therefore I think 'tis but a just design,
> To cuckold him, and pay him in his coin.
> Besides he ne're was marry'd to your Mother,

He first whor'd her, and then he took another.
What kindness or respect ought we to have
For such a Villain and perfidious Knave?
This should not trouble, but provoke us rather
With all the speed we can to lye together.
I am no kin to you, nor you to me,
They call it Incest but to terrifie.
Lovers Embraces are Lascivious Tricks
'Mongst musty Puritans and Schismaticks.

This is that 'Anglo-Saxon irreverence' that Michael Billington mentioned in his review of *Phaedra Britannica*. One sees it too in Stevie Smith's poem 'Phèdre'. And very necessary it is too, though it scarcely helps to recreate the Racinian mode in modern English. We read such pieces in early rehearsals, partly for the couplets, but also to draw the fire of cheerful vulgarity before we tackled the main text. It's an irreverence not confined to our attitude to inaccessible foreign classics, and I associate it in my mind with one of my culture heroes, the comedian 'Professor' Leon Cortez, who offered his own cockneyfications of Shakespeare, reducing the high-flown poetry of kings to an earthy demotic. Nor is such irreverence purely Anglo-Saxon, even towards Racine. Far from it. In June 1974 I saw a production of *Phèdre* I have already referred to, directed by Régis Santon at the Théâtre Essaion, which played the Racinian text as vulgar farce, a compound of Bunuel, Racine and Feydeau, with *Tristan and Isolde* as background music, and a vaguely Latin American setting, something like Torre Nilsson's film *La Casa del Angel*. The production had simply given up the struggle to present the play on its own terms, and enjoyable as it was as a lively piece of juvenile iconoclasm, very necessary for the French classic theatre, it gave no help whatsoever to one desperately seeking access to the play for equally, if not more, irreverent English audiences. With this constant sense of total subversion I had, even more carefully, to consider solutions to the play which would place the problem in a society where the sense of transgression was once more an agonising burden. Sexual problems do not occur in a vacuum, in a theatrical never-never land, but are created by social codes. The period I chose eventually, after many false starts and crablike researches, envisaged a particular society, early Victorian Britain, with a rigid code made even more formally defensive by being placed in the alien environs of sensual India.

The politics of the play are also obscured by genealogical complications, with which we no longer have any spontaneous rapport, and distanced by our distaste for the absolute monarchy of the court of Louis XIV. Even the translator cannot shirk his responsibility for historical criticism.

Everywhere in the imagery of seventeenth-century poetry, prose and drama, in England and France, the psychological structure of man is seen as an interiorisation of the political. 'The Government of Man', writes the Cambridge Platonist, Benjamin Whichcote, 'should be the Monarchy of Reason; it is too often a Democracy of Passions.' Passions are elsewhere in Dryden

> unreasonable things
> That strike at Sense, as Rebels do at Kings.

When Dryden came to paraphrase the famous Latin hymn *Veni Creator Spiritus* the simple lines:

> infirma nostri corporis
> virtus firmans perpeti

become a typical piece of the politically expressed psychology I mean:

> Our Frailties help, our vice controul;
> Submit the Senses to the Soul;
> And when Rebellious they are grown
> Then lay thy hand and hold 'em down.

The alignment of political synonyms in such imagery is: Reason/King/Rule/Monarchy/(to which series we can add *raj* = rule) on the one hand and what they restrain on the other: Passions/Mob/Democracy/('the Natives'). As Martin Turnell, the best English commentator on Racine, points out: 'there are only two classes in Racine: masters and servants, the rulers and the ruled, royalty and the people'. Elsewhere, discussing the psychology of Corneille and Racine, he writes that 'reason has to operate *tyrannically* and repress by force an uprush of the senses'. Hence 'the rule of law'; the use of words like 'seditious' and 'mutinous' of the passions, hence also the time of the piece, defined as taking place a few years before the Mutiny. As I used the prospect of *les événements* of 1968 in Paris as a political, historical 'measure' of the realities of my setting of *Le Misanthrope* and of Alceste's status as a critic of society, so in *Phaedra Britannica* I imagine the tensions of the play continuing into the Indian Mutiny, 1857 (the year also of the Obscene Publications Act). My text demands that the political realities of Racinian society are reinterpreted physically, realised literally in 'black and white'. I sought to re-energise critically the political content by aligning it with the British 'Imperial dream', which like Goya's dream of reason, 'produces monsters'.

V

Aphrodite speaks in Euripides. In Seneca, Venus is merely addressed. But even in Euripides the gods are, as his translator Philip Vellacott puts it, 'no more than dramatic fictions'. The gods in Racine, as Martin Turnell points out, are 'projections of basic human impulses which means that in *Phèdre* they belong to the realm of psychology rather than theology'. '*Venus, c'est Phèdre, c'est Hippolyte . . . Neptune est dans Thésée,*' writes Jean-Louis Barrault in his production notes. The British projected their own suppressed nature on to the continent they subdued, personifying a destructive INDIA, devastating to those who gave in to its powers, who were seduced by its nakedly obvious allure. Personification is general throughout the literature and memoirs of British India. Everything psychologically alien or suppressed becomes 'India' or 'the dark gods' or, not detached enough to be theologically accurate, an apostrophised Hindu deity like Siva or some other menacing god from a bewilderingly diverse pantheon. Here, for example, is an Englishwoman writing about the 'hot weather':

> One has to experience the coming of the Hot Season to understand something of the worship of Siva – Creator and Destroyer – the Third Person of the Hindu Trinity. For its approach – swift, relentless and inevitable – is like that of a living and sensate force – like the visible work of that terrible yet withal beneficent God who destroys and tramples all things beneath His feet in an ecstatic harmonious dance, that He may create them anew. For in a sense there is a necessity for the hot weather. The intensity of the sun's power cracks and cleaves the dry, obdurate earth, in order that the blessed rains of the Monsoon may irrigate and revivify the whole, jaded, exhausted face of the land.

And as Jean-Louis Barrault speaks of the tragedy of *Phèdre,* giving the arc and cathartic trajectory of the play the same kind of cumulative, meteorological image, as *'un de ces orages de fin août',* it seems to make Siva, as present in the British imagination, particularly fitted to preside over the passion of *Phaedra Britannica.* The same woman goes on to describe her feelings of helplessness in the Indian heat (which another woman Mrs E. M. Croker likens to some 'cruel vindictive animal') in terms which, typically, create the sense of powerful alien forces:

And finally there is the close, hot evening, and an airless night of tossing and turning, of trying to find one cool spot in one's bed, giving it up in despair, and lying in still resignation to look up at the uncaring stars above the gently flapping punkah, helpless beneath the destroying feet of Siva.

Such projections onto an alien divinity are very common in Anglo-Indian writing, and they tend to stand for those things that are felt to be outside the sphere of reason, order and justice (or the current concepts of them) which it is the function of tragedy, according to George Steiner, to reveal as 'terribly limited'. It was to insist on the role of the gods as projections that I conflated the functions of Venus and Neptune in Racine. The sea which in Racine is the symbol of the uncontrolled, the formless, becomes in my version 'the jungle', almost a synonym for chaos. I have unified the psychological projections represented in Racine and ascribed them both to Siva, as he was imagined by the British, not necessarily as a complex component of the Hindu pantheon. Contemplating the attributes of Siva, though, one can see that the god can well bear the parallels, being at once the god of regeneration and sexuality, and of destruction. He contains opposing forces. He is associated both with aescetism (Hippolyte) and yet is everywhere reverenced under the symbol of the phallus or *lingam*. He is Destroyer/Creator, birth and death, Apollo *and* Dionysus to use the Nietzschean pair that forge the tragic dialectic. Even the minor parallels can be maintained, to authenticate the transfer, as Siva has a bull as a vehicle, and as a weapon the *trisula* or trident. But the matchings at this level hardly matter, even if they aid the metamorphosis. What matters is the function of projection, the use of pagan gods in a culture that dramatises itself as an age of reason, and its equivalent in the British apostrophisation of the dark gods of India.

VI

I don't remember the exact point at which I decided on a nineteenth-century Indian setting, but in retrospect there seem to have been catalysts and clues about me from the start, though I did begin with versions ostensibly in Ancient Greece and in the period of Louis XIV. Of all the many elements I now can recognise the following as particularly prominent:

1. Maria Casarès, who played Phèdre in Jean Vilar's production at the TNP in 1957, said of her character: '*j'ai toujours imaginée étendue dans l'ombre d'un chambre close, dans un lieu où le soleil explose*'. India! The all-pervading presence of the sun, either seen as light or felt as heat in a darkened room, became also a physical counterpart for Phèdre's mythological kinship in the original.

2. There was an equivalent, felt intuitively at first and then researched, between the way critics write about the character of the confidante, Oenone, and the way in which Anglo-Indian memoirs and fiction write of the ayah figure. Jean-Louis Barrault calls Oenone the '*valeur noire*' of Phèdre, and in my version she is literally that (the Anglo-Indians used the inaccurate and deliberately insulting adjective *black* of Indians). Racine also speaks, too aristocratically and high-handedly for my liking, of the *bassesse* of Oenone, and the servile propensities which make *her* able to accuse Hippolyte, and not her mistress as was the case in the Euripides version. As I have made it a Memsahib and ayah relationship, it is a way of absorbing into my version, without doing violence to the sense, my social reservations about Racine, and it makes the Memsahib's final outburst of racialist rejection of her faithful servant a terrible one, and one that is linked to the outside world of alien domination of which the psychological is a mirror aspect.

3. I felt the need of making the Amazon mother of Hippolyte physically present in the son, a constant reminder of the past of Thésée. My Hippolyte, Thomas Theophilus, becomes a 'half-caste' embodying the tensions between Britain and India within himself, as much as he embodies the two conflicting selves of his father. The occurrence of marriage between British men and Indian women was by no means uncommon in nineteenth-century India and, if we need historical authentication, it is enough to cite only the more well-known examples like James Achilles Kirkpatrick, Resident at Hyderabad, Job Charnock, who rescued a Brahmin widow from suttee and lived with her happily until her natural death fourteen years after, Colonel Gardiner, and Sir Charles Metcalfe who had three Eurasian sons by an Indian princess probably related to Ranjit Singh. The railways were to bring the Memsahibs to India and put a stop to that. I have assumed that transition in *mores* to be taking place, creating a new distance between ruler and ruled that was to harden to a more rigid apartheid after the Mutiny of 1857. The Victorian male couldn't permit his women the same intimate insights into India which he had allowed himself before his ladies made the crossing over the 'black water'.

4. Assailed as the British felt on all sides by an irrational India with its dark sensual gods and 'primitive' customs, they created in their imagination defensive roles for themselves as the inheritors of rational civilisation. They constructed residencies and public buildings in classical style, attempting to realise in external marble what they felt unable to realize internally in their far from securely stable minds. The books of the period are full of engravings showing proud classical façades in clearings in dense jungle, with creeper and mangrove festooning the edges of the scene. It is an eloquent juxtaposition. Mark Bence-Jones in his *Palaces of the Raj* (London, 1973) describes

the Residency at Hyderabad, with its Durbar Hall lined with Ionic columns, and a staircase which 'was adorned with sculpture: the Apollo Belvedere, Leda and the Swan' (not Pasiphaë and the Bull to complete the circle but almost there!) and 'Venus Rising from the Sea'. 'The mirrors in neoclassical frames, reflected the Durbar Hall to infinity.' It reads almost like the description of a traditional set for *Phèdre* at the Comédie Française!

It is more than a convenient point of contact. It represents the effort of one era, with its values threatened, to define itself in terms borrowed from another, which would seem best to support and prop up what was felt to be most shaky. The drama of Britain and India was constantly seen in these terms. Even as late as 1924 (the year of *A Passage to India*) Bennet Christian Huntingdon Calcraft Kennedy could write: 'We are here to govern India as delegates of a Christian and civilised power. We are here as representatives of Christ and Caesar to maintain this land against Siva and Khalifa.' And the cleaned-up classicism of the corresponding architecture, deriving as it does from Greece and Rome via Palladio and Wren, is still, as David Gerhard writing about Lutyens's New Delhi Residency, has it, 'a favourite political symbol in our century ranging from the megalomania of Albert Speer and Hitler to the New Deal of Roosevelt'. This belief in our being the chosen heirs of Greece and Rome gives a special poignancy to those pictures of the classical façade of the Lucknow Residency after the Mutiny, shattered by rifle-fire and shell, and littered with skulls. This kind of Residency and the life lived within it seemed to fit almost exactly Martin Turnell's summary (in *Jean Racine: Dramatist*) of the dramatic and political function of the palace in the plays of Racine. They are 'not simply impersonal buildings which provide a setting for the tragedy . . . They represent a particular *order* . . . '

We are aware from the first of an almost suffocating tension in the air combined with a desperate effort to maintain some sort of control which frequently breaks down. The tension is pervasive; it is also contagious. It is the atmosphere which produces fascinating and frightening revelations about human nature – about ourselves.

The palaces vary in style . . . they have one thing in common. There is something of the prison about them. We have the impression that the community is somehow confined within their walls. The sense of confinement is partly psychological, but in some parts of the palaces we shall find one or two members of the community are literally prisoners . . .

The palaces are huge, dark, claustrophobic. They give the occupants the alarming impression that they are constantly being watched, that their lives are in danger in that disaster may overtake at any moment.

There are winding corridors with innumerable rooms leading off them. But we, the visitors, are only admitted to a single room. The whole of the drama is concentrated inside it . . . at the same time we are aware that the room, or more accurately, the palace, is a world within a world it is trying to dominate.

VII

Couplets keep the cat on the hot tin roof. Each spirit has its own custom-built treadmill. After the metronome, the comic pace-maker of the *Misanthrope* couplet, I wanted a more organic model for my iambics. I wanted to return the iamb back to its sources in breath and blood. In the silences one should hear the heart beat. Jean-Louis Barrault writing of the Alexandrine in *Phèdre* says:

*Le coeur, qui egrène, jusqu'à la mort, les deux temps de
son tam-tam obsédant: systole-diastole; systole-diastole.
Brève-longue; brève-longue etc:* le coeur bat l'iambe.

It was this heartbeat, this bloodthrob that marked the
time of my metric. The heart as '*tam-tam obsédant*' leads
us straight back too to British India, where, another
woman writes in her memoir, 'the throbbing tom-toms
became almost like our heartbeats':

> I sensed the gods of India were there
> behind the throbbing heat and stifling air.
> Heart beat like a tom-tom, punkah flapped
> backwards and forwards and my strength was sapped.
> I felt you mocking, India, you brewed
> strange potions out of lust and lassitude,
> dark gods mocking, knowing they can claim
> another woman with the Judge's name,
> picking off the family one by one,
> each destroyed by lust and Eastern sun.

[1975]

Phaedra Britannica (after Racine) was first performed by the National Theatre Company at the Old Vic on 9 September 1975 with the following cast:

Governor Michael Gough
Memsahib Diana Rigg
Thomas Theophilus David Yelland
Burleigh Robert Eddison
ADC Daniel Thorndike
Lilamani Diana Quick
Tara Illona Linthwaite
Ayah Alaknanda Samarth
Chuprassie Ishaq Bux
Servants Talat Hussain, Jagdish Kumar, Albert Moses

Director John Dexter
Designer Tanya Moiseiwitsch
Assistant to Designer Timian Alsaker
Lighting Andy Phillips
Staff Director Harry Lomax
Vocal Coach Catherine Fleming
Production Manager Richard Bullimore
Stage Manager Diana Boddington
Deputy Stage Manager John Caulfield
Assistant Stage Managers Tim Spring, Karen Stone
Sound Sylvia Carter

Act One

*The scene is the Durbar Hall of the Governor's Residency
in British India, a few years before the Indian Mutiny.
Thomas Theophilus and Burleigh stand behind the
classical colonnade inhaling what is left of the fresh
night air, and listening to the bugle from the Fort
offstage playing reveille.*

THOMAS

No! No! I can't. I *can't*. How can I stay?
I've got to go at once. At once. *Today!*
The Governor's been gone now half a year,
I can't stay loitering and loafing here
frustrated and ashamed I'm not the one
directing the search-parties, me, his son!
It's almost up, the dawn. I must prepare.

BURLEIGH

And where will you start looking? Where?
The Company's had sepoys scout as far
as Jalalabad and Peshawar
north to the very outposts where its *raj*
is constantly beset by sabotage.
Unpacified child-murdering marauders
make it a certain death to cross our borders.
You know the Governor! He might have strayed
into those areas still unsurveyed.
Thomas, you know as well as I that soon
the search'll be called off for the monsoon.
Could even come today, the first cloudburst.
This damned hot weather's at its very worst.
Who wouldn't give a coffer of rupees

to lower the mercury a few degrees?
Besides, perhaps for reasons of his own
H.E. prefers his whereabouts unknown.
One knows his nature, ready to pursue
anything that's savage, strange, or new,
his 'curiosity' how wild tribes live,
his 'scholar' 's passion for the primitive.
Frankly it would be no great surprise
if he were living somewhere in disguise,
and, cool as ever, 's ready to embark
on some fresh enterprise that's best kept dark,
absorbed, preoccupied both day *and* night,
let's say 'researching' some strange marriage rite!
Leading some new unfortunate astray!

THOMAS

Show some respect. Be careful what you say!
Father's the Governor. He's good. He's great,
no loose romancer and gross reprobate.
My father's in some danger and not caught
in any trammels of that trivial sort.
When he was new out here and young, perhaps
there *was* the occasional moral lapse.
Not now, though, Burleigh. All that's of the past.
The Governor's heart is constant and steadfast.
No footloose fancy. No inconstant vow.
His life revolves round 'the Memsahib' now.
I'm going for two reasons: one, to find
my father; two, leave *this place* far behind.

BURLEIGH

'This place!' 'This place?' O surely that's not how
your childhood paradise seems to you now?
If 'this place', as you call it, 's lost its savour
where else I wonder will you find to favour?
Not Britain. No! Completely unimpressed!

There all you felt was homesick and depressed.
What's the real reason why you want to go?
Fear? Of what? Surely you can let me know!

THOMAS

Yes, Burleigh, paradise it may have been . . .
until 'the Memsahib' came on the scene.
The Judge's daughter's presence soon destroyed
that carefree, tranquil life we all enjoyed . . .
a judge so unimpeachable and just
to have a wife destroyed by bestial lust
and daughters . . .

BURLEIGH

Yes. Indeed. Of course one knew
that things were far from well between you two.
The storybook stepson/stepmother thing!
She wasn't long in starting harassing.
No sooner had she seen you, you were sent
to school in Britain, i.e. banishment!
That particular storm's blown over though.
The old obsession's gone, or doesn't show.
Besides it seems His Excellency's wife
has quite succumbed and lost all hold on life.
Her nerves seem whittled down to fraying strings.
She's given in and lost all grip on things.
What happened to the mother years before 's
enough to give alarm for much less cause.
The India we'd all like to ignore
struck at the Judge's family twice before,
bestial India, that undermined
his own wife's body and first daughter's mind.
Now she won't eat, can't sleep, and seems in pain,
though what it is no one can ascertain.
As to its nature she's quite sealed her lips.
A very strange complaint Her Ladyship's,

not common fever with its heat and chills
but one of India's obscurer ills.
How can an ailing woman cause your flight?

THOMAS

It's not the Memsahib. Or her vain spite.

Pause.

Remember the revolt? Ranjit and six sons
so bloodily destroyed by redcoat guns?
The daughter of that line that raised the war
against the Company and rule of law
under the strict restraint of house arrest . . .
She's the reason . . .

BURLEIGH

    Come! Can you detest
poor Lilamani so much, you as well
as the Governor want her life made hell?
And she so innocent! Would she have known
about her father's plans to seize the throne?
I don't believe she knew about their plot
to overthrow the Sahibs. Surely not!
Politics! Rebellion! I don't suppose
she's even acquainted with words like those.
She seems so full of charm. At least to me.

THOMAS

If it were hatred, would I need to flee?

BURLEIGH

A little tentative analysis
from me, your oldest friend, can't come amiss.
I've watched you struggling, I know for you
the Governor's character's not one, but two.
As law-enforcer, hunter; fine! But pride
has hardened your nature to his 'darker' side.
How long for I wonder? Are you still

fighting off love's *raj* with iron will?
India's spirits stung by your disgust
will never rest until you've kissed the dust.
And blood will out! Have the dark gods won?
And are you, after all, your father's son?
I've watched you struggle with yourself. My guess
(now don't flare up) 's capitulation. Yes?

THOMAS

If you're my oldest friend you ought to know
I'd never let myself descend so low.
Still at the breast I started to drink in
chaste principles and pride and discipline.
Think of my Rajput mother who would ride
fearless through danger at the Governor's side.
Think of her merits. She surpassed most men.
Then say 'capitulation'. Think again.
And you know very well you played your part
stamping the Governor's image on my heart.
Your schoolroom stories of my father stirred
my blood to emulate the things I heard,
a giant cannibal fought hand to hand,
the cripplers grappled with, mutilation banned,
dacoits encountered, and suppressed by law,
rebellions put down, and so much more.
Like hunting tigers! All the rest in trees
he goes on foot as coolly as you please,
waits till it's almost on him, doesn't shoot,
but drives a bayonet through the pouncing brute!
All the maneaters that he's bayoneted!
A pyramid of heads! A pyramid!

Pause.

As for that other self, so swift to swear
his plausible empty love-vows everywhere . . .
Oudh! Hyderabad! Kabul! Each of those
stands for some scandal the whole province knows,

145

scores of 'incidents' throughout Bengal,
O far too many to recall them all –
the purdahs plundered, the zenanas sacked,
many an infamously flagrant act –
the young girl daubed with kohl and henna dye
snatched from a Parsee caravanserai.
The Judge's daughters! Both! The sister's mind,
after her heart was broken, soon declined.
Disowned. A drunkard. Died. And then the other
became the Memsahib and my stepmother!
But she was fortunate in that at least
she had the benefit of rites and priest.
How many times I wanted to cut short
the countless details of that sordid sort.
If only time's recorder could erase
those blots and leave untarnished praise!
Will the gods humiliate me and extort
submission from me of that loathsome sort?
The Governor has exploits he can set
against those foibles and make men forget.
In me, with no such honours, they'd despise
the deliquescence of a lover's sighs.
What trampled monsters give me right to stray
even a little from the narrow way?
And if my pride were, somehow, overcome,
it's not to Lilamani I'd succumb.
Could I be so distracted to dispute
the Governor's veto for forbidden fruit?
She's quite untouchable. A strict taboo
falls like a scimitar between us two.
Prohibited. The Governor rightly fears
heirs to that family of mutineers.
And so she lives life out, for ever barred
from wedlock, and the like, and under guard.
Am I to brave his wrath, espouse her cause,
and show the natives I despise his laws?

BURLEIGH

You may protest. I fear it makes no odds
once your fate's been settled by the gods.
And I could see it happening. The more
he tried to blinker you the more you saw.
Hostility fed love. Your father's spite
bathed its victim with an added light.
Love's sweet, so why resist it, so why shy
from feelings common to humanity?
Such stubborn scruple in the face of love
which even your great heroes aren't above!
Siva's avatars subdue sahibs. Few
escape love's clutches. Why should you?
Submit, poor Thomas, pay love your salaams,
yield to the Princess's delightful charms.
The Governor yielded to your mother too
and from their mutual warmth created you.
Without their union you would not be,
you who wrestle against love to struggle free.
So why keep up this pitiful pretence?
Everyone has seen the difference.
For days now, even weeks, you have become –
how should one put it – well, less 'mettlesome'.
Nobody has seen you on 'the morning ride'
racing your ponies by the riverside.
You don't play polo, you no longer train
wild Arab horses to accept the rein.
Your weapons rust. No more the hue and cry
we made the jungle ring with, you and I.
Like someone drugged on *bhang,* all heavy-eyed,
sick of some passion that you seek to hide,
it seems so obvious. You're all ablaze,
dazed and bewildered in a lover's maze.
The little Princess is it? Lost your heart?

THOMAS

I'm going to find my father, and must start.

BURLEIGH

I rather think her ladyship expects
before you go your 'filial' respects!

THOMAS

Present 'the Memsahib' with my salaams.

Exit Thomas Theophilus. Enter Ayah.

BURLEIGH

Good morning, ayah! Well, no new alarms?

AYAH

The Memsahib! She seems to *want* to die.
Her days and nights are spent in agony.
There's nothing I can do. She never sleeps,
but stares all through the night and sighs and weeps.
First wants the jalousies wide open, then
almost at once they must be closed again.
She wants the punkah fast, the punkah slow,
too high, she says, to cool her, then too low.
For hours she gazes at the silver thread
that marks hot weather, wishing herself dead;
she points and says: *Ayah, when it reaches there
my lungs will have exhausted all the air.*
Now she wants to see the day. It seems
her brief siestas bring her dreadful dreams.
She asks, nay, sahib, she commands no eye
shall gaze upon her in her agony . . .

Exit Burleigh. Enter Memsahib.

MEMSAHIB

. . . no more . . . I can't. Must stop.
No strength! . . . Can't move another step.

Dazzled. My eyes. O ayah, I can't bear
the sudden brightness. Sun. Light. Glare.
Can't, ayah, can't bear the light. The heat.
I don't seem able to stay on my feet.
Aaaggghhh . . .

Sits.

AYAH
Heaven hear our desperate prayer.

MEMSAHIB
These stifling rags! . . . give me air!
My hair piled up? Wound round? and who did that?
Cumbered my reason with a lumpish plait?
It weighs like stone. What meddling little maid
burdened my leaden brain with this huge braid?
Aaah all things weary me, and make me vexed!

AYAH
Your wishes change one minute to the next.
Tired of your boudoir, you it was who said:
The sunrise, ayah. Help me out of bed.
You wanted dressing, wanted your hair done
to be presentable to see the sun.
You said: *Let in the sun, I want to see.*
Now you shrink from it in agony.

MEMSAHIB
That's where it all started, that red fire. . . .
. . . blinding, consuming . . . Ayah
its light sinks in, right in, to scrutinise
the sordidness concealed behind my eyes.
This is the last time that I'll have to gaze
on those all-seeing, penetrating rays.

AYAH
O all you ever talk about is dying . . .

149

MEMSAHIB

The jungle clearing, watching dustclouds flying . . .
horse and boy one animal, the hard sound
of hoofbeats on the baked hot-weather ground . . .
nearer . . . nearer . . .

AYAH

Memsahib?

MEMSAHIB

Mad! Oh no . . .
Wandering! Letting reason and desire go.
Your gods, the gods of India possess
my darkened mind and make it powerless.
I can feel my whole face hot with shame
blushing for dreadful things I daren't name.

AYAH

Blush, Memsahib, but blush that you stay mute
and make your sufferings much more acute.
Scorning pity, to all our pleas a stone,
do Memsahibs die loveless and alone?
You're letting yourself die. Three times the night
has dropped its purdah and obscured the light
without you tasting food. You pine away.
In letting go, Memsahib, you betray
your husband, children, and the source of life.
The Governor Sahib needs his faithful wife!
Think when the children come and you're not here,
the Governor away, have you no fear
of what the Rajput woman's son might do
to helpless children out of hate for you?
Your children in Belait, have you no thought
for them being subject to the half-breed's sport?
Thomas Theophilus . . .

MEMSAHIB

God!

AYAH
(*triumphant*)
                    Still feel then?

MEMSAHIB
Ayah, never refer to him again.

AYAH
If I thought that it would rouse you I'd recite
Thomas Theophilus day and night.
Live, Memsahib, live. Mother-love demands.
Live and save your children from his hands.
To let that half-breed Rajput colt control
those who survived you should affront your soul,
that cruel, heartless half-breed who can't feel
grind Sahib's pukka sons beneath his heel?
No time to waste. Each moment of delay
Memsahib's precious lifeblood ebbs away.
While there's an ember left that still glows red,
fan life into flame. Come back from the dead.

MEMSAHIB
My guilty life has dragged out far too long.

AYAH
Guilt! Guilt! Your guilty life! What guilt? What wrong?
What blood of innocents have those hands spilt?
How could Memsahib's hands be stained with guilt?

MEMSAHIB
They're not. My hands are clean enough. You're right.
I would to God my heart were half so white.

AYAH
What horror did that heart of hers hatch out
that Memsahib's so penitent about?

MEMSAHIB
Better to let my heart's dark secret go
with my dead body to the earth below.

AYAH

Pray do, pray do! But if Memsahib dies
she must find someone else to close her eyes.
Memsahib's life fades fast. Before it fades
her ayah goes down first to warn the shades.
Doors to oblivion are all unbarred.
One knocks and enters. It is never hard.
When all one's hopes and longings have been wrecked
despair can guide one to the most direct.
Has ayah's faithfulness once failed the test?
The Memsahib was nursed upon this breast.
I left my little children and my man
far, far behind me in Baluchistan
to care for you. I even held your hand
crossing black water to the Sahib's land.
Daughter of Judge Sahib, will you repay
love and devotion in this cruel way?

MEMSAHIB

Don't, ayah. Stop insisting. It's no good.
This unspeakable truth would chill your blood.

AYAH

Is truth so terrible, Memsahib? *Wai*,
could anything be worse than watch you die?

MEMSAHIB

I'll die in any case. With twice the shame
once guilt, that's better nameless, gets a name.

AYAH
(*on her knees*)

Memsahib, by these tears that wet your dress
rid ayah of her anguish, and confess.

MEMSAHIB
(*after a pause*)

You wish it? Then I will. Up, off your knees.

Pause.

AYAH

Memsahib made her promise. Tell me. Please.

MEMSAHIB

I don't know what to say. Or how to start.

Pause.

AYAH

Tell me, Memsahib. You break my heart.

MEMSAHIB
(*sudden vehemence*)

Mother! Driven by the dark gods' spite
beyond the frontiers of appetite.
A *judge's* wife! Obscene! Bestialities
Hindoos might sculpture on a temple frieze!

AYAH

Forget! Forget! The great wheel we are on
turns all that horror to oblivion.

MEMSAHIB

Sister! Abandoned . . . by him too . . . left behind . . .
driven to drugs and drink . . . Out of her mind!

AYAH

Memsahib, no. Don't let black despair
flail at your family. Forbear. Forbear.

MEMSAHIB

It's India! Your cruel gods athirst
for victims. Me the last and most accursed!

AYAH
(*truth dawning*)

Not love?

TONY HARRISON

MEMSAHIB
Love. Like fever.

AYAH
Memsahib, whom?

MEMSAHIB
Witness once more in me my family's doom.
I love . . . I love . . . I love . . . You know the one
I seemed to hate so much . . . the Rajput's son . . .

AYAH
Thomas Theophilus? The half-breed! Shame!

MEMSAHIB
I couldn't bring myself to speak his name.

AYAH
Wai, Memsahib, all my blood congeals.
Love's a running sore that never heals.
Our India destroys white womankind,
sapping the body, softening the mind . . .

MEMSAHIB
It's not a sudden thing. This black malaise
struck at the very heart of hopeful days.
My wedding day in fact. The very day
I gave my solemn promise to obey
the Governor Sahib, turning down the aisle,
I glimpsed his son. That steely, distant smile!
I saw him, blushed, then blenched. I couldn't speak.
Things swam before my eyes. My limbs felt weak.
My body froze, then blazed. I felt flesh scorch
as Siva smoked me out with flaming torch.
I sensed the gods of India were there
behind the throbbing heat and stifling air.
Heart beat like a tom-tom, punkah flapped
backwards and forwards and my strength was sapped.
I felt you mocking, India, you brewed

154

strange potions out of lust and lassitude,
dark gods mocking, knowing they can claim
another woman with the Judge's name,
picking off the family one by one,
each destroyed by lust and Eastern sun.
I tried to ward them off. I tried to douse
my heart's fierce holocaust with useless vows.
Tried the *bazaar*! Besought a Hindoo priest
to placate his deities. But nothing ceased.
I saw that sacrifice was offered at the shrine
of every god you Hindoos hold divine –
Siva, Kali, Krishna . . . that shaped stone . . .!
essayed their names myself, but could intone
only young Thomas's. He was my Lord.
He was the deity my lips adored.
His shape pursued me through the shimmering air.
I tried to flee him. He was everywhere.
O most unspeakable – In Sahib's bed
the son's eyes staring from his father's head!
Against every natural impulse of my soul
I played the stepmother's embittered role,
and had him hounded, and got Thomas sent
back home to Britain into banishment,
forced from his father's arms, his father's heart.
My husband and his favourite prised apart.
At first, relief. I started breathing. With him gone
I put the mask of Governor's Lady on.
I led a wholesome and quite blameless life,
the model mother and submissive wife,
grand lady and efficient châtelaine
adopting public roles to stifle pain.
Useless distractions, purposeless pretence!
The pain, when he returned, was more intense.
The old foe face to face and no escape.
The scars of love's old wounds began to gape,
the old sores fester, the flesh weep blood.

Nothing staunches love or stems the flood.
No longer veins on fire beneath the skin,
ravenous India had her claws deep in.
Ayah, ayah, O I utterly detest
this cancerous passion that consumes my breast.
I was about to die, and hide away
this sordid secret from the light of day.
But your entreaties wouldn't let me rest.
I gave in to your tears and I confessed.
Save your tears for after. Please don't try
to stir me back to life. I want to die.

Enter Governor's ADC.

ADC

Your Ladyship, alas, no one would choose
to bring Your Ladyship this bitter news,
but someone had to. It's already known
by almost everyone but you alone.
His Excellency, the Governor of Bengal,
is dead. Or killed. His death deprives us all.

Silent agony from Memsahib.

AYAH

Wai!

ADC

I regret there's nothing we can do
to bring him, or his relics, back to you.
The 'son' already knows. The news was brought
by scouts returned from searching to the Fort.

More silent agony.

Your Ladyship, I fear that there is more.
Bazaar talk mentions riot, even war.
Down from the mountains a murderous horde
have put a frontier outpost to the sword.

And Ranjit's daughter under house arrest
may be the focal point for fresh unrest.
There's panic in the quarters. What we need
is Your Ladyship herself to give a lead.
Most vital in such times a figurehead,
someone to look to in the Governor's stead,
an example to the others, brave and calm,
someone to salute to and salaam.

Pause.

The Governor's (mm) 'son' 's about to go . . .
Commands a following . . . could overthrow
the rule of law . . . ambition thwarted, rank
from both his strains, own future pretty blank . . .
nobility on one and on the other
Rajput royal blood from his wild mother.
With disaffection rife he might decide
to throw his lot in with his mother's side.
Some of us consider that it's right
not to let the boy out of our sight.

AYAH

The Memsahib has noted your report.
Now allow her time for grief and thought.

Exit ADC.

To think I thought it all a waste of breath
trying to talk Memsahib back from death.
I'd almost given up, prepared to go
with Memsahib to the world below.
His Excellency Sahib is no more.
The bazaar is humming with these threats of war.
His widow must put on the bravest front
for all the sahibs in the cantonment.
Memsahib, live! Fling guilt and shame aside.
Forget this pact with death, this suicide.

The Governor Sahib journeying beyond
releases you from shame and breaks your bond.
Death has condescended to remove
all barriers. Your love's a normal love.
Memsahib need no longer veil
a love which Death has placed within the pale.
It's likely that the half-breed Rajput colt
will swing to the other side and will revolt,
unite with Lilamani and make war
against the Company and rule of law.
Try to persuade him loyalty is best.
Soften the stubbornness within his breast.

MEMSAHIB

Very well! Your arguments prevail. I'll try,
if there are means to help me, not to die.
If duty to my kin in this dark hour
can give me back one spark of vital power.

    Exit Memsahib and Ayah. Enter Lilamani with Tara,
    her attendant.

LILAMANI

In here? The Governor's son? I don't believe . . .
To speak with *me*, you say? To take his leave?
Can this be true? Is this happening to me?

TARA

The first of many blessings. You'll soon see.
Those suitors that the cruel tyrant banned
will soon flock unopposed to seek your hand.
Soon, Rani Sahiba, soon your royal due,
freedom and empire will devolve on you.

LILAMANI

I thought it all bazaar talk, but now, no.
I see from your glad face it must be so.

TARA

The brute who loosed the redcoat cannonade
on Rani's noble brothers joins them as a shade.

LILAMANI

So, the Governor is dead. How did he die?

TARA

The most fantastic stories multiply –
much speculation, but one rumour's rife
how, yet again unfaithful to his wife,
he helped another Sahib violate
the Maharani of a native state,
cloaking the nature of his real pursuit,
licentiousness called 'law-enforcement'. Brute!
Some say beyond the frontier, beyond
the forbidden river, Indus, into Khond.
They disappeared (they say in the bazaar)
into the place where ghosts and dead souls are,
the two white sahibs standing without dread
among dark multitudes of silent dead!

LILAMANI

It's not possible! A living man descend
among the ghostly dead before his end.
He must have been bewitched. The evil eye!

TARA

You seem to doubt his death, Your Highness, why?
Everyone believes what I have said.
The Governor is dead, Your Highness, dead.
The Memsahib, with sahibs from the Fort,
anxious for their skins, are holding court,
worriedly debating under swinging fans
potential chaos and contingent plans.
They must be organised before the rain.

LILAMANI

Do you suppose his son is more humane?
Would he look on my plight with more regard?

TARA

I'm sure he would.

LILAMANI

No. No. He's very hard.
She'd be most foolish the woman who expects
kind treatment from a man who hates our sex.
Haven't you noticed how he'll never ride
anywhere near us but reins aside?
You know what people say about how stern
he is, a piece of ice that will not burn.

TARA

Too much phlegmatic Britain in his veins
dampens the Rajput warmth his blood contains.
I know the *myth*: ascetic, cold, severe,
but not, I've noticed, with Your Highness near.
The reputation made me scrutinise
this paragon's cold face and flint-like eyes.
I saw no coldness there. His inmost heart
and what they say of him are poles apart.
He was enslaved the first time both your eyes
exchanged shy glances, and although he tries
in your presence to turn his eyes away,
his eyes stay riveted, and won't obey.
To call him lover would offend his pride
but looks tell everything that mere words hide.

LILAMANI

You've known me all my life, would you have thought
this shadow puppet of harsh fortune brought
into a world of bitterness and tears
should ever feel such love and its wild fears?
I, last of Ranjit's noble household, forced

to watch my brothers face the holocaust.
My father bayoneted! The redcoat guns
killed my six brothers. All my father's sons.
The eldest, proud and strong, a bloody mess
blown from a cannon into nothingness.
Smoking smithereens! India's red mud
churned even redder with her children's blood.
A state with no new Rajah on the throne.
Only I survive, defenceless and alone,
and drag my life out under strict taboo,
constant surveillance, what I think, say, do,
everywhere I go the Sahib's spies
watch all my movements with their prying eyes.
What is he afraid of? That love's warm breath
might bring my angry brothers back from death?
As if weak love-pangs such as mine could fan
long burnt-out cinders back into a man.
You also were aware I could despise
the wary Sahib and his watchful spies,
indeed, love meant so little to me then
I almost could have thanked the Governor's men
for taking so much trouble to provide
external aids for what I felt inside,
that scorn I had of love. Until my eyes
first saw his son, and I felt otherwise.
It's not the handsomeness and blazoned grace
that Nature's lavished on his form and face
(which he's unconscious of, or quite ignores)
it's not entirely those that are the cause,
but something rarer and more precious still:
his father's good's in him without the ill,
the strengths that earned the Governor his great name
but not those weaknesses that mar his fame.
And what I love the most, I must confess,
is his obdurate scorn, his stubbornness.
The Memsahib made Governor Sahib fall –

grabbing a heart available to all.
You can't call conquest waiting in the queue
until the 'conquered' one gets round to you.
No sense of victory where many more
have planted standards in the field before.
No, but to triumph over and subdue
a heart subject to no one until you,
to captivate and make a man of steel
know the pangs of love and learn to feel,
to make a man half-gladdened, half-forlorn,
finding himself in chains he's never worn,
chafing the harness that he half wants on,
fretting for freedom, but half glad it's gone,
that's what I call triumph, that's the kind
of hard-won victory I have in mind,
the uphill struggle it's a thrill to win –
breaking the wild, unwilling stallion in.
Whatever am I thinking though?
He's obstinate. He'd sneer at me I know.
Then perhaps you'll hear my outraged cries
against that haughty pride I eulogise.
That rod of iron bend?

TARA
           You soon will know.

He's coming now.

Enter Thomas Theophilus ready to travel.

THOMAS
           Madam, before I go
I wanted a few words with you to say
your position might well alter from today.
My father's dead. My presentiment was strong
that fate, not folly, kept him gone so long.
No, nothing less than death could overthrow
my noble father, no mere mortal foe.

Only some darker superhuman force
could quench the hero's meteoric course.
My father *was* a hero. Fate sees fit
to take his brilliance and extinguish it.
Acknowledge his great virtues, even you,
and give the good in him its proper due.
Learn from a son's deep love to moderate
your just resentment and your family's hate.
Were I the Governor I'd countermand
the law forbidding men to seek your hand.
If I were on this dais you'd dispose
of self and heart exactly as you chose.
If I were my dead father I'd revoke
his interdictions, lift that cruel yoke . . .

LILAMANI

And even that you think of doing so
moves me more deeply than you'll ever know.
The ties of generosity like yours
bind me more strictly than your father's laws.

THOMAS

No, let me finish. If I had any say
you'd be a *reigning* princess. Now. Today.
Your country gagged on blood. Blood, so much blood,
even the sun-baked earth was turned to mud,
your brother's bloody gobbets and splashed gore
splattered like catsup from the cannon's jaw.
Though I'm ambitious I can never rise
because of my mixed blood, my dual ties.
Though my ambition's balked I can aid yours,
and, if I may, I'd gladly serve your cause,
in the only way I can, behind the scenes –
the mediator's role, the go-between's!

LILAMANI

Can I believe my ears? Is all this true?

What friendly deity persuaded you?
To put your future into jeopardy,
your precarious existence! All for me!
It's quite enough to see you moderate
your hate for me and . . .

THOMAS

                Hate you, madam? Hate!
So self-respect and pride can brand a man
as some unpacified barbarian?
Wasn't my mother human just like yours?
Am I some jungle freak that snarls and roars?
In any case, by standing at your side,
the wildest savage would be pacified.
If anything is magic then you are.

LILAMANI

Sir, I beg you . . .

THOMAS

           No, I've gone too far.
Reason's unseated. Nobody can rein
runaway passions into line again.
My confession is so pressing, once begun
I have no other course but going on.
Look at this object. Shed tears for its sake,
watch iron bend, and adamantine break,
this monument to pride with feet of clay,
this sun-baked stubbornness that's given way,
this is the victim, me, who used to scoff
at lovers bound in chains they can't throw off,
who saw love's storms sink thousands in the sea
and felt secure and said: *This can't touch me*,
now humbled by the lot that most men share
I find myself adrift, I don't know where.
One moment only killed a lifetime's pride.
I submitted to my fate and my will died.

I fled and thrashed about, tried to subdue
the pain that was inside me caused by you.
Shadow, sunlight, dense forest, open space –
it didn't matter where – I saw your face.
I was the hunter once, but now I feel
more like the beast that flinches from the steel.
This prisoner before you vainly tries
to find some shred of self to recognise.
My weapons are beginning to corrode.
I've quite forgotten that I ever rode.
My idle mounts relaxing in their stall
no longer recognise their master's call.
My crudeness must astound you. You'll regret
having this monster snarling in your net.
You should value even more your praises sung
by such a novice and unpractised tongue.

Enter Burleigh.

BURLEIGH
Her ladyship desires an interview.
I'm really not sure why.

THOMAS
          With me?

BURLEIGH
                    With you.
I'm not sure of the reason. All I know
's she wishes a few words before you go.

THOMAS
How can I face her now, or she face me?

LILAMANI
I beg you lay aside your enmity.
She shares in your bereavement. Try to show
a little sympathy before you go.

THOMAS
I need some too. From you. Give me some sign
of your reactions to those words of mine.
My offers? Heart? What *am* I to believe?

LILAMANI
That I am just as willing to receive
as you to give. Your gift of love alone
is worth all worldly powers or mere throne.

> *Exit Lilamani making the gesture of* namaste *to
> Thomas Theophilus.*

THOMAS
(*to Burleigh*)
Soon the sun'll be too high for us to start.
Please tell the men we're ready to depart,
then come back in a breathless hurry, say
how the men are anxious to be on their way.
I could dispense with farewells of this sort.
Friend, I depend on you to cut it short.

> *Exit Burleigh. Enter Memsahib and Ayah who
> remains behind the colonnade.*

MEMSAHIB
I'm told, sir, that you're anxious to depart.
I'd hoped to shed the grief that's in my heart
and blend my tears with yours, and to declare
that, with this sense of danger in the air,
now that we know for sure your father's gone,
I scarcely have the will to carry on.
The spirit of unrest extends and grows . . .
I'm expendable to you, though, I suppose.
It wouldn't worry you, stepmother fed
to vultures, dogs . . . I'm sure you wish me dead.

THOMAS
I've never wished you anything so bad.

MEMSAHIB

I could have understood it if you had.
To all appearances I seemed hell-bent
on causing you much suffering and torment,
stepmother on the warpath, out for blood,
wreaking devastation where she could.
To all appearances! How could you know
the sad reality that lay below?
My schemes and subtle hints had one design
to keep your person far away from mine.
Suffocated by proximity,
stifled by contact of the least degree,
I wanted space between us, and so much
not even the lands we lived in came in touch.
Only with you in Britain, only then
could I begin to live and breathe again.
If penalties are gauged to the offence
and your hostility's my recompense
for what seemed mine to you, were you aware,
you'd know that punishment was less than fair.
No other woman ever fitted less
the type of stepmother aggressiveness . . .

THOMAS

A mother, madam, as is too well known,
rejects outsiders to protect her own.
It's said to be a not uncommon fate
of second marriages, this kind of hate.

MEMSAHIB

O I must be the one exception then
that proves your rule. Or you must think again.
The feelings of your own stepmother are . . .
rather different . . . different by far . . .

THOMAS

Madam, it's still too early to succumb.

It's still just possible that news may come.
Your grief, perhaps, is somewhat premature.
Somewhere your husband is alive, I'm sure.
My father will come back. His life seems charmed.
India's dark gods won't have him harmed.
I've often thought that Siva and his crew
favoured my father, somehow, haven't you?

MEMSAHIB

There is no voyage home from where he's gone.
No gods that anyone can call upon.
Even the gods of India give way
once greedy Death has fastened on its prey.
What am I saying? Dead? How could he be
when I can see him now in front of me?
I feel my heart . . . Forgive me. My distress
makes me, I fear, too prone to foolishness.

THOMAS

I see that through desire a loving wife
can bring the man she longs for back to life.
As if you see him when you gaze at me!

MEMSAHIB

I pine, sir. Yes. And smoulder. Desperately.
I love your father, anxious to forget
the fickle social butterfly who'd set
his cap at almost anything in skirts.
That's one side of your father that still hurts.
I see the Governor's womanising ghost
ravish the consort of his present 'host'!
When I say I love him I don't mean
the womaniser and the libertine,
no, I remember the attentive him,
still diffident, one might say almost grim,
yet so attractive, fresh, he could disarm
everybody with his youthful charm,

whether they were sahibs or Hindoo.
In all his youthful pride he looked like you,
your bearings, eyes, the way you sometimes speak,
the same aloofness and the same . . . physique.

Pause.

Mother was 'ill', and outbreaks of bad crime
kept Father on the circuits all the time;
my sister and myself felt lonely, *then*
your famous father swam into our ken.
A wild maneater of prodigious size
began most dreadfully to terrorise
the province that we lived in, and it claimed,
O . . . scores of victims, eaten, mauled and maimed.
A hunter even then of great repute
your father was called in to kill the brute.
He'd taken on so many beasts like these
he seemed like Theseus or like Hercules.
With his adventurous, eccentric life,
his exploits, books, his loves, his Rajput wife,
all this, to us two sisters, made him seem
the complete answer to a young girl's dream.
We fell in love with him right from the start,
two sisters rivals for the same man's heart!
A pity you weren't there, that you weren't one
sent out to help. Too young to hold a gun!
The younger daughter might have been less slow,
less prone to stand back for her sister. No!
I would have taken the initiative.
Everything she gave, I too would give.
I would have led you to exactly where
the monstrous tiger had its tangled lair.
I would have shown you every little twist
to where the jungle's deep and gloomiest.
I sense your shots sink home with a soft thud!
The stillness of the beast! The smell of blood!

But for a few dim stars, the endless drone
of chirring insects we are quite alone.
Palpable jungle darkness all around.
Would I have cared if we were lost or found?
With you beside me and the night so black
who would ever want the daylight back?

THOMAS

Madam . . . I don't think ever in my life . . .
Have you forgotten you're my father's wife?

MEMSAHIB

Forgotten? I? What leads you to infer
that I no longer value honour, sir?

THOMAS

Forgive me, madam. I acknowledge to my shame
an unpardonable slander on your name.
I didn't understand . . . I couldn't tell . . .
I think . . .

Turns.

MEMSAHIB

You understood me very well!
I love you. Love! But when I spell out love
don't think that it's a passion I approve.
Do you suppose I wouldn't if I could
banish this fever throbbing in my blood?
I'm more hateful in my own than in your eyes.
India's chosen me to victimise.
I call on India to testify
how one by one she bled my family dry,
the gods of India whose savage glee
first gluts itself on them and now on me,
my mother and my sister, now my turn
to sizzle on love's spit until I burn.

You know very well how much I tried
to keep my distance, O I tried. I tried.
Keeping my distance led me to devise
a barrier of hate built up of lies –
I faked hard-heartedness, I cracked the whip,
filled you with hatred for Her Ladyship,
was everything they say stepmothers are
until the Memsahib was your *bête noire*.
What use was that? I made you hate me more
only to love you fiercer than before.
I found you even harder to resist –
you were most beautiful when wretchedest.
You'd soon see if you looked at me! I said,
if for a second you could turn your head,
and, just for a moment, look into my eyes.
I think that even you would realise.
Aaggh! Revenge yourself. Go on, chastise
me for foul passions you despise.
There were many monsters that your father slew.
He missed the 'maneater' in front of you.
How did he ever let this vile beast pass?
YOU give this animal the *coup de grâce*!
Yes, take the sword he gave you and destroy
the Governor's widow who dare love his boy.
Get your father's sword out. Thrust! Thrust! Thrust!
Kill the monster while it reeks of lust.
Or if you think that I'm too vile to kill,
and will not strike, give me the sword. I will.

Struggles with him.

Give me it!

*Enter Ayah emerging from colonnade and snatching
the sword away.*

AYAH

Stop, Memsahib. Come away.
Think if you're noticed in such disarray.
Someone's coming. Memsahib! The disgrace!

*Exeunt Memsahib and Ayah still carrying the sword.
Enter Burleigh.*

BURLEIGH

Her Ladyship? Dragged off? My boy, your face!

THOMAS

We've got to get away from here. We must.
I feel such nausea, and such disgust.
I feel so utterly polluted . . . she . . .
No. Consign the horror to eternity.

BURLEIGH

Thomas, the men are ready to depart.
We'd best be off before the troubles start.
Your father's death is felt as the first blow
of widespread insurrection from below.
Some rumours though insist he isn't dead.
Seen somewhere near the frontier. So it's said.

THOMAS

Nothing must be ignored. Sift every clue.
Anything we find we'll follow through,
I don't care what the sources of it are –
returning scouts, or spies, or the bazaar.

Exit Burleigh.

But if he's dead, I'll help to bring this land
under a cleaner, less corrupted hand.

Exit Thomas Theophilus.

Act Two

Bugle-calls offstage. Enter Chuprassie and Servants.
Enter ADC. Enter Memsahib and Ayah.

MEMSAHIB

Tell the chuprassie, please, the answer's NO.
The Memsahib's not fit to go on show.

Exit ADC ushering Chuprassie and Servants out.

Hide me from the world 's what they should do,
conceal my raw desire from public view.
Such thoughts which never ought to even reach
the conscious mind I've put into plain speech.
And how he heard it all, that block of wood,
making as if he hadn't understood!
I pour out my secret, inmost heart
and all he wants to do is to depart!
He pawed the ground, and had no other thought
than how he could best cut my ravings short.
The way he stood and shuffled with bowed head
could only make my shame a deeper red.
And even when I had his swordblade pressed
all ready to be plunged into my breast,
did he snatch it back? Made no attempt!
Just stared at me! Such coldness! Such contempt!
I touch it once, that's all, and in his sight
it's been polluted by some dreadful blight.

AYAH

Self-pity, Memsahib, the way you brood,
nourish a passion that is best subdued.
What would the Judge Sahib your father say

if he were still alive and here today?
He'd say: 'Find peace in duty, daughter, find
some public service to assuage your mind.
Duties a Governor's widow can perform
to help the Sahibs ride the coming storm.'

MEMSAHIB

The storm's already raging in my soul.
The Memsahib's no touchstone of control!
My reason's a torn punkah that can't move
the airless atmosphere of febrile love.
O reason soon seems sapped and comatose
shut up in passions so stifling and close!

AYAH

You could go home.

MEMSAHIB

And leave him here? O no!

AYAH

You had him sent away.

MEMSAHIB

Yes, years ago.
It's too late now. He knows. He knows. I've crossed
the frontier of virtue and I'm lost.
Hope, for a moment, caught me unawares
and all my shame was bared to his cold stares.
When I was quite prepared for my demise
you dangled life and love before my eyes.
All your native guile and honied speech
put the unattainable within my reach.
I wanted, *wanted* O so much to die.
You had to come and stop me. Why? Why? Why?

AYAH

Innocent or guilty, Memsahib, I'd do
even more than that if it's for you.

Spare your ayah though. Can you forget
that face of his, indifferent and hard-set?

MEMSAHIB

Perhaps it's innocence and virgin youth
that makes his ways seem clumsy and uncouth.
Look at the stations where he's had to live
among the most far-flung and primitive.
Let's try to understand. Perhaps that's why.
It's the novelty of love that makes him shy.
So perhaps we shouldn't condemn him yet.

AYAH

His Rajput blood, Memsahib, don't forget.
His mother was barbarian, half-wild.

MEMSAHIB

Half-wild or not, she loved. She bore this child.

AYAH

He hates all women and would never yield.

MEMSAHIB

Good, his hostility helps clear the field.
If love is something that he'll never feel
let's search elsewhere for his Achilles heel.
Ambition! Dual parentage frustrates
all hopes he might have had in both his states.

Listens.

Listen! Horses! Go make the boy believe
in greatness I could help him to achieve.
Say how my father's name would help provide
some useful access on the legal side.
O tell him now the Memsahib has schemes
by which he'll realise his inmost dreams.
Ayah, anything! Urge, implore him, cry.
Say the Memsahib's about to die.

And if it seems that you must grovel, do.
Do anything. My life depends on you.
Anything!

Exit Ayah.

   India, you see it all
watching the haughty stoop, the mighty fall.
Your gods possess dark powers no man can flout.
How much more blood of mine can you squeeze out?
How much further down can I be brought?
If you want more, you'll find much better sport
hunting a quarry harder to destroy,
fleeter of foot, a virgin. Hunt the boy!
O India! There's much more good pursuit
chasing the suppler, more elusive brute.
It's your sensual nature he ignores.
Avenge yourself. We have a common cause:
to make him love . . .

Enter Ayah.

    So soon? the answer's no.
He wouldn't listen even. Let him go.

AYAH

Silence those feelings. Never let them stir.
Remember your old self and who you were.
Banish such thoughts for ever from your head.
Your husband, Governor Sahib, isn't dead.
The people cheer, those few who recognise
the Governor Sahib in his new disguise.
Any moment now he will appear.

MEMSAHIB

The Governor! Alive? And almost here!
If he's alive, all I can do is die.

AYAH

Again you talk of death, Memsahib. Why?

MEMSAHIB

And had I died this morning as I planned
and not let your persuasion stay my hand,
I might have earned some tears, and saved my face.
All I deserve's dishonour. Death. Disgrace.

AYAH

Death! Death!

MEMSAHIB

What have I done? What have I done?
The Governor will be here, and with his son.
The one who saw her grovel with cold eyes
will watch Her Ladyship resort to lies,
tears of frustration just shed for the boy
turned so deceitfully to wifely joy,
the wife still burning for her husband's son
go through the motions of reunion,
the still flushed consort desperate to convince
the husband she betrayed not minutes since.
There's just a chance that he's so overcome,
so anxious for his father, he'll stay dumb.
Or maybe he'll tell all through sheer disgust
at seeing his father's wife display her lust.
And if he does keep quiet, I'm not one
to shirk the consequence of what I've done.
I can't forget things. I'm not one of those
frequenters of mess balls and evening shows,
who can commit their crimes and uncontrite
are never troubled by a sleepless night.
My conscience hurts me. Hurts. Each word I said
keeps echoing and booming through my head.
Those beastly heads his study's full of roar
as we enter *adulteress* and *whore*.
I see the hand of judgement start to scrawl
graffiti of my guilt on every wall.
Death's the only answer. Death. A swift release

from pain. For me and for my conscience, peace.
Is it so much to die? To one who's racked
by great torment it's a very simple act.
The only fear that lingers in my mind
is for my children. The shame I leave behind.
So many generations of blood-pride
obliterated by my suicide.
Think of the children, orphans, forced to face
those stories (all too true) of my disgrace.

AYAH

I do. I weep for them. They'll suffer hell.
I fear those things will happen you foretell.
But why, Memsahib, why must you expose
your little children to such ills as those?
If you die, all that's likely to be said
's she couldn't face her husband, so she fled.
What greater sign of guilt could you provide
than plunging headlong into suicide?
Memsahib, think! This suicide of yours
does more than lawyers to defend his cause.
Your death saves him. Your tragedy becomes
a camp-fire story for his hunting chums.
Without you here, there's no more can be done.
I'm a poor ayah. He's the Governor's son.
My word against his son's! Huh, take my part
against a cherished favourite of his heart!
Then all India will hear and quite ignore
in all the din against the one voice for.
Memsahib, I would rather die with you
than live to hear such stories, false or true.
Thomas Theophilus, Memsahib? How
do you feel about the half-breed now?

MEMSAHIB

His head should be mounted along with all
the monsters on the Sahib's study wall.

AYAH

Then don't give in submissively. Don't lose
without a struggle, Memsahib, accuse
the boy before the boy accuses you.
Who will contradict you if you do?

Takes up sword.

And this, Memsahib, look. Here's evidence:
the weapon in your hands, you, shaken, tense.

MEMSAHIB

Purity put down? Innocence oppressed?

AYAH

Only keep silent and I'll do the rest.
I suffer fear as well. I feel remorse.
I'd rather die but see no other course.
What are one poor ayah's scruples worth
with her Memsahib buried in the earth?
I'll speak, but making sure his anger goes
only to bitter words and not to blows.
And just supposing guiltless blood were spilt
to save your honour and to spare your guilt,
aren't these the measures that we have to take
when it's a question of your name at stake?
Honour must be saved at all expense
even the sacrifice of innocence.

*Enter Chuprassie and Servants. The Governor pushes
through them and enters, disguised as an Indian.*

GOVERNOR

Fortune relenting has turned foul to fair
and returned me to your arms . . .

MEMSAHIB

                                        Sir, stay there!
Don't desecrate your joy. I've lost all right

to claim the eagerness of your delight.
You have been wronged. Fate brings you from the dead
but spits its venom at your wife instead.
No longer fit to bear the name of wife!

Memsahib hurries off closely followed by Ayah.

GOVERNOR

And this my welcome! The dead brought back to life.

THOMAS

Your wife's the one to question. Only she
can help you clarify this mystery.
If desperation moves you, Father, then
heed that of this most desperate of men,
and permit your shaken son to live his life
in some locality not near your wife.

GOVERNOR

What? Leave?

THOMAS

As long as you, sir, were away,
I'd no alternative except to stay,
protecting those entrusted to my care,
against my will: your wife; and Ranjit's heir.
I did my best, but now with your return
I need no longer stay, sir, and I yearn
to prove myself your son and blood my spear
on prey far grander than wild boar or deer.
By my age, single-handed and alone,
you'd toppled a cruel Sultan from his throne,
shot scores of grim maneaters dead, and quelled
banditry in savage districts, held
the passes against unpacified Afghans
and made the highroads safe for caravans.
How many villagers you went to save
from dacoits or maneaters came to wave

and shout: *Jai! Sirkar ki jai!* around your tent
Glory and victory to the Government!
So many trophies on your walls by then
to satisfy the lifetimes of most men.
Old heroes could retire because they knew
the rule of reason was secure with you.
Obscurity! The undistinguished son
of such a father, and with nothing done!
Even my mother did more things than me.
Father, I feel trapped in this obscurity.
Let me have your weapons. I'll pursue
the fiercest monsters as you used to do.
I'll have the Residency walls and floors
covered with trophies just as wild as yours.
From private bedroom to official throne
carpeted with beasts I've overthrown.
Or make my going such a noble one
the world would know at last that I'm your son.

GOVERNOR

What's this? What contagion of insanity
makes my (so-called) loved ones flee from me?
Why did I ever come back from the dead
to find my family so filled with dread?
Of me? Myself the object to strike fear
into the ones I trusted and held dear!

Pause.

O India got into us somehow!
Absolute madness when I look back now,
part imbecility, part foolish prank
and probably the simpkin that we drank,
well anyhow, the upshot of it all
was a midnight entry, via the palace wall,
into a harem. My colleague, ADC
in charge of the suppression of Thuggee

(he's more hot-blooded than you'd think, that man),
forced the favourite of the local Khan.
And, put it down to India, I'm afraid
that I 'assisted' in his escapade.
Taken by surprise, no time to draw,
the tyrant had us seized and bound . . . I saw . . .
He kept . . . God knows what the monsters were.
I tell you even I was frightened, sir.
He kept . . . these somethings hungry in a pit.
I heard my friend thrown screaming into it.
My captor was a beast, obscene, perverse,
given to practices I won't rehearse,
to crude carnalities that overrode
every natural law and human code.
He'd draw the line at nothing. No taboo
would stop him doing what he wanted to.
I was shut up in a hole, a living tomb
so dark it seemed like Hell's own ante-room.
Chained naked like a beast – six months in there,
barely a spark of light or breath of air!
Then India relented, I suppose.
I broke the sentry's neck and stole his clothes
and made a quick escape, but not before
your father settled his outstanding score
with that black tyrant who'd devised all this.
I dropped him piecemeal down his own abyss,
that devilish despot and foul debauchee
chewed by his pet, flesh-starved monstrosity.
Disguised, I left that hell-hole far behind
restored to light and air, and my right mind.
Anxious to resume my shaken hold
on normal life I find the world turned cold.
This is my hearth and home and surely where
I have some right to breathe a cleaner air.
A season spent in hell, I've no desire
for whiffs of brimstone from the household fire.

I still smell prisons, yet I'm among
the very ones I yearned for for so long.
I see my dear ones with averted face
shunning the welcome of my warm embrace,
my presence striking terror in their soul
and wish I were still shut up in that hole.
I want the truth from you. I want it now.
What wrong has my wife suffered? When? Who? How?
Why isn't the culprit under lock and key?
You're in it too! Why don't you answer me?
Speak, why can't you? My flesh and blood! My son!
Is everyone against me? Everyone?
Ah India, I've given you my life.
Deliver up the man who's harmed my wife.
I'll get to know, by fair means or by foul,
what manner of strange monster's on the prowl.

Exit Governor.

THOMAS

O this unventilated atmosphere!
Burleigh, my blood runs cold with sudden fear.
What if Her Ladyship, while still a prey
to her strange frenzy, gives herself away?
Instead of a warm son and welcoming wife
my father finds a foul infection rife,
some plague that makes his hearth and home unclean;
like victims sickening in quarantine,
the wife and son to whom he's been restored,
shivering with symptoms in this fever ward.
As in the jungle when the beaters' ring
closes round the beast that's panicking,
I feel that sense of menace and my heart
thumps as the undergrowth is forced apart.

*Enter Ayah displaying the sword of Thomas
Theophilus, and followed by the Governor.*

183

GOVERNOR

ANIMAL! . . . Now it all comes out!
The reversal everybody spoke about!
The lower self comes creeping up from its lair
out of the dismal swamps of God-knows-where.
It lumbers leering from primeval slime
where it's been lurking, biding its own time.
How could his kind absorb our discipline,
our laws of self-control, our claims of kin.
I've expected far too much. It's in his blood.
Control himself? I don't suppose he could.
One should have known the worst. One ought to know
that India once hooked in just won't let go.

Takes the sword.

And this the weapon! One he couldn't lift
when I first gave it him. His father's gift!
I don't suppose his sort acknowledge sin.
Don't blood-ties count? To violate one's kin!
And the Memsahib? Why did she allow
this animal at liberty till now?
Her silence makes his foulness almost fair.

AYAH

It was the Sahib's grief she wished to spare.
The Memsahib, so sickened with sheer shame
was she at kindling his lustful flame,
her desperate feelings turned to suicide,
and but for me, Sahib, she would have died.
I saved her, Sahib. I preserved your wife
in the very act of taking her own life.
In pity for her sorrow and your fears
I now explain the meaning of her tears.

*The Governor drives the sword into the dais on
which the throne stands.*

GOVERNOR

Barbarian! No wonder that in spite
of all his efforts I could sense his fright.
His chilly welcome took me by surprise,
felt frozen by the scared look in his eyes.
When did my son first show himself so foul?
When did this animal first start to prowl?

AYAH

At the beginning of your married life
the boy already had disturbed your wife.

GOVERNOR

And in my absence things came to a head?

AYAH

Everything occurred as I have said.
We must not leave her on her own too long.
Allow me to return where I belong.

Exit Ayah.

GOVERNOR
(*seeing Thomas enter*)

Good God! Wouldn't anyone be taken in
by looks so seemingly devoid of sin?
No mark of his lascivious offence
sullies that subtle mask of innocence.
A beast in human shape! I'd like to brand
ANIMAL on his flank with my my own hand!

THOMAS

May not a sympathetic son be told
what makes his father's look seem hard and cold?

GOVERNOR

After dishonouring your father's name,
still reeking of your lust and smirched with shame,
the animal still has the brazen face

to stand before his father in this place!
Instead of running far away from me
back to the jungle and its savagery,
beyond our influence and rigid laws
back to the world of bestial lusts like yours.
Unless you want to share the fate of those
whose lawlessness I crushed with iron blows,
unless you want the Governor to show
his famous skill in killing monsters, GO!
India! Remember how I cleared
your countryside of monsters that all feared.
Now in return I ask your gods to take
swift vengeance on this monster for my sake.
If you cherish me in your dark heart,
India, tear this animal apart!

THOMAS

Her Ladyship brands me with that foul sin?
It's too revolting even to take in.

GOVERNOR

I think I can see through your little game.
Your lust kept secret through the lady's shame.
You loathsome animal, you put your trust
in her reticence to conceal your lust,
That's not enough. You should have had the sense
not to have left behind this evidence,

*Taking sword and displaying it to Thomas
Theophilus.*

or been more systematic, and instead
of leaving her just speechless, left her dead.

THOMAS

Why do I stand and hear so black a lie
and not speak truths I'd be acquitted by?
Sir, there are dreadful things I could disclose

186

nearer to yourself than you suppose.
I could blurt secrets out. I could . . . but no,
give me some credit for not doing so.
I cannot wish more agony on you
but please consider what I am and who.

Thomas Theophilus takes sword from Governor.

A man first breaks small laws, then treads taboos
basic to all men beneath his shoes.
Like virtue vice develops. It takes time
for petty to turn into heinous crime.
Impossible! The twinkling of an eye
turn innocence to bestiality!
My mother's chastity was her renown.
That and her courage. I've never let her down.
I made restraint a virtue and subdued
mutinous passions into servitude.
My shibboleths were bridle, curb and bit.
Lust! Bestiality! I mastered it!
I'm the one who took restraint so far
that I'm a laughing stock in the bazaar.
You know the sobriquets they call me by,
good-natured, and obscene, as well as I.
I never thought of women, now I'm faced
with charges of black lust. I'm chaste, sir. Chaste!

GOVERNOR

Your foul obsession must have taken hold
from very early on to make you cold
to every female influence but one.
Wouldn't some black concubine have done?

THOMAS

Father! Sir! It's too much to conceal,
I have to tell the truth. My heart *can* feel.
It feels a chaste emotion, but for one
you yourself placed interdictions on.

It's Lilamani. Under house arrest.
She's stormed my stubborn heart. There, I've confessed.
Despite myself I contravened your law
and this is what I need forgiveness for.

GOVERNOR

Very clever! You're ready to confess
to that to hide the worse lasciviousness!

THOMAS

For six months now no matter how I've tried
I've loved. I've loved her, and I'm terrified,
and came to see you now to tell you so.
Sir, how much further do I have to go?
I swear by . . .

GOVERNOR

          O the guilty always flee
as a desperate resort to perjury.
Enough! Enough! No more tedious harangues,
if it's on stuff like this your story hangs.

THOMAS

You think my story's false, and full of lies?
Your wife, sir, in her heart knows otherwise.

GOVERNOR

Animal! How dare you? Don't say any more.

THOMAS

I'm to be sent away? Where? And how long for?

GOVERNOR

Across the Indus, the 'forbidden river',
and beyond our frontiers. For ever!

THOMAS

Charged with such crimes, and your curse on my head,
who will welcome me, or give me bread?

GOVERNOR

Peoples exist without *our* discipline,
the lesser breeds, perhaps they'll take you in.
Hospitality in the far North-West
means laying down your wife for any guest.
You should feel welcome there. I'm sure you'll find
depraved men, debauchees, of your own kind!

THOMAS

Debauchery! Compare my mother's, my own life
with that of the woman who conceived your wife.
Think of my parentage, then hers, and choose.
Decide whose blood is coming out, sir. Whose?
Think of my mother, Father! Think! At least
she wasn't serviced by a slavering beast!

GOVERNOR

Go! Get out of my sight. Or else I'll shout
for the sentries and have you frog-marched out.

Exit Thomas Theophilus.

Like shivering and chill preceding fever
I sense the presence of avenging Siva.
My spine's an icicle, my innards knot
with pity for this monster I begot.
God, I feel stifled by my wretchedness!
How did I come to sire a beast like this?

Enter Memsahib.

MEMSAHIB

Your shouting could be heard through all the doors.
It made me terrified to hear those roars
and bull-like bellowing. I feared far worse
might follow on your homicidal curse.
You still have time to call him back. You could.
O do, I beg you. He's your flesh and blood.
Spare some thought for me. How could I survive

knowing that, but for me, he'd be alive?
Could I live with the knowledge I'm the one
who turned a father's hand against his son?

GOVERNOR

No, not a father's hand. A darker force
than any man's ensures death takes its course.
India owes me some destruction.

MEMSAHIB
                    No!

GOVERNOR

Her gods are swift in paying what they owe.
And now, in all its blackness, tell me all
before the mercury of anger starts to fall.
I want each little detail.

*The Governor turns and walks to the colonnade.
A pause in which it seems the Memsahib has the
truth all ready to disclose.*

                        You've not heard
half of the guilt your stepson has incurred.
He launched into a great frenzy against you.
Implied that all you'd said just wasn't true!
And in his own defence he swore that . . . Guess!
He swore he loved the Indian princess!
Lilamani . . .

MEMSAHIB
            Swore? What?

GOVERNOR
                    Tried to confuse
the issue. Lies all lies. A desperate ruse.

Suddenly tense.

I hope whatever happens happens soon.

Leaving.

Then everything washed clean by the monsoon!

Exit Governor.

MEMSAHIB

And just when I was coming to his aid!
This thunderclap! This stunning cannonade!
Stung by remorse and guilt I flung aside
my ayah's arms and left her terrified.
O God knows just how far I might have gone
if I'd have let repentance drive me on.
If he hadn't cut me short . . . God knows
I had the truth all ready to disclose.
And Lilamani (*Lilamani!*) stealing
the little boy from me who has no feeling.
The one who'd walled himself completely in
against invasions of the feminine!
Perhaps his heart's accessible to all,
and he has hundreds at his beck and call.
Women pawing him from every side
and I'm the only one he can't abide.
The charms of any native concubine
are no doubt more agreeable than mine.
The only one to whom he *can* say no!
Too old, too white for his seraglio!
Chastity? Surfeit! And I'd come to claim
his innocence, and ruin my own name!

Enter Ayah.

Ayah, have you heard the latest? Guess!

AYAH

Memsahib, ayah comes to you in real distress.
I wondered why you'd torn yourself away.
I was very much afraid what you might say.

MEMSAHIB

Ayah, there's competition. And, guess who?

AYAH

Memsahib . . .

MEMSAHIB
He loves another. Yes, it's true.
This fierce quarry no one could hunt down,
who countered blandishments with a cold frown,
this tiger frightening to stand beside,
gentle as a lamb, quite pacified.
That princess . . .

AYAH
Her?

MEMSAHIB
Yes *her*. Agh how much more
persecution has India in store?
As if being torn apart by two extremes,
first shivering despair, then fevered dreams,
as if the final insult of his cold rebuff
and all my sufferings were not enough.
Lovers? Them! What native sorcery has thrown
this smokescreen round them? When were they alone?
How? When? Where? You knew all along. You knew.
You could have told me sooner, couldn't you?
Exchanging glances. Talking. Furtiveness.
Where did they hide, hm? In the forest, yes.
To follow one's feelings through nature's course
without recriminations and remorse,
not to feel criminal, and meet as though
the sun shone on one's love and watched it grow!
Ah! Every day they must wake up and see
vistas with no black clouds, and feel so free!

AYAH
They'll never meet again, Memsahib. Never!
Their love . . .

MEMSAHIB

will survive for ever and ever.
Though they were twenty thousand miles apart
heart would heliograph to exiled heart,
across the Himalayas if need be.
Nothing can come between them. Even me!
Kisses! Promises! Touching one another!
scorning the fury of the mad stepmother.
Their happiness feeds off my jealousy.
That green-eyed monster is destroying me.
That mutinous family! No reason why
the Governor should show her leniency!
The father bayoneted, the brother shot
from a cannon. She should die too. Why not?
She's of their blood. They died. Why should she live?
Her crime is even harder to forgive.
How smoothly one progresses from the first
tentative transgressions to the worst.
My first steps taken, sick with vertigo,
I inched towards dishonour, now I go
with eyes wide open and with one bold stride
into the black abyss of homicide.
O, those white hands, remember? If I could
I'd plunge them elbow-deep in guiltless blood.
How can I bear to have the sun's light pry
through every cranny at my misery?
There's nowhere, nowhere dark enough to hide.
No, everywhere the sun can get inside.
Close the shutters and black out the glare
you feel it then as heat, and everywhere:
the mercury a hundred in the shade,
the grass screens sprayed with water, and resprayed,
the hopeless, winnowing thermantidote –
heat like some animal that claws one's throat.
There's no escape from that all-seeing eye,
that presence everywhere, except to die.

My Hell is India, always at high noon,
with no relief of night, and no monsoon,
and under that red sun's remorseless stare
mankind's grossest secrets are laid bare.
My Hell is such exposure, being brought
a guilty prisoner to my father's court.
I see the Judge's phantom with shocked face
jib at the details of his daughter's case,
hearing his once-loved flesh and blood confess
to crimes of monumental loathsomeness.
Aghast but relentless he applies the Law
to horrors even he's not heard before.
His task is Judgement. Judges give no quarter,
and merciless he sentences his daughter.
Father, forgive me. Please forgive me. Try.
Harsh India's destroyed your family.
The same gods in your daughter. Recognise
the lust they kindled blazing in her eyes.
Repentance never lets up its pursuit.
I've broken laws, but never reaped the fruit!
Harried by ill luck till my last breath
all that seems left me is a dreadful death.

AYAH

You are in love. And that's your destiny.
You're in the power of some evil eye.
Is love unheard of, even in these parts?
Memsahib, millions have human hearts.
Are you the first or last of us to fall?
Memsahib, love is common to us all.
Weakness is human, Memsahib, submit
to your humanity. Give way to it.
Even the gods, we Hindoos say, who fright
mere mortals sometimes, know delight.
Not only men, Memsahib, gods above
partake of pleasures and the joys of love.

MEMSAHIB

You reptile! Spitting still! The snake still tries
to poison the Memsahib with black lies.
Your evil whispers drugged my sense of right.
The boy I shunned you urged into my sight.
Who gave you leave? Who gave you orders? Why
did you have to brand him? Now he'll die. He'll die.
His father mouths strange curses and implores
vengeance and justice from those gods of yours.
Let what agonies you've earned spell out the fate
of those low persons who corrupt the great.
You take our weaknesses and give them scope
and grease the incline of the downward slope.
Her Ladyship debased, demeaned, brought low,
down to the level of your blackness. Go!

*Exit Ayah. Memsahib is left alone with the sense of
India closing in. Exit Memsahib.*
    Enter Lilamani, followed by Thomas Theophilus.

LILAMANI

No! No! Your keeping silent's suicide!
This sacrifice you make to spare his pride
in normal circumstances would be one
that's most becoming in a loyal son,
but now with danger like a dangling sword
it's more a luxury you can't afford.
If, without much thought for me, you can consent
and so submissively to banishment,
then go; leave me to languish and to grieve.
But at least defend yourself before you leave,
defend your honour. There's still time yet
to persuade your father to retract his threat.
If you keep silent then the scales will tip
wholly in favour of Her Ladyship.
Tell everything . . .

THOMAS
                    Tell everything and show
my father his own shame, I couldn't, no.
Could I bear exposing his wife's lust
and watch his whole life crumble into dust?
The fullest horror's known to only you
and those who witness all we say and do.
If I didn't love you would I have revealed
obscenities to *you* I'd want concealed
even from myself! You gave your word
never to pass on what you have heard.
And even if it proves at my expense
I have to make you swear to reticence.
That gesture of respect for him at least.
From every other tie I feel released.
Remember too that right is on our side.
Sooner or later I'll be justified.
Her Ladyship will surely not elude
the consequences of gross turpitude.
Leave this prison, and its poisoned air,
and follow me to exile, if you dare.
I can offer you the means you need to flee.
Even the guards on watch are all with me.
We could count on powerful allies in our fight
to win you back your throne, your lawful right.
My mother's tribe, the warlike Rajput clan,
have sworn allegiance to us to a man.
Mountain chieftains and the Rajah's court
send secret guarantees of their support.
The Memsahib! Why should such as she
prosper by destroying you and me?
Now's the time. Everything is on our side.
And yet you look afraid and can't decide.

LILAMANI
There's no dishonour in escape, indeed

I feel it only right I should be freed.
My family's heroes struggled to set free
our subdued people from white tyranny.
Your father is a tyrant and I owe
him no obedience. I'm free to go.
But I'm of royal blood, and many wait
for me to reassume the reins of state,
the last upholder of my father's name.
My followers permit no hint of shame . . .

THOMAS

Nor I! My mother's gods are yours. Suppose
we swear our loyalty in front of those?
Near where my royal mother's buried, she
and all her ancient Rajput family,
there stands a shrine, a very holy place
where no perjurer dare show his face.
To stand in for our fathers we'll invoke
the gods, whose shrine it is, to join our yoke.

LILAMANI

(seeing Chuprassie enter with three Servants)
The Governor's chuprassie! Go, please, go.
I'll stay a while so nobody will know.
Send someone I can trust to be my guide
to lead me to the shrine to be your bride.

She makes the gesture of namaste *to Thomas Theophilus
who, after a pause, returns the gesture and exits.
Enter Governor, who first confers with Chuprassie.*

GOVERNOR

I'm told my son's been taking leave of you?

LILAMANI

We said farewell. Your 'intelligence' is true!

GOVERNOR

Those lovely eyes! It's their work, then, all this?
First to hypnotise that stubbornness!

197

LILAMANI

The truth is something that I can't deny.
He doesn't seem to share your enmity.
He's never treated me like a pariah.

GOVERNOR

It doesn't operate like that, desire.
I suppose he swore his love 'for ever more'.
You're not the first. He's said it all before.

Lilamani remains silent.

You should have kept him on a tighter rein.
Doesn't the competition cause you pain?

LILAMANI

It should pain you to vilify your son,
especially so pure and chaste a one.
Have you so little knowledge of his heart?
Can't you tell innocence and guilt apart?
Don't listen to that snake, Memsahib's nurse.
Take back, Sahib, your rash assassin's curse.
Our gods may well give ear to your wild wish
because they find you brutish, devilish.
Sometimes it's anger makes the gods say yes
and gifts may be the gods' vindictiveness.

GOVERNOR

You're trying to throw dust into my eyes.
Love's blinkered you to his depravities.

LILAMANI

Take care, Sahib. Your manly strength and skills
have notched up many monsters in your kills.
Their glazed eyes watch us talking, but not all
have their heads hung on your study wall.
Your great collection is still missing one . . .
But I'm forbidden to go further by your son.
Strangely enough, his love for you's not gone

and his respect prevents my going on.
Unless I leave your presence I'll forget
myself and say things that we'll both regret.

Exit Lilamani. The sound of thunder.

GOVERNOR
They're both in league to throw me off the track.
A conspiracy to stretch me on the rack.
In spite of my resolve some doubt still gnaws.
A still small voice cries mercy, and I pause.
Deep in my hardened heart to my surprise
pity still sends out its feeble cries.

Resolved again.

I want it all made absolutely clear.

Shouts.

Chuprassie!

CHUPRASSIE
Sir!

GOVERNOR
Memsahib's ayah. Here.

Exit Chuprassie. Enter ADC.

ADC
Sir! Her Ladyship! Something's very wrong.
She's gripped by God knows what and can't last long.
Whatever thoughts are passing through her head,
she seems, Your Excellency, almost dead.
Her face is ghastly pale, her bloodless lips
seem more a corpse's than Her Ladyship's.
The ayah's been sent packing by your wife.
Fled to the forest careless of her life.
Went to earth where none would give pursuit,
a region best relinquished to the brute.

No blacks and none of us (but you)'d give chase
into that swampy beast-infested place.
The jungle swallowed her. No search would find
much more than shreds of sari left behind.
What drove the woman there nobody knows.

GOVERNOR

What's this?

ADC

        Her Ladyship finds no repose.
She hugs the children's likenesses, which seems
to calm her for a while, but then she screams
and pushes them away as if she could
no longer bear the thought of motherhood.
She walks or rather lurches to and fro,
not knowing where to sit or where to go.
She looks at one but seems to stare right through.
She knows there's someone there, she's not sure who.
She sat down at her desk three times and wrote
but each time changed her mind and burnt the note.
For pity's sake, sir, go and see your wife.

GOVERNOR

The ayah dead! My dear one sick of life.
Someone fetch my son. I'll hear his case.
Let him defend himself before my face.

*Exit ADC. The Governor listens to the distant
thunder of the coming monsoon.*

O God what if the thing's already done?

*Thunder. Wind blows through the room. Enter
Burleigh.*

Ah! Burleigh, you. What's happened to my son?
You've been his tutor how long now? Well nigh . . .
But what's this, man? My God, you're weeping. Why?
My son! What's happened?

BURLEIGH
                    Now you demonstrate
anxiety on his behalf. It's all too late.
He's dead.

GOVERNOR
          No!

BURLEIGH
          The gentlest boy I knew!
And, if I may say so, the most guiltless too.

GOVERNOR
My son dead? No! The moment I extend
my arms to him, THEY hound him to his end.

BURLEIGH
We moved like a slow cortège out of the town.
Even the horses jogged with heads hung down.
He rode his finest white Arabian steed
at little more than normal walking speed.
The sepoy escort all looked just as grim
and sullen out of sympathy for him.
We're hated, but obeyed because we're feared.
He was almost one of them; admired; revered.
Then from the jungle came a dreadful cry.
Birds and old dry leaves began to fly.
And dust, like blood turned into powder, floats
in huge spirals, blinds us, scours our throats.
The wind got up, increased. The jungle trees
first leant a little to a light stray breeze
then began bending violently and then
just as suddenly sprang straight again;
then bent with force that made the palm leaves crack.
Then all of a sudden all the sky went black,
and from the deepest darkest part a cry
like the first but lower rent the sky.
Our hearts stand still. Blood freezes in our veins.

Hair stiffens on our frightened horses' manes.
The forest begins heaving like the sea,
and seems to open up, and, suddenly,
we see, festooned with seared lianas, IT,
some horrifying, monstrous composite,
like one of those concoctions that one sees
in dark recesses on a temple frieze.
An old woman told the sepoys it was Siva
in his avatar of monster. They believe her.
You know how sceptical I am, but there
is the monster, and its bellows fill the air.
The whole earth shudders as it moves its feet
and shambles forward through the shimmering heat.
An epidemic smell, the beast exhales
a stink like cholera from its gold scales.
Then everyone starts running, everyone
except, that is, your son, your fearless son.
We all take shelter in a shrine nearby.
He reins in his horse and does not fly.
We see him all alone, without a fear,
grab that ordinary, native spear
he sometimes went hog-hunting with, and fling
the weapon with sure aim into the thing.
It gushes blood, breathes fire and smoky heat,
squirms and writhes before the horses' feet.
The thing with wide jaws like an open sluice
disgorges gore and vomits blackish juice.
The horses panic. A regular stampede!
He calls out to his own. They take no heed.
The one he's riding bolts and all in vain
he shouts *whoa, whoa*, and tugs hard on the rein.
He wastes his strength. From each champed bit
flies froth and slaver and blood-red spit.
The sepoys say that maddened Siva sank
a sharpened trident into each scorched flank.
They gallop, riderless but one, towards the rocks –

the snap of broken bones and cracked fetlocks,
as they collide and sprawl, and he
trails tangled in one stirrup helplessly.
Excuse my lack of self-control, these tears.
That cruel sight will haunt me all my years.
I saw him with my own eyes, sir, saw him towed
by the stallions he'd tamed himself and rode
in the cool of the morning, saw your son
dragged by the ponies he'd played polo on.
I hear him try to check them, *whoa there, whoa.*
It terrifies them more and still they go.
His body drags and twists, his clothes all tear.
He leaves a terrible trail of blood and hair.
That once fine handsome beauty with the look
of something dangling off a butcher's hook!
There was really nothing left to call a face.
At last the maddened horses slow their pace.
Staggering they slow down to a halt,
near where his princely forebears have their vault.
I follow, panting, sobbing. Sepoys wail.
Strewn flesh and bloodstains left an easy trail.
Rough rocks bearded with the boy's fine hair,
flesh on the sharp bamboo shoots! Everywhere!
Thomas, I say. He takes my hand. He tries
to open wide what once had been his eyes.
Dear friend, he gasps, *something has been sent
to snatch my life away. I'm innocent.*
When I am gone, look after her for me,
little Lilamani, lovingly.
Perhaps one day when Father's disabused
and pities the dead son he once accused
beg him treat her kindly and restore . . .
With that his head fell back. He said no more.
The brave boy died, and left in my embrace
a lump of mangled flesh without a face.
Your 'gods' glut anger on the blameless one.

I doubt if you would recognise your son.

Thunder.

GOVERNOR

Son, my son! All consolation in you gone.
I've murdered my own future. Thomas! Son!
India, you've served me all too well.
My life will be dragged out as one long hell.

Enter Memsahib unnoticed.

BURLEIGH

Then Lilamani came, afraid of you,
and what your enmity would make you do.
She stares, gripped by some suffocating dream
at blood-red undergrowth and sickly steam.
She sees (what an object for a lover's eyes)
that mess that was her loved one and denies
the evidence before her, clings to doubt.
She sees the pile of flesh but looks about
and asks for him. How could she face that grim,
raw, featureless heap, and think it him?
At last she's certain and pours out her hate
on all the gods the Hindoos venerate,
then cold and moaning, sickened, almost dead
she crumples by the corpse she should have wed.
Relaying his last wish fulfils my vow.
My joy in life's all gone. I loathe it now.
It's blighted at the root. It's meaningless.
Your son is dead and

Indicating the Memsahib.

there's his murderess!

GOVERNOR

Good evening, madam. Well, it seems you've won.
You've won your victory. I've lost my son.

Now new suspicions and misgivings start
sending tremors through my broken heart.
But what's the use? No, take your spoil. Enjoy
the harsh destruction of my gentle boy.
Relish it, and gloat. Go on, lick your lips.
The triumph (so far) 's all Your Ladyship's.
I'm willingly blinkered. Don't want to know.
I'll think him a criminal if you say so.
There's been more than enough to make me weep
without my stirring up that murky deep.
Now I see it all. Given all my fame
so that the world can better see my shame.
This time there's no escape. No new disguise
will ever shield me from their staring eyes.
I want to cast off everything and run
from you, from India, my mangled son,
the very universe, and leave behind
the frontiers marked out for humankind.

MEMSAHIB

No sir! Silence will no longer do!
These accusations! They were all untrue.
He's innocent . . .

GOVERNOR

        You were the very one
whose testimony made me curse my son.
You . . . !

MEMSAHIB

      Richard! Listen! I need to reassure
a father that his son died chaste and pure.
The guilt was mine. For which I now atone.
The inordinate desire was mine alone.
The ayah took advantage of my state
of shock and faintness to incriminate
your son to you, and of her own accord

205

accused him. She's had her just reward.
Like her, I wanted instant suicide
but wished to clear his name before I died.
I wanted, needed to confess, and so
I chose another, slower way to go –

The Memsahib sinks to her knees.

– there's poison in my veins, and beat by beat
the heart that once was blazing loses heat.
It's all as if I saw you through dark gauze,
through rain beginning like a slow applause.
I hear it starting now, the rain, cool rain
giving the blood-red earth new life again.
Rain. Rain. Like purdah curtains. When I die
the dawn will bring you all a clearer sky.

Memsahib dies.

ADC

She's dead!

GOVERNOR
                    But her black actions, they won't die.
They'll blaze for ever in the memory.
Clearer than day it all comes home to me.
Now let me force myself to go and see
what's left of him, and try to expiate
my dabbling with strange gods I've come to hate.
He must be buried with all honours due
his mother's and my rank . . .

Enter Lilamani.

                              and as for you –
Your family were mutineers. I realise
I seem some savage brute to your young eyes.
Your family mutinied. They raised the war.
I had to administer the rule of law.

Your family, now mine, have borne the cost
of crossing certain bounds best left uncrossed.
Now try to ford, though times force us apart,
those frontiers of blood into my heart.

*As the Governor speaks the Chuprassie and Servants
kneel and begin a chant which gradually becomes
dominant. The sound of rain like slow applause.*

THE PRINCE'S PLAY

Le Roi s'amuse
by Victor Hugo
in an English adaptation
by Tony Harrison

Introduction

THE FANATIC PILLAGER

'*Harrison, fanatique pillard.*'
        Victor Hugo, 'Preface' to *Cromwell* (1827)

I

Rigoletto was the first grand opera I ever saw, when I'd hitch-hiked to Paris in my teens and queued for the gods at the Paris Opéra, the Palais Garnier, topped by a gilt Apollo brandishing his lyre like a winning team captain in the FA Cup. Somewhere on that day the seeds of both *The Trackers of Oxyrhynchus* and *The Prince's Play* were sown without my knowing it. I've never forgotten the experience, though I have seen countless productions since. The impression that the final scene made was profound. The storm, the stabbing of Rigoletto's daughter Gilda, the jester exulting over the sack he thinks contains the Duke of Mantua:

> *Quest' e un buffone, ed un potente e questo!*
> *Ei sta sotto i miei piedi! E desso! oh gioia!*

The lightning flash, the thunder machine that Verdi specifies in the score, affected me more than any theatre I'd seen since the comedians, magicians, verse pantomimes and forties and fifties variety in Leeds which first made me love and want to create theatre. The success of Verdi's opera eclipsed Hugo's play (which was banned after only one performance in 1832), and is often used to belittle the original drama by critics like George Steiner, for example, who wrote that 'Victor Hugo's *Le Roi s'amuse* is an insufferable piece of *guignol;* as *Rigoletto,* it is enthralling.'

It seems to me enthralling before it was ever set to music. Verdi had better dramatic instincts and thought *Le Roi s'amuse* 'perhaps the greatest drama of modern times', and Triboulet 'a creation worthy of Shakepeare' and, in another letter, 'a character that is one of the greatest creations that the theatre can boast of, in any country and in all history' (23 April 1850). He writes to his librettist Piave of his flash of inspiration:

> Oh, *Le Roi s'amuse* is the greatest subject and perhaps the greatest drama of modern times. Triboulet is a creation worthy of Shakespeare . . . I was going over several subjects again when *Le Roi s'amuse* came into my mind like a flash of lightning, an inspiration . . . Yes, by God, that would be a winner.
>
> (8 May 1850)

When years later I read Hugo's play from a copy I'd come across on the stalls of a *bouquiniste* on the Seine, it had the same effect on me but instead of being created by the music, it was induced by the unadorned verse of Hugo, who for the same scene, where Verdi draws on the resources of a huge orchestra, and a distillation of Triboulet's speech, has a much longer magnificent tirade in his own brand of the Alexandrine. It was the Hugo version of the Alexandrine I'd always wanted to explore since my earlier immersion in those of the comic Moliere and the tragic Racine for the Old Vic, using the same metre for different ends, and in need of radical renewal by the Romantics. The cumulative venom of the verse is redistributed in the opera to horns and strings with the baritone Rigoletto left with only a simplified Italian couplet or two from Triboulet's French *tirade*. The unaccompanied verse works by the venomous accretions of crowing vengeance. The Jester drags the sack in which he believes he has the dead King down to the Seine:

TRIBOULET *Il est là! – Mort! Pourtant je voudrais*
 bien le voir.

Here, according to Hugo's stage directions, Triboulet
touches the sack:

C'est égal, c'est bien lui – Je le sens sous ce voile
Voici ses éperons qui traversent la toile. –

Now Triboulet puts a triumphant foot on the sack.

Maintenant, monde, regarde-moi.
Ceci, c'est un bouffon, et ceci, c'est un roi! –
Et quel roi! Le premier de tous! Le roi suprême!
Le voilà sous mes pieds, je le tiens. C'est lui-même.
La Seine pour sépulcre, et ce sac pour linceul.
Qui donc a fait cela?
  (Croisant les bras.)
                    Hé bien! oui, c'est moi seul. –

Hugo makes the Alexandrine perfectly conversational, stopping and starting to accommodate action, and then comes
up with a beautifully balanced line like

La Seine pour sépulcre, et ce sac pour linceul

and at once completes the couplet with prosaic address.
  His plays represent a total reworking of the neoclassical
Alexandrine. It was this speech that I went to when I
wanted to persuade Richard Eyre that it should be done at
the National Theatre. I offered him the choice of two plays
by Victor Hugo, *Le Roi s'amuse*, or *Torquemada*, another
powerful play on the dangers of ideology, with the In-
quisitor swearing he'll burn everyone to save them from
Hell, lighting bonfires from here to the stars. Both plays
are well worth the resources of the National Theatre.
Richard Eyre went for *Le Roi s'amuse* probably because
I already had an idea for a London setting for the play.

II

The Comédie-Française actor Ligier who was to play Triboulet wept through the whole of Act V, which contains the speech I quoted from above, when Hugo read *Le Roi s'amuse* to the company. Hugo records what Ligier said to him afterwards: 'Ligier me disait hier à la répétition que je reconstruisais le théâtre français.' What sort of reconstruction of French theatre was it exactly? How did Hugo and the Romantics throw off the restraints of neoclassical verse drama? Central to the endeavour was the example of Shakespeare, who combined high and low, sublime and grotesque, poetic and prosaic. Shakespeare's example stultified subsequent English drama but helped to reanimate both the German and French stages. In some ways the ghost of Shakespeare prevented English Romantic poets being quite as radical as Hugo, who was inspired by his dramaturgy but was not obliged to imitate his language. The English failure to do this is mocked by Coleridge:

> As the ingenious gentleman under the influence of the Tragic Muse contrived to dislocate 'I wish you a good morning, sir! Thank you, sir, and I wish you the same,' into blank verse heroics:

> 'To you a morning good, good sir! I wish.
> You, sir! I thank: to you the same wish I.'
> *Biographia Literaria*, xviii

As Hopkins wrote to Robert Bridges in 1885: 'The example of Shakespeare . . . has done ever so much harm by his very genius, for poets reproduce the diction which in him was modern and in them is obsolete.'

It was a great loss to English theatre when the great all-accommodating flexible blank verse of Shakespeare lost its theatrical energy and poetry adopted neoclassical 'rules'.

What Thomas Nashe could call the 'drumming decasillabon' in 1589 would become in the hands of Shakespeare and the Jacobeans one of the most flexible and varied metres in any language and richer than almost any other dramatic medium. That it encompassed a greater scale of language than anything else also depends on the heterogeneous audience, and audiences became more restricted after the age of the Globe. The blank verse eventually became the style parodied above by Coleridge, and we can see the process in its earlier stages in the work of Sir John Denham as early as 1642 with his play *The Sophy* which shows, according to the Rev. Gilfillan, 'here and there an appreciation of Shakespeare – shown in generous though hopeless rivalry of his manner' (1857). The year 1642 saw not only the closing of the theatres but also the publication of Denham's *Cooper's Hill* with the beginning of the monotonously regular couplet, losing the blank verse of the drama, where dramatic situations create the variety of invention in the verse, scansion being as much a question of dramatic character as metronome. Half a century later John Dennis is regretting what has been lost and what he calls 'the Harmony of Blank Verse', whose

> Diversity distinguishes it from Heroick Harmony, and bringing it nearer to common Use, makes it more proper to gain Attention, and more fit for Action and Dialogue. *Such Verses we make when we are writing prose; we make such Verse in common Conversation.*
>
> (1712)

It was dramatic sensitivity that gave immense variety to what could be monotonous dramatic blank verse.

Verse always needs to return itself to 'prose and common conversation'. Returning verse to the realities of prose is also to acknowledge the truth of dramatic situation. When they drift apart we tend to have our culture falling into the mutually exclusive categories of high and low.

Verse and prose. Sublime and grotesque. As the constantly perceptive Granville Barker says, the lines of Shakespeare and the Jacobeans 'are to be scanned – and can only be scanned – *dramatically and characteristically*'. Perhaps it is even better expressed by Coleridge in *Biographia Literaria*: 'Every passion has its proper pulse, so it will likewise have its characteristic modes of expression.'

I remember having a conversation about this with Richard Eyre, who was to direct *The Prince's Play,* during a rehearsal of *The Changeling*, which he was directing at the National Theatre. He had invited me to talk to the actors about verse, as it is a sad truth that even experienced actors often have little familiarity with verse – even Shakespeare – as their careers (and mortgages) are dependent on the intimate techniques of TV and film. To illustrate the truth of Granville Barker's observation, we could look at examples from the play they were rehearsing:

> ALSEMERO   Even now I observ'd
>   The temple's vane turn full in my face,
>   I know 'tis against me.
> JASPERINO   Against you?

The servant completes the five-stress line with an utter disbelief prosodically expressed in the three equally stressed syllables: 'Against you?' His surprise and mocking disbelief are part of the metre. His bunched stresses question his master's sanity. Something similarly simple at the end of the play when De Flores is confronted:

> TOMAZO Ha! my brother's murderer?
> DE FLORES   Yes, and her honour's prize
>   Was my reward; I thank life for nothing
>   But that pleasure; it was so sweet to me
>   That I have drunk up all, left none behind
>   For any man to pledge me.

The defiant sexual relish of De Flores before Alsemero the husband of Beatrice Joanna and Vermandero is metrically flourished in 'was so sweet . . . '. It's a similar dramatic stress to what we find in Wyatt's line from his sonnet 'They flee from me that sometime did me seek', so misunderstood by his editor Tottel:

It was no dream; I lay broad waking.

Tottell, who edited the poem, didn't understand the dramatic stress of 'I lay broad waking' and printed the line as:

It was no dream, for I lay broad awaking.

Almost all critics and academics who review poetry or the theatre are afflicted with a bad case of Tottel's ear. In one of the very few good scholarly books on theatre poetry, *The Poetics of Jacobean Drama*, Coburn Freer condemns most of his colleagues when he says:

As far as the bulk of published criticism on English Renaissance drama is concerned, including criticism of Shakespeare, the plays might as well have been written in prose . . . when the verse is noted at all, it is made to sound like a background Muzak.

What the rare perceptive critic could see in Jacobean verse could also be applied to Molière:

The opinion, still often encountered, that Molière wrote 'carelessly' or 'awkwardly' usually overlooks the fact that he was a *dramatic* poet, and that Alexandrines that are criticised for their ungainly style may, in their dramatic context, be the apt expression of a character's evasiveness, embarrassment, anger or pedantic self-importance, as the case may be.

> W. G. Howarth,
> *Molière: a Playwright and his Audience* (1982)

We can see in *The Misanthrope* the headlong angry impetus of Alceste and that of the mollifying Philinte trying to apply the brake, and the insinuation of Arsinoe. The variations on the basically similar metrical base both distinguish the characters by a bespoke tempo and also bind them in a united fate emblemised by the shared metrical code. No one understood this fact better than Victor Hugo himself and as he himself puts it in the great gauntlet-throwing preface to *Cromwell* (1827): 'Molière est dramatique.'

III

So while the influence of Shakespeare stifled English theatre, because it came removed from its English, it vivified German and French theatre in different ways. In Germany the example of Shakespeare, whom they also adapted for Weimar, helped Goethe and Schiller to create a new German drama. Goethe's *Götz von Berlichingen* (1773) 'used . . . for the first time since Shakespeare . . . a dramatic language which ranged from the coarse expressions of the soldiers' camp to the heights of poetic rhetoric.' A contemporary review termed the work 'the most beautiful, the most captivating monstrosity'. It was monstrous, of course, because it shattered every rule of French classical dramaturgy. It was in fact 'Shakespearean', and to those who cleaved to the ideals of neoclassical French that was repellent. Frederick the Great of Prussia was one such, and even in 1780 called it *'une imitation détestable de ces mauvaises pièces anglaises'*.

Significantly this early stage work of Goethe was written in *prose* which could pass from high to low with greater facility than the neoclassical verse derived from Corneille, Racine and Voltaire. The increasingly classicising world of Weimar found itself less able to accommodate the Shakespeare who encompassed both low and high. Goethe's later practice was to convert a first prose version into blank verse, creating blank verse derived from Shakespeare by the rules of French neoclassical drama. As Michael Hamburger observes, 'At their most Shakespearean, Goethe and Schiller wrote their plays in prose.' As Goethe and Schiller became more self-consciously 'classical' they tried to omit from Shakespeare those aspects, the low characters and language, which were the very things that inspired the French Romantics to throw off the restraints of Racine. Both Goethe and Schiller adapted Shakespeare more to the taste of Weimar. The porter in *Macbeth* was an obvious casualty in Schiller's version. So was Mercutio in Goethe's *Romeo and Juliet*. By 1815 Goethe had come to the opinion that Shakespeare was better read than performed.

The French had their own neoclassical verse drama with its Aristotelian unities of time and place and rarefied language and in the regular Alexandrine, which a renewed acquaintance with Shakespeare helped to overthrow. Shakespeare was rediscovered by the French Romantics during the visit to Paris of Charles Kemble's company in 1827 with Harriet Smithson (1800–1854) – who played Ophelia and Juliet and later married Hector Berlioz in 1833 – a member of the appreciative audience, which also included Gautier, Dumas *père,* Delacroix and Victor Hugo, for whom Shakespeare became the inspiration to overthrow the restrictions of neoclassical drama in France with its unities and its diction that excluded everything prosaic. Verdi thought the creation of the hunchbacked jester Triboulet 'worthy of Shakespeare', and for Hugo Shakespeare was 'the deity of the theatre, in whom the three characteristic geniuses of our own stage, Corneille, Molière, and Beaumarchais, seem united, three persons in one' ('Preface' to *Cromwell*).

Hugo was not, like Goethe and Schiller, anxious to delete or devulgarise the porter in *Macbeth* or exclude the Fool from *Lear.* Far from it! In his groundbreaking but rarely performed *Cromwell* Hugo gives the Protector no less than four fools, Trick, Giraff, Gramadoch, and Elespuru! It is in the great 'Preface' to this huge play that Hugo sets out his credo for the theatre of his time. Again we find verse being renewed by plunging it into the constant flow of conversational prose, the language of real situations.

What Hugo says in his 'Preface' to *Cromwell* is that, like Shakespeare, he wanted to run the whole poetic gamut from the high to the low, from the most elevated ideas to the most vulgar, from the most comic to the most serious, without ever leaving the confines of the spoken scene. This is the sort of poetry a man would write if a spirit had endowed him with the soul of Corneille and the head of Molière. 'Il nous semble que ce vers-là serait bien *aussi beau que de la prose*' (Hugo's italics). 'I have flung classical verse to the black dogs of prose!' he writes in a wonderfully combatant manifesto poem which can be set beside the 'Preface' to *Cromwell* as a central French Romantic text. Both 'Preface' and poem bristle with Hugo's phenomenal energy:

> Je fis souffler un vent révolutionnaire,
> Je mis un bonnet rouge au vieux dictionnaire.
> Plus de mot sénateur! plus de mot roturier!
> Je fis un tempête au fond de l'encrier,
> Et je mêlai, parmi les ombres débordées,
> Au peuple noir des mots l'essaim blanc des idées . . .
> Je massacrai l'albâtre, et la neige, et l'ivoire;
> Je retirai le jais de la prunelle noire,
> Et j'osai dire au bras: Sois blanc, tout simplement.
> Je violai du vers le cadavre fumant;
> J'y fis entrer le chiffre; O terreur! Mithridate
> Du siège de Cyzique eut pu citer la date . . .
> J'ai dite aux mots: Soyez république! Soyez
> La fourmilière immense, et travaillez! croyez,
> Aimez, vivez! – J'ai mis tout en branle, et, morose
> J'ai jeté le vers noble aux chiens noirs de la prose.
>
> Réponse à un acte d'accusation (1834)

The old dictionary flaunts the red liberty cap of the revolutionary. (I have one of Jocelyn Herbert's Fury masks from the *Oresteia* on my OED!) Arms are simply white not 'alabaster' or 'ivory'. He will use prosaic calendar dates as he did when he flung down the gauntlet in the very first line of *Cromwell*:

> *Demain, vingt-cinq juin mil six cent cinquante-sept* . . .

Words will be republican and *work*. The distinctions between high and low are abolished. This is not a theatrical sensibility that would shy away from *le mouchoir* of Vigny's *Othello,* even if the grand actress Mlle Mars would find it utterly objectionable and ask for the genteel circumlocutions of neoclassical verse at its worst – Mlle Mars (1779–1847), past whose somewhat stern and disapproving bust I walk when I go to see anything at the Comédie-Française or even when I just pass by. Her stare looks through the glass doors of the Comédie-Française whenever I walk from my favourite little hotel, next to the statue of Molière, to any of my favourite brasseries. She was not hospitable to assaults like Hugo's on '*le vers noble*', being renowned for rejecting Vigny's *mouchoir* from his *Le More de Venise* (1829), the handkerchief of Shakespeare's *Othello*. She would have accepted the periphrastic euphemism of *fatal tissu* or *lin leger*. Snotrag was still a century away. The handkerchief became the kitchen sink of French Romantic drama. Oscar Wilde in *The Truth of Masks* talks about the French Shakespearean translator Jean François Ducis (1733–1816), who had to adapt the plays so that they conformed to the 'unities' of French neoclassical taste. He had great difficulty also with the handkerchief and tried 'to soften its grossness by having the Moor reiterate "*Le bandeau! Le bandeau!*".' And a sack with a king's body in it? Unthinkable!

In 1829 a production of Hugo's earlier verse drama *Marion de Lorme* was planned with Mlle Mars as Marion.

But the Ministry of the Interior refused to authorise its performance, on the grounds of its suspected allusions to Charles X. So Hugo turned from the Comédie-Française to the boulevard theatre. The actress Marie Dorval (1798–1849), unlike Mlle Mars, came from boulevard theatre and was unused to the grand verse style and found the Alexandrine uncongenial. Marie Dorval played at the Théâtre de la Porte-Saint-Marin, which was not subsidised by the state and less hassled by censorship. Its staple was melodrama, its audience more mixed than that of the Comédie-Française. One reason for this was that its prices were a good deal cheaper, and the writer who wrote most plays for it was Pixérécourt (1773–1844), 'the Corneille of Melodrama', who always claimed that he 'wrote for those who cannot read'.

A year before *Le Roi s'amuse* Hugo had given his *Marion de Lorme* to this theatre and Marie Dorval had played the title role. Romantic drama shocked this public less than the elite at the Comédie-Française. What is interesting about this experience for Hugo, who wanted to bring her to the Comédie-Française for *Le Roi s'amuse,* is that a study of the emendations made by Hugo during the rehearsals for *Marion de Lorme* reveal the influence of the boulevard actress pushing Hugo further along the road of his manifesto aims in the 'Preface' to *Cromwell*. The manuscript as studied by the scholar M. Descotes shows that the actress was frequently inducing Hugo towards making his verse more broken up, more jagged, in short more *prosaic*. This is the kind of change that I am also used to making in rehearsals. Hugo clearly valued the experience as the manuscript contract with the Théâtre Français for *Le Roi s'amuse* makes clear in the controversial point that it was Hugo himself and not Alfred de Vigny, who was her lover, who insisted on the engagement of Marie Dorval 'sur l'expresse demande de M. Hugo'. Hugo even threatened to take the play elsewhere if she could not be hired. She was unavailable on this occasion. Mlle Mars refused. Marie Dorval wasn't to appear at the Comédie-Française until 1834 in the role of Kitty Bell in *Chatterton* by Alfred de Vigny (1797–1863), her lover, with whom she turned up for the première of *Le Roi s'amuse*. So did Mlle Mars, who had refused a role in the play and whose jealousy eventually was to drive Marie Dorval from the Comédie-Française back to the boulevards.

IV

This impulse to bring the energy of natural prose into verse is a constantly renewing strategy, as natural colloquial speech which changes rapidly can leave successive poetic styles marooned, and when poetry reconnects with prose it reanimates itself. Sometimes it means that the inherited form struggles to accommodate itself to the freedom of conversation and sometimes, as in the case of Ibsen, it means an abandonment of poetic drama entirely. To consider the case of Ibsen is crucial for anyone who wants to write poetry for the theatre. Ibsen, who was a great dramatic poet, did not re-energise his verse by tempering it in douches of prose, but deserted the medium entirely for prose because, as he wrote to Lucie Wolf in 1883:

> The stage is for dramatic art alone, and declamation is not dramatic art . . . Verse has done immense injury to the art of the theatre . . . It is most unlikely that the verse form will be employed to any extent worth mentioning in the drama of the immediate future; for the dramatic aims of the future will pretty certainly be incompatible with it. It is therefore doomed to extinction. For art forms die out, just as the preposterous animal forms of prehistoric times died out when their day was over . . . I myself, for the last seven or eight years, have

hardly written a single verse, but have cultivated exclusively the incomparably more difficult art of poetic creation in the plain unvarnished speech of reality.

Henrik Ibsen, letter to Lucie Wolf, May 1883

This is a daunting text for the dramatic poet of our day, though I comfort myself by noting he refers to the *immediate* future. It is also some comfort to know that Ibsen told C. H. Hereford, who translated *Brand* into English, that he would probably write his last play in verse 'if only one knew which play would be the last'. *When We Dead Awaken* was his last, but I can imagine Ibsen not wanting to fulfil his promise to Hereford because he would never want to face the fact that anything he was writing could be his last. But his English translator and biographer Michael Meyer wrote that he thought that *When We Dead Awaken* 'would have been a much greater play if he had written it in poetry – as he nearly did'.

V

Hugo's *Le Roi s'amuse* had its first and *last* performance on 22 November 1832. It was 'suspended' by the Ministry. Contemporary accounts speak of the tumult in the house following Triboulet's

> *vos mères aux laquais se sont prostituées.*

A review which history has dragged out of its timid anonymity and shown to be by Lucca described *Le Roi s'amuse* as one of the 'most grotesque abortions of French dramatic literature'. A supercilious critic said that the much vaunted revolution in drama had met its Waterloo:

> *La révolution dramatique a été battue avant-hier à la Comédie-Française, elle est en pleine déroute: c'est le Waterloo du Romantisme.*

It wasn't played again until 1882, and a witness noted that the respectful silence was a hundred times more cruel than the hostile cries of 1832. The actor Got, who played Triboulet fifty years after Ligier, noted in his journal that there was above all '*froideur*' and '*ennui*' in the audience. Edmond Bire: '*Le grand poète offre au peuple, au mauvais peuple, un tableau jacobin.*' He condemns not only *Le roi s'amuse* but also *Lucrece Borgia* as belonging to the 'prolonged revolution'.

Lucrece Borgia (1833) was Hugo's next play after the disappointment of the banned *Le Roi s'amuse*. He speaks in the 'Preface' of the two plays as a 'bilogy' conceived at the same time, but with the important difference that he wrote *Lucrece Borgia* in *prose* for the boulevard theatre, the Porte-Saint-Martin. Graham Robb in his wonderfully full, engrossing and often funny biography of Hugo records how the old claque of Romantics, who came as vociferous supporters to both *Hernani* and *Le Roi s'amuse*, were horrified to know that the characters of the new play would speak prose and demanded an explanation of Hugo. He convinced them that 'it was the duty of Romanticism to renovate prose just as it had smashed the old Alexandrine mould'. And that in itself, if he had done nothing else, was a great achievement, even for this ninetenth-century giant.

VI

How could I bring the 'Waterloo of Romanticism' to Waterloo? As with the Paris of de Gaulle in *The Misanthrope* with street unrest and disturbance round the corner in 1968, or with the Indian Mutiny hovering over *Phaedra Britannica*, I was looking for a way of setting *Le Roi s'amuse* in a more familiar period that would re-energise the social tensions and clarify the corruption and anti-royal tirades of Triboulet. I wanted to bring it a little nearer home, and came up finally with the mid 1880s, the London of Jack the Ripper, with its answering *guignol*, and constant rumours of royal scandal round Eddie the Duke of Clarence. It was the world of that earlier Bloody Sunday of 13 November 1887, when an estimated 20,000 unemployed demonstrated in Trafalgar Square. Sir Charles Warren opposed them with 4000 constables, plus Life Guards and Grenadier Guards. And it was a time of Royal affiliations with actresses, chorus girls, comedians like Dan Leno, known universally as 'the King's Jester'. The King's Jester in my version eventually became a Glaswegian music-hall comic. I didn't begin to finalise the comic's speeches, even though they were the ones I was first naturally drawn to, until I knew who we would find to play him. I would always seek to use the natural first accent of the actor, so had not decided whether the comic was a Cockney or a Northerner, a Lancashire Ian McKellen or a Geordie, like Alun Armstrong, or, as it finally turned out, a Scot, when Richard Eyre cast Ken Stott. I made him a working-class Glasgow comic who found success in London and was patronised by His Royal Highness. Ken Stott, who proved utterly brilliant in the role, bridging the comedy and tragedy with an ease that would have gladdened the soul of Hugo, became Scotty Scott, with a tartan hump made to look like the bag of a bagpipe bristling with chanters. He became like a bitter version of Harry Lauder with no chance whatever of being dubbed a knight. The way he has to ingratiate himself on stage and off to the set that hangs around HRH eats like a canker in his soul. On the other hand the 'Poet Laureate', whom I made the equivalent of Hugo's Clement Marot, poet to the court of Francis I, although like Scotty Scott also of humble origin, had totally transformed himself, modelling his accent and behaviour on the gang of witless aristocrats hanging round HRH. He becomes a genteel version of the jester, writing the romantic chat-up lines for a prince who can't think them up himself. Verdi and Piave don't bring the Poet into *Rigoletto*. But, unbelievably, we still have a Poet Laureate, and a monarchy! It should be pointed out that I created this character out of the Marot of Hugo and it was some five years before I wrote my poem *Laureate's Block*!

The period we chose to set the play in was also a time when, as now, the Prince of Wales was a great asset to republican propagandists. Ramsay MacDonald, looking back at the period, writes in the journal *Democracy* in 1901, 'the throne seemed to be tottering . . . the Queen and the Prince of Wales had no hold on the popular mind; there was a spirit of democratic independence abroad; the common man believed in the common man', but is forced to add: 'That has gone.' Even Queen Victoria wrote to the Lord Chancellor when the behaviour of the Prince of Wales was increasing that democratic independence 'of these days when the higher classes, in their frivolous, selfish and pleasure-seeking lives, do more to increase the spirit of democracy than anything else'. Democracy is, of course, a dirty word. It's no surprise that when the Queen saw Tom Taylor's adaptation of Hugo's play, *The Fool's Revenge*, she was not amused: 'a dreadful play', she notes in her journal, 'adapted from Victor Hugo's *Le Roi s'amuse,* and the same subject as *Rigoletto,* only altered. It is a most immoral, improper piece . . . '

My aim was to bring that immorality and impropriety the unamused monarch saw underneath the play out into the open. In *Cromwell* Hugo gives Harrison, the fanatic pillager, the following lines:

Il ne reste plus rien des biens de la couronne.
Hampton-Court est vendue au profit du trésor;
On a détruit Woodstock, et démeublé Windsor.
          Victor Hugo, *Cromwell*, Act I, Scene ix

[2001]

The Prince's Play was first performed in the Olivier Theatre at the Royal National Theatre on 19 April 1996 with the following company:

Scotty Scott, the Comic Ken Stott
HRH the Prince of Wales David Westhead
Barmaid Catherine Tate
Lord Tourland Andrew Havill
Lord Gordon William Chubb
Lady Gossett Michele Moran
Lord Gossett Robert Swann
Lady Coslin Kathleen McGoldrick
The Poet Laureate Iain Mitchell
The Duke of Peen Joseph Bennett
Sir Percival Dillon Dugald Bruce-Lockhart
Montgomery Martin Chamberlain
Lord Bryan Simon Markey
Waiter at the Café Royal Thierry Harcourt
Lord Kintyre Michael Bryant
The Diddicoy Sean Chapman
Equerry Patrick Baladi
HRH's Bodyguard Anthony Renshaw
Becky, the Comic's daughter Arlene Cockburn
Mrs Bryden June Watson
Magdalena Rachel Power
Woman Judith Coke
Carter Edward Clayton
Doctor Paul Benzing

Other parts played by members of the company.

Director Richard Eyre
Designer Bob Crowley
Lighting Jean Kalman
Music Richard Blackford
Director of Movement Jane Gibson
Dialect Coach Joan Washington
Sound Paul Groothuis
Stage Manager Trish Montemuro
Deputy Stage Manager Fiona Bardsley
Assistant Stage Managers Valerie Fox, Andrew Speed

Grateful thanks are due to Marion Holland for invaluable assistance with research.

T. H.

Act One: Lord Kintyre

SCENE ONE

We hear the sound of someone being followed in a cobbled street. The sound intensifies to the sound of dancing clogs, which are then seen dancing in a narrow circle of spotlight. The spotlight widens to reveal the comic (Scotty Scott) dressed as a woman, doing a clog dance in a London music hall with a golden proscenium.

HRH the Prince of Wales with various aristocratic hangers-on is in a box near the stage. The act ends. Scotty Scott curtsies to the 'royal box'. HRH throws him a bouquet, which Scotty Scott picks up and clasps to his bosom and curtsies again.

Exit Scotty Scott to change for the next number. It is the interval. A Barmaid brings in champagne and glasses for HRH's party. HRH gooses the Barmaid as she pours his champagne.

BARMAID

Your Royal Highness!

Exit Barmaid.

HRH

Fillies, eh? And fizz!
Is there more to life? Don't think there is.
Fillies and fizz! What else is there beside?
And I've found a filly I can't wait to ride.
Nothing like the hunt! My sights are set
on game I haven't had much luck with yet,
but I won't be happy till she's in my snare.
An obvious pleb, of course, born God knows where,
but so damnably enticing!

LORD TOURLAND
Is it her
you've followed to chapel these past Sundays, sir?

HRH
(*laughing*)
A Cheapside chapel! Praying in my pew!

LORD TOURLAND
You've been up to this at least a month or two.

HRH
I know.

LORD TOURLAND
And she lives where, this present belle?

HRH
Close to Lord Gossett's.

LORD TOURLAND
Gossett's, know it well.
Splendid mansion! Somewhat spoiled by views
over a rather squalid little mews.

HRH
That's Bussy Street, that unlit cul-de-sac.

LORD TOURLAND
Ah, so that's where you've tracked your quarry back.
Have you had the chance to get inside?

HRH
No, not at all, although I've really tried.
There's some old Scottish crone
who guards her day and night as chaperone.
All she's allowed to say, to see, to hear
's decided by this dragon overseer.
But they've all got their price. I might just grease
the door ajar with a 'wee bag of bawbees'.

There's this dragon and at night a shape,
wrapped and muffled in an ink-black cape
which makes him merge with shadows, goes inside.

LORD TOURLAND
If he does, why can't you?

HRH
God knows I've tried!
I'd love to get inside. I've tried to, but
the door's immediately closed fast and bolted shut.

LORD TOURLAND
And has this filly given Your Highness cause
to think she welcomes this pursuit of yours?

HRH
Not uninterested 's my frank surmise.
No obvious revulsion in her eyes.

LORD TOURLAND
Is she aware that she's a prince's prey?

HRH
No, wouldn't do to give the game away.
I cultivate the homespun studious looks
of a poor student who spends his life with books.
Sallow, skinny, studious, and skint.

LORD TOURLAND
Probably some Bishop's secret bint!

*A roll of drums and from behind the curtain the skirl
of bagpipes being played. The curtain rises revealing
Scotty Scott in full Scottish tartan, kilt and sporran,
playing the bagpipes.*

HRH
(calling out to Scotty Scott on the stage)
Give us a wise ruling from the boards
on how the ladies should be handled by these Lords.

233

Silence is the secret. My advice on this is:
seal your lips if you seek stolen kisses.
What's your opinion? Am I right or wrong!

SCOTTY SCOTT

Right, Your Highness. But listen to my song.

*Music. Scotty Scott goes into his routine song
of 'The Ladies! The Ladies!'*

SCOTTY SCOTT
(singing)

Pity this poor Glasgow lad
come to London in his plaid.
The Ladies can't stand my pipes' lilt
and when I sport my sporran
they spurn me as foreign
and I've never once lifted my kilt.

My tartan tirade is
the Ladies, the Ladies,
the Ladies I love just won't stay.
The Ladies, God bless 'em,
I long to possess 'em
but Ladies, they all fly away.

The Ladies, God bless 'em,
we long to possess 'em
but Ladies, they all fly away.

The Ladies, God bless 'em,
we long to possess 'em
but Ladies, they all fly away.

Where the soldiers parade is
where you'll see the Ladies
watching fine soldiers on show,
but when stout lads present
(you know what is meant!)
the Ladies, the Ladies they always say NO!

BUT . . .

There's a lad with more luck in
these matters of . . . [friendship]
one groomed for a very posh job,
phenomenally firm in fine ermine
he's known as the nation's top nob!

HRH and his troupe join in on 'top nob'.

The Ladies, God bless 'em,
we long to possess 'em
but Ladies, they all fly away.

The Ladies, God bless 'em,
we long to possess 'em
but Ladies, they all fly away.

The Ladies, the Ladies
the one who's got it made is
the man who can love 'em then flee
and there's said to be royals
who don't have the toils
and troubles the Ladies, the Ladies give me!

The dancer, the Duchess
och, all that he touches
whatever the Lady, och aye,
the Wizard of Windsor's wand wins her
he never, like Scotty, need sigh . . .

The Ladies, God bless 'em,
I long to possess 'em,
but Ladies, they all fly away.

*Scotty Scott invites the audience and aristocrats to
engage in a singing competition using some of the
following couplets.*

(1)

You in the cheap seats, let's hear you outsing
this choir of cronies of your future King!

(2)

Your Royal Highness and your noble train
versus the plebs in singing my refrain:

*If the audience does seem louder than the aristocrats
then Scotty says:*

(1)

Your Royal Highness, your team's below par
they need a shot of champers from the bar!

(2)

Your Royal Highness, your Dukes and Lords
need more *Veuve Cliquot* on their vocal cords.
Give 'em a gargle and let's see
if they can't sing my song with more *esprit.*

*If the audience fails to respond to Scotty's cajoling,
HRH should address his subjects as follows:*

(1)

I hereby command you as your future King
to pull your fingers out at once, and sing.

(2)

All our future subjects now before us
are forthwith commanded to join in the chorus.

SCOTTY SCOTT

The Ladies, God bless 'em,
we long to possess 'em,
but Ladies, they all fly away.

The Ladies, the Ladies,
the one time I strayed is
the time when the wife was away.

But the wife came back early
caught me and my girly
dreadf'ly indecorous and *déshabillé*!

Och, I know what the French is
for wenches, for wenches,
the wenches in French are all *filles*.
No *fille* ever winces at princes
but wenches all wince to meet me.

The Ladies, God bless 'em,
I long to possess 'em,
but Ladies, they all fly away.

The Ladles, God bless 'em,
we long to possess 'em,
but Ladies, they all fly away.

The Ladies, the Ladies,
one Lady who stayed is
one that I wished had took flight.
And O God Almighty,
the wife in her nighty
will make sure I'm in bed tonight.

> *Applause and the curtain comes down, the audience
> exit.*

SCENE TWO

*Backstage of the same music hall, with dressing rooms
in a long corridor with fans and aristocratic stage-door
Johnnies lining the walls waiting for chorus girls etc.*
  *HRH and retinue are loitering about watching the
women pass, straining to catch a glimpse of stocking in
the women's dressing rooms.*

LORD TOURLAND
I'd love her in my bed. She's so divine.

LORD GORDON
Either of that pair would do for mine.

HRH
(*calling over to the Lords*)
Gorgeous Lady Gossett's got my choice!

LORD GORDON
(*indicating Lord Gossett,
one of the fattest men in England*)
The husband's over there, sir, watch your voice!

HRH
The husband, for all I care, can go to hell.

*HRH pursues Lady Gossett. Lord Gordon talks
to Scotty Scott.*

LORD GORDON
Wasn't Lord Kintyre's daughter this month's belle?
Seems there's a new one now. Who'd think he'd tire
so quickly of the daughter of Kintyre?
She dropped her pantaloons to save her pater
only to get the push-off three weeks later.

SCOTTY SCOTT
Yes, now she's pretty shattered and heartbroken.

He hasn't written to her, hasn't spoken
for at least a week . . .

LORD GORDON

                    Perhaps he'll pack
her off to her husband if he'll have her back.
After all she's paid the Prince the dues
no daughter in her place could well refuse
when he lent his influence to sway the Bar
and get her father off.

SCOTTY SCOTT

                   All most bizarre.
But what possessed Kintyre to have her wed,
to pack off a beauty like her to the bed
of that bloated Birmingham Lord Mayor?

LORD GORDON

Lord Kintyre's odd! I followed the affair
and for the whole duration sat in court.
Not knowing his acquittal had been bought
for a price his precious daughter had to pay
the Prince in kind, I heard Kintyre pray
to God to bless the Prince of Wales, his friend.
Now, apparently, he's really round the bend.

HRH
(passing with Lady Gossett)

Leaving London? You'll tear my heart in two!

LADY GOSSETT

My husband's adamant, what can I do?

HRH

What can you do? I beg you, just say no.
The whole of London cries 'Don't go! Don't go!'
The name most often on the poets' lips,
most toasted by lieutenants, is Your Ladyship's.
You make the city glow. You shine so bright

239

your leaving will plunge London into night.
You'd scorn your future monarch, scorn
the devotion of the best and noblest born,
the meteors of the metropolitan Heaven
to be a dazzling star in darkest Devon!

LADY GOSSETT
(*with one eye on her watching husband*)
Your Highness, sshhh!

HRH
London with you not here 's
like a ballroom when the brightest chandelier 's
been snuffed, or bright stars leave the skies.

LADY GOSSETT
(*pulling away from HRH as her husband approaches*)
My husband's watching us.

HRH
O damn his eyes!

Lord Gossett shepherds his wife away.

HRH
(*to Scotty Scott*)
I wrote that idiot's wife a passionate ode.
It's odd our new Poet Laureate never showed
my little effort to you.

SCOTTY SCOTT
God forbid!
Frankly I'm relieved he never did.
I can't stand verses. His are bad enough
without Your Highness churning out the stuff.
Let the Laureate make the verses, you make love.
Only poets rhyme carnality with dove.

HRH
Rhyming for women lifts the heart. It sings.
It gives my royal dungeon soaring wings.

SCOTTY SCOTT

Makes Windsor like a windmill! Then you'd find
you did nothing else all night and day but grind!

*For a moment HRH is offended. Scotty Scott's gone
too far.*

HRH

I think that you've just earned a dose of whip . . .

*HRH sees Lady Coslin passing by and says loud
enough for her to hear:*

if I weren't enamoured of Her Ladyship.

SCOTTY SCOTT
(*bitter from the whipping threat*)

Fickle as the wind! The feller flirts
with everything that flounces by in skirts.

Lord Gordon comes up to Scotty Scott.

LORD GORDON

Watch Lady Gossett. I think we'll get
the old dropped-glove routine now. Want to bet?

*Scotty Scott nods and he and Lord Gordon watch
Lady Gossett as she drops her bouquet. HRH leaves
Lady Coslin whom he has been flirting with and
retrieves the dropped bouquet, and begins to chat
to Lady Gossett.*

LORD GORDON

What did I tell you? Trapped and no escape.

SCOTTY SCOTT

The ladies, they're demons in human shape.

LORD GORDON
(*noticing the husband of Lady Gossett approaching*)

The husband!

LADY GOSSETT
(*also noticing her husband*)
Your Highness, please! No more!

SCOTTY SCOTT
What's old jealous fat-guts come here for?
Old Lord Fatso's wobbling wattles all aquiver
because he sees his wife and *who* is wiv 'er!

LORD GOSSETT
Are they whispering about me over there?

LORD TOURLAND
She's very beautiful, your wife. Take care!

Lord Gossett backs away.

LORD GORDON
Why are you always so preoccupied,
continually glancing from side to side?

*Lord Gossett backs away from Lord Gordon and
finds himself face to face with Scotty Scott.*

SCOTTY SCOTT
It's the pressure of perpetual suspicion
that gives such mad persistence to his mission.

*Lord Gossett bustles his wife away from HRH, who
returns to his cronies.*

HRH
(*to Scotty Scott*)
The Ladies, the Ladies! Eh, my friend!
My Heaven 's the Ladies laid end to end.
What about you?

SCOTTY SCOTT
                    Me, I'm the sort of bloke
who's been made to feel that life's just one big joke.
You gallivant, I glower, you cavort, I crack

the black jokes of the scathing, scorned hunchback.
Balls and sports and love affairs are best
when seen, with due detachment, as a jest.

HRH
I bless the day Her Majesty the Queen
conceived me. With Lord Gossett off the scene
I'd be ecstatic. What's your view of him?

SCOTTY SCOTT
Not only a deformity but dim!

HRH
Indisputably a dampener! His jealous bile
has rather cramped the roving royal style.
I can want what I want, and what I want I get
except for Lord Gossett's wife who's not mine, yet.
But how wonderful it is just to exist!
The world's so happy!

SCOTTY SCOTT
                    And the Prince so pissed!

*HRH and Scotty Scott watch Lady Gossett,
chaperoned closely by her anxious husband.*

HRH
Her eyes! Her arms! How beautiful she is!

Then to Scotty Scott, leaning on him:

Escort us to more fillies and more fizz.

*Scotty Scott supports the tipsy HRH and they sing,
as they exit to the Café Royal, a few choruses of
'The Ladies! The Ladies!'*

SCENE THREE

The Café Royal. The same mixture of nobles and notables.

POET LAUREATE

What's the news?

LORD GORDON
                    His Royal Highness is at play.

POET LAUREATE

That's not news. It happens every day.

LORD GOSSETT
(*restlessly pacing the room*)

It's very bad news for some. The Prince's sport
's fine for the catcher, less fine for the caught.

LORD GORDON

Poor fat Lord Gossett makes my spirit wince.

POET LAUREATE

His wife's the latest plaything of the Prince.

LORD GORDON

Ah, here's the Duke!

Enter the Duke of Peen.

DUKE OF PEEN
(*excited, breathless*)
                    You'll die! You'll die!

It's something you'll be flabbergasted by,
It's sensational, hilarious, sublime.
It craves the permanence of verse and rhyme.
It needs immortalising. A limerick
from the Laureate here would do the trick.

POET LAUREATE
(*haughty and offended*)

I don't do limericks.

DUKE OF PEEN

Oh what a toffee-nose!
You'll wish you did write limericks when I expose
the hunchback's little secret!

SIR PERCIVAL DILLON

He's lost his hunch!

POET LAUREATE

They're going to serve his body up for lunch,
his head on a platter, as befits a boar,
and a great big apple jammed into his jaw.

DUKE OF PEEN

No, nothing like that, no, the hunchback's got . . .

MONTGOMERY

The pox!

LORD BRYAN

A secret hoard of money.

SIR PERCIVAL DILLON

Not . . .

no, *not* a knighthood. That would be obscene.
I'd have to return *my* knighthood to the Queen.

DUKE OF PEEN

No, you won't believe it. Your sides will split . . .
The hunchback 's got himself a fancy bit!

ALL
(*laughing*)

No! Never! Get away!

DUKE OF PEEN
                    No, honestly, I swear.
He keeps her hidden and I've found out where.
Got her installed in grubby Bussy Street,
pretty dilapidated but at least discreet.
He goes there every night wrapped in a cloak
and not looking like a man who likes a joke,
sombre and intense, more like a poet,
and nobody would ever even know it,
if I hadn't been myself . . . out for a stroll . . .
I've got a little plan. Don't tell a soul.

POET LAUREATE
Yes, only a limerick could include
the paradox of him and love. I'll make it rude.

   Lord Tourland joins them.

SIR PERCIVAL DILLON
Talking of dark ladies what about the Prince
who started prowling too some eight weeks since?
Like someone searching for a buried treasure.

MONTGOMERY
What's he up to?

LORD TOURLAND
                    The pursuit of pleasure.
You know how it always is with him –
the wind blows and he gets a sudden whim,
this time to go about dressed in the kind
of clothes that keep him out of sight and out of mind
until he's in some bedroom, God knows whose.
But I'm not married. I've no wife to lose.

LORD GOSSETT
It's a very old established royal habit
to see happiness in others and then grab it.
Those I feel sorry for, the men I pity,

have daughters, wives and sisters in this city
to fall ready victims to the roving eye
of the future king they'll be dishonoured by.
Exercising royal power for power's sake 's
twice as thrilling the more waste it makes.
All His Royal Highness's great gay guffaws
just show the vicious teeth that fill his jaws.

LORD TOURLAND
He really fears the Prince.

SIR PERCIVAL DILLON
       His wife much less.

POET LAUREATE
His fear 's engendered by her fearlessness.

LORD GORDON
I think it's the duty of a Duke or Lord
to make damn sure the Prince is never bored.

DUKE OF PEEN
Yes, when he's bored, his boredom casts a cloud
all over Britain. So boredom's not allowed.

SIR PERCIVAL DILLON
Keep him amused by any means you know.

*They hear HRH and Scotty Scott still singing snatches
of 'The Ladies! The Ladies!'*

Here comes the Prince with 'lover-boy' in tow.

*Enter HRH and Scotty Scott. The nobles stand for
HRH.*

SCENE FOUR

The same. Scotty Scott looks round the company with
obvious distaste for the literati and university dons.

SCOTTY SCOTT
Too many intellectuals (so called!)
around tonight, Your Highness, I'm appalled.

HRH
The family rather think a poet or prof
might profit me. Something might rub off.

SCOTTY SCOTT
Your Highness, as one less drunk than you,
I've got the better judgement of the two
and as one less befuddled, with a clearer brain,
rather than intellectuals I'd entertain
diarrhoea!

HRH
      You overstep the bounds!
Educating me for when I'm crowned 's
important.

SCOTTY SCOTT
      You'd do better in the Zoo
than chatting to that academic crew.
or meet with the mad Mahdi in Khartoum,
or trapped with twenty bishops in one room,
or officially bound for hours to be nice to
some Flemish-speaking Belgian Burgomeister,
or talk to your ancestors in stone or bronze
than listen to those droning Oxford dons.
What has scholarship to offer when the room
reeks with the Ladies' irresistible perfume?

HRH

But, supposing, my advisors say,
(perish the thought though) that there'll come a day
when the Ladies aren't enough, that's when I'd need
to study all those books I ought to read.

SCOTTY SCOTT

If things got as bad as that I'd not prescribe
the tedious ramblings of some boring scribe.
The ailment's tragic but the cure far worse –
no more Ladies, only libraries of verse.
Bad advice, Your Highness, family or not.

HRH

Away with the highbrows, then. I'll dump the lot.
I suppose that I could keep some poets though.

SCOTTY SCOTT

Your Royal Highness, *all* the poets should go.
You and poetry, sir, I'd say they mix
as well as the Devil and a crucifix.
I'd keep poetry as much at bay
as Satan keeps the holy water spray.

HRH

Half a dozen?

SCOTTY SCOTT

    One Poet Laureate's enough!
Don't overdose on it. It's poisonous stuff.

POET LAUREATE

Charming!

  Aside.

      One day he'll rue that jest.

SCOTTY SCOTT

The Ladies, Your Highness, and to hell with the rest!

It's the Ladies, the Ladies that light up a party,
Your Highness, the Ladies, not limp *literati*!

HRH

Yes, the Ladies, the Ladies. Bookworms blight
all ladies bring us of dreams and delight.

*There is laughter from a group of three men at
another table.*

HRH

Are those noble bullies making cruel fun
of my comedian?

SCOTTY SCOTT
(*listening*)
No, sir, the other one.

HRH

Which other comic's been invited? Who?

SCOTTY SCOTT

The comic that they're laughing at is you.
It won't be long, they say, before you're reigning
but, in actual fact, Your Highness, they're complaining
that Your Royal Highness is most likely to disown
his former cronies once he's on the throne.

HRH

You see the types they are?

SCOTTY SCOTT
Aye!

HRH
Bloody shower!
I've done everything that's in my power
to give them advancement, either a command,
or a baronetcy with a lot of land,
and that ungrateful sod's my Household Squire

but they moan and whinge and want promoting higher.
Such ingratitude!

SCOTTY SCOTT
I'd say there still was scope
to raise them higher.

HRH
How?

SCOTTY SCOTT
The hangman's rope!

*The three in question have overheard the conversation
as Scotty Scott intended. The Duke of Peen addresses
them.*

DUKE OF PEEN
Did you hear what he said, that gross buffoon?

LORD GORDON
I did.

LORD TOURLAND
The bastard!

SIR PERCIVAL DILLON
We'll get even soon.
We'll get that crass comedian destroyed.

SCOTTY SCOTT
In your heart, Your Highness, is there no a void?
Don't all your easy conquests make you wish
you'd more angling to do to land your fish,
some catch with real passion, but impressed
more by your person than your royal crest?

HRH
How do you know there's no one in this town
who loves me for myself, and not my crown?

SCOTTY SCOTT

Who doesn't know your rank?

HRH

                  I have a 'friend'.
She lives in a cul-de-sac in the East End.

SCOTTY SCOTT

Not a pleb?

HRH

      Why not?

SCOTTY SCOTT

           Not plebs, sir, do beware.
Loving beneath you 's a dangerous affair.
The plebs when passionate get wild and hot.
Give them an inch of you, they'll take the lot.
Princes (and comics) should be content to bed
the wives and daughters of the better bred.

HRH

I long for Lord Gossett's wife tonight in mine.

SCOTTY SCOTT

Why not? Why not?

HRH

           All very well and fine
to say why not, but how?

SCOTTY SCOTT

           Abduction, say?

HRH

And what of the husband when she's dragged away?

Scotty Scott draws his hand across his throat.

HRH

Don't do that! He can see.

SCOTTY SCOTT

                Speak to the Queen.
Pay him with promotion. Know what I mean?
Speak with Her Majesty. He can get his Garter,
you get both his wife's. A gentlemanly barter!

HRH

His jealousy 's like one much lesser born's.
He'd shout out from the roof and show his horns.

SCOTTY SCOTT

Awkward customer! But if he can't be bought
there are countless ways a cuckold can be caught.
Either get him some ermine as a small reward
or get him convicted for indecency or fraud.
I'd've thought to throw this idiot in jail 's
not beyond the powerful Prince of Wales.
Your Royal Highness shouldn't find it hard
to lean on some sycophant from Scotland Yard.
Concoct some serious offence and get him life
so you can have your freedom with his wife.

*Lord Gossett has overheard the last part of Scotty
Scott's suggestion.*

LORD GOSSETT

The demon!

HRH

(to Scotty Scot)
You're pushing him too far!

SCOTTY SCOTT

Well, what's the point of being who you are
if you can't indulge your slightest princely whim.

LORD GOSSETT

(attacking Scotty Scott with a champagne bottle)
If I'm to hang, by God I'll swing for him.

SCOTTY SCOTT

With all your weight I think the rope would snap.

LORD GOSSETT

I'll see you damned!

SCOTTY SCOTT

You don't scare me, old chap,
I scourge the mighty with my comic act.
I stick my neck out, but my head's intact.
All I'm afraid of 's if my hump were where
your belly is. That would make me care.
Then I'd be really ugly.

LORD GOSSETT

You common Glasgow bore!

HRH

(*suddenly severe*)

That's enough. From both of you. No more!

*HRH's Bodyguard and others restrain Lord Gossett
and HRH leads Scotty Scott away from the fracas.*

LORD GORDON

HRH finds everything so droll.

SIR PERCIVAL DILLON

He laughs at anything. Got no control.

POET LAUREATE

Strange for me to see our Prince at play.

LORD BRYAN

That comedian. We've got to make him pay.

ALL

Hear, hear!

POET LAUREATE

But how? It's very hard
to get at him. He's under 'Royal guard'.

SIR PERCIVAL DILLON

Notwithstanding all the people he 's offended
the vile buffoon's immune as he's befriended
by the Prince who finds the clown amusing
although it's mostly us he keeps abusing.
Everybody here 's got cause to bear
the joker grudges, but get him, how and where?

DUKE OF PEEN

I know a way. And I suggest we meet
later on tonight in Bussy Street,
close to Lord Gossett's.

POET LAUREATE
(*seeing a chance to get his own back*)
I get the idea!

ALL

Agreed! You're on!

SIR PERCIVAL DILLON
But sshhh! The clown might hear!

SCOTTY SCOTT

Who can I torment now, what target hit,
straight to the bullseye with my bolts of wit?

A *Waiter approaches Scotty Scott.*

WAITER

An elderly gentleman in formal black attire
demands to see His Highness. Claims he's Lord Kintyre.

SCOTTY SCOTT
(*recognising an opportunity for sport*)
Ah, ha! Lord Kintyre! By all means
show him in. Oh *now* we'll have some scenes!

THE VOICE OF LORD KINTYRE
(*from outside the room*)
Only His Highness! I will address
only His Royal Highness, no one less!

HRH
Who the devil 's that?

THE VOICE OF LORD KINTYRE
I will remain until
I see His Highness . . .

> *HRH recognises the voice of one whose daughter*
> *he has seduced and signals that he must not be let in,*
> *but Lord Kintyre bursts through the crowded room*
> *and confronts HRH.*

SCENE FIVE

LORD KINTYRE
Speak to you I *will*!

HRH
Lord Kintyre!

LORD KINTYRE
Lord Kintyre, in fact.

SCOTTY SCOTT
(*to HRH*)
Sir, let me read this gent the Riot Act!

Turning on Lord Kintyre.

They would have locked you up and lost the key
if His Highness hadn't schemed to get you free.
Since those delinquencies you're even dafter.
Are all of us to fall about with laughter
or look at your madness with astonished awe?

Appealing to the crowd.

This gent wants grandsons from . . . his son-in-law!

Outburst of general cackling.

Sired by his son-in-law! I mean
he's the ugliest monster that I've ever seen.
Hairy, pasty, stunted and half-blind,
deformed like him in front, like me behind.
Your gorgeous daughter and your son-in-law,
conjugally speaking, make the world guffaw.
If the Prince had not seen fit to intervene
what a brood of monsters you'd have seen:
ginger-haired, gap-toothed, and gross deformity,
in front like My Lord, behind like me.
If you want grandsons with no handicap
to pull your beard and clamber on your lap,
the way to get such grandsons on your knees is
to let the Prince play how and when he pleases!

*This final flourish causes general hoots of laughter
among HRH's hangers-on.*

LORD KINTYRE

More affront! Sir, you are a prince, a title
which obliges you to hear my sad recital.
Not long ago when I was brought to trial
and, most unexpectedly, saw Fortune smile,
my foolish dream had led me to believe
the Prince of Wales had worked for my reprieve.
Bear in mind my noble forebears (mine
is an ancient, honourable line)
when I tell you, sir, I'd rather languish
in a cell till death than feel the anguish
I feel now, go to the gallows even, rather
than feel the pain I feel now as a father,
knowing, as I do, that, to clear my name

257

my daughter bought my honour with her shame.
Her slandered father could be soon acquitted
provided, she'd been told, that she submitted
to your callous lust that could well spread its stain
over the country, if you ever reign.
My reprieve and pardon were a Prince's plan
to drag my daughter to his soiled divan.
If we lived in an age when monarchs' power
had enemies beheaded in the Tower
(and with fathers and husbands who obstruct your joy
you'd like the headsman's axe in your employ)
and, as one such obstruction, I myself had been
a headless innocent on Tower Green,
beheaded at your behest, I swear my ghost
would haunt you everywhere where you played host
to revellers and roués, and other royal rakes,
and, in the name of fathers, for our daughters' sakes,
the head I carried in my hands would cry:
The man my daughter was dishonoured by.
That head with bitter tongue and bloodied beard
would be the phantom that you always feared,
when ogling, or groping, guzzling, glad or gay –
my ghost would sour your every suave soirée,
still the spectre at your feasts who will proclaim
the roué prince pollutes his Royal name!

HRH
(*choking with rage*)

Have you forgotten whom you stand before?

To Bodyguard.

Throw this fellow out and call the Law!

SCOTTY SCOTT

He's either barmy or been on the booze.

LORD KINTYRE

I curse you both! Mock me if you choose,
but it's quite unpardonably vulgar, sir,
to have me snapped at by your mongrel cur,
like an old lion forced down to its knees
by the yapping of a pampered Pekinese.

Turning on Scotty Scott.

I curse you, and forecast a future hour
when your sycophantic satire will turn sour.
All this frivolous fun you're paid to poke
won't seem so funny when your fate 's the joke.
Your unfortunate but fitting malformation
puts you beyond the pale of procreation,
but if you were capable my curse would be
to know, as I did, proud paternity,
to sire, as I did, a beloved child,
who'd be, as mine was, shamefully defiled.

To HRH.

Your crown is of gold, mine these hairs of white.
Both crowns should have respect and proper right.
A prince takes his own vengeance. Mine
is in the far more powerful hands of the Divine!

Act Two: The Diddicoy

SCENE ONE

SCOTTY SCOTT
I'm bothered by it, that old fellow's curse.

THE DIDDICOY
(*emerging from the shadows*)
Evening, sir!

SCOTTY SCOTT
(*assuming that he's being robbed*)
I've nothing in my purse.

THE DIDDICOY
Who said I wanted it? You do me wrong.

SCOTTY SCOTT
Then I hope that you won't detain me long.

THE DIDDICOY
You're hasty in your judgement, sir, my trade
's professional services, with a blade.

SCOTTY SCOTT
A cut-throat. God!

THE DIDDICOY
I've watched you every night,
restless and worried, looking left and right.
Not like I've seen you on the boards
'working the house' from humble folk to Lords,
nah, more like a nervous man whose eyes survey
every shadowy street and alleyway.
It's my guess that a Lady is the cause.

SCOTTY SCOTT

What's that to you?

THE DIDDICOY

My interests are yours.
You seem like a bloke who might need to employ
the blade-craft and discretion of the Diddicoy.
Maybe some swell or blackguard's blowing kisses
or making sheep's eyes at the missus,
you'd like seeing to?

SCOTTY SCOTT

What are you saying?

THE DIDDICOY

Seeing to, assassinating, slashing, slaying!
A modest honorarium would guarantee
your missus's molester's R.I.P.
I'm a bloke to whom the ladies can apply
to have their honours well protected by.

SCOTTY SCOTT

So what would you charge to execute a
persistent pest like an unwanted suitor?

THE DIDDICOY

Depends on who you're doing in. Degrees
of danger or of class adjust the fees.

SCOTTY SCOTT

So if the man's of rank?

THE DIDDICOY

Nobs cost double.
Disposing of your nobs is far more trouble.
They might have minders and so killing nobs
is riskier than ordinary jobs.
With assassination your sliding scale 's
from paupers (cheap!) to top-price Prince of Wales.

SCOTTY SCOTT
(*laughing*)
Top-price Prince of Wales! And is your blade
in much demand?

THE DIDDICOY
Never short of trade.
But hiring assassins is a hobby which
requires your hirer to be rather rich.
It's a luxury most people can't afford.
You've got to be loaded like a Duke or Lord.
Or blokes like you, sir, who have made their pile
and can affect the gentlemanly style.
Self-made men with secrets hire my skill.
Half down-payment, half after I kill.

SCOTTY SCOTT
Risky if you're caught.

THE DIDDICOY
Nah, some golden grease
works wonders on the palms of the Police.

SCOTTY SCOTT
So much a head?

THE DIDDICOY
Yer, but I couldn't oil
their palms enough if I'd done like, say, a Royal.

SCOTTY SCOTT
How do you go about it?

THE DIDDICOY
Right on the street
or back at my place.

SCOTTY SCOTT
That sounds more discreet!

THE DIDDICOY

My sister helps me. She's the baited trap.
She knows all the ways there are to tempt a chap.
But before he gets his wicked way, sir,
I'm in there brandishing my whistling razor.

SCOTTY SCOTT

I see.

THE DIDDICOY

Minimum of fuss. No noise. No stir.
I aim to give good, decent service, sir.
Give me your custom and I guarantee
you'll have full satisfaction for your fee.
I'm not a gang whose way to get things done
's to mob the man in question ten to one.
I operate alone with the discretion
best suited to a man in my profession.
I'm not your ordinary East End chivver,
those windbags who can brag but don't deliver.
Me, and my honed helper, yours to summon
to stop that feller pestering your woman.

SCOTTY SCOTT

There's no woman, so I don't require
the services you're offering for hire.

THE DIDDICOY

Bear me in mind. If you ever want to meet
come to The Fiddlers, Lower Dorset Street.
Ask for the Diddicoy.

SCOTTY SCOTT

And join the queue!

THE DIDDICOY

Don't despise me.

SCOTTY SCOTT
We've both got jobs to do!

THE DIDDICOY
At least I give a service for my pay.
I'm not on the welfare, skiving off all day.
I've got four kids to bring up and support.

SCOTTY SCOTT
And you want to raise them as a father ought.
I wish you well.

THE DIDDICOY
(*holding up his razor*)
Your humble servant, sir. *Adios!*

Exit the Diddicoy.

SCOTTY SCOTT
(*watching him disappear into the night*)
The cut-throat and the comic are quite close!
He works with a well-honed razor, me,
I wound my victims with sharp repartee.

SCENE TWO

SCOTTY SCOTT
The old man damned me. Even as he spoke
and yelled his curse at me I made a joke.
I mocked him. I was my wicked self all right,
but inside my soul was shuddering with fright.
Cursed. Damned. Nature and society combined
have shaped me with a warped and grudging mind.
Comedy and crippledom have made me bitter.
I'm tired of making titled dim-wits titter.

Even in dreams when I escape
out of my world I still wake up this shape.

All I'm good for, all my life and worth,
depends on moving men I loathe to mirth.
It's so humiliating. All men have the right
to shed their tears, even troops who fight
massed together round the tattered rag
they flatter with the name of national flag,
the convicts chained together who've been sent
to Australia, scorn laughter and lament.
The prisoners cooped for life in Pentonville
can break down in their cells and weep their fill.
They're captive creatures, yet they're free
to sob their hearts out fully, but not me.
All men who suffer weep, and only I,
the constant comic, have no right to cry.

There's nothing in a hump to make you proud,
I burn with envy at the well endowed.
All the surrounding sparkle and gay glitter
only makes me blacker and more bitter.
I've no sooner found some corner to console
my inner anguish, and my grieving soul,
when up he comes, His Highness, full of vim
(he's powerful, he's loved by women, him),
young, handsome, Britain's noblest born,
up His Highness comes, and with a yawn
gives me a kick when I'm quite lost in grief,
and says, 'Come on, I need some light relief.'

Bloody Court jester! I've a human heart
that doesn't always want to play the part.
All my dark feelings, anger, envy, rage,
all the vitriol I should fling on the age,
that boiling tar of passions in my breast,
when he clicks his fingers, gets suppressed.
One flick from the Prince of Wales's whip
I stifle my suffering, and crack a quip.
Up, down, left, right, no matter whether

I jump or run or sit I feel my tether.

Humiliation from the men 's a constant hell,
and when I think I might get better from some belle
who encourages my interest, all I get 's
the sort of patronising pat they give to pets!
Women who I'd like to take to bed
treat me like a dog and pat my head.
Beyond the pale of passion I suppose
they even let me see them with few clothes.

I hereby warn each patronising peer
every slight on me will cost you dear.
You Lords, I loathe you all. Each time you laugh
you add a letter to your epitaph.
I'll be whispering in the Prince of Wales's ear
spoiling the prospects of some pushy peer.
Just when he thinks his fortunes start to flower
because of his proximity to power,
I'll nip the budding bloom and shred
every petal from its drooping head.

You Lords brewed all this venom and this bile.
Like a Borgia with a belladonna phial
I let some droplets fall on every joy
I choose to shrivel, sour, or destroy,
the comedian as canker, the poisonous Pierrot
making gall and vinegar out of *Veuve Cliquot*!

The spectre at your feasts who'll dump malaise
into the middle of your merriest soirées,
the baleful shadow whose black bulk blots
the sun out of all blissful, sunlit spots.
What kind of life is this I've chosen
where every generous impulse in me 's frozen?
Anything more pensive, soulful, sadder,
gets jingled out by jester's bells and bladder.

Scotty Scott approaches the door into the house.

The corruption that I castigate at Court 'll
vanish once I'm through this blessed portal.

Everything that I denounce, lampoon, deplore
disappears the far side of this door.
And like a change of costume I transform
from the cruel satirist to someone warm.

I cast aside the quips and play a role
that gladdens my sad heart and cheers my soul.
I shed my loathing and my deep disdain
for that hateful world I'm forced to entertain.

The old boy cursed me.

                        Maybe I'm just mad?

*Scotty Scott enters the house and embraces his
daughter, Becky.*

Oh lass! oh lass! Come here and hug your dad!

More beautiful than ever. Everything all right?
Come here, lassie. Hug your old da tight.

BECKY
You're a good father, Dad.

SCOTTY SCOTT
                        Nay, what would I do
with no daughter in my life, no you?
I'd be lost, love.

Scotty Scott sighs.

BECKY
                Such sighs! So sad!
Can't you tell me why you're sighing, Dad?
So many secrets! It's a secret why
you felt just now the need to heave that sigh,
and it's a secret who's my family.

SCOTTY SCOTT
No secret, there's no family but me.

BECKY
Father's the only name for you I've had.

SCOTTY SCOTT
That's all you need to know – that I'm your dad.

BECKY
In the glens before you came to claim
your daughter back, 'little orphan' was my name.

SCOTTY SCOTT
It'd've been far better if I'd left you there.
But I needed someone, someone who would care . . .
I couldna cope without.

Scotty Scott breaks down.

BECKY
Dinna fash yersel',
only tell me what you want to tell.

SCOTTY SCOTT
Never gang outside.

BECKY
I stay in every day
except Sundays when we go to church to pray.

Tell me about my mother.

SCOTTY SCOTT
Best not to stir
those perfect memories I have of her.
It'll remind me that I once had in my life
a woman, beyond all others, as a wife.
For all my misery and malformed physique
your mother loved this pitiable freak.
When she died her secret perished too:

how to give a man like me a love so true.
Her love was a flash of lightning in the night,
a ray of paradise that cast its light
right into the hell my life had been
and is again, without her on the scene.
I hope the earth lies softly on the breast
I leaned my head on once for peace and rest.
You're all I have. Thank God that I have you.

Scotty Scott weeps.

BECKY

Don't cry, Dad. It tears my heart in two.
I hate to see you crying in this way.

SCOTTY SCOTT

And if you saw me laugh what would you say?

BECKY

Can you no tell me what it is and share
with your daughter all this constant care?

SCOTTY SCOTT

No! No! God in Heaven be thanked
I have one haven that's still sacrosanct.
This one small corner of the universe is
where I'm free from scoffers and from curses.
Here there's innocence. Here I'm just your dad,
the holiest title a feller ever had.
Father. Father. That consecrated word
's the only honour that I'd want conferred.

BECKY

Daddy! Daddy!

SCOTTY SCOTT
                          O where else could I find
another heart so caring and so kind?
The fiercer that I loathe the world, the more
you're all that's in it that I could adore.

269

What else can matter in the whole wide
repulsive world but that we're side by side.
What else need enter into heart or mind
than that we're sitting here with hands entwined.
O lass, the sole blessing Heaven above
has deigned to grant me is a daughter's love.
You're all I have where many others
have friends and relatives, wives or brothers,
vast families, a long ancestral line.
Men have many mainstays. You alone are mine.
Some people put their faith in what they own
but I put all of mine in you alone,
no gold or silver, I have Heaven to thank
you're the wealth my soul has in the bank.
Some have a God who prospers their affairs,
a God they plead to with perpetual prayers.
I'm as devotional as them, but dare I say,
you are the one I worship and obey.
Some men have their looks but I think you'll agree
Beauty has blessed you and by-passed me.

You're my family, mother, sister, daughter, wife.
You're my universe, my being, my whole life.

Everywhere else my soul 's bruised by despair.
Suppose I lost you – but that doesn't bear
thinking about a moment even. Give
your da one of those smiles that help him live.

    Becky smiles.

So like your mother's. Beautiful like you.
You're so alike in many ways, you two.
She did that gesture that you're doing now,
sweeping your hand like that across your brow.
She did that too, so nothing came between
her and the innocence she kept serene.

You radiate an angel's light, so bright
I'd still behold it if I had no sight,
and, if I were blind, my sightless gaze
would feel the radiance of your healing rays.

BECKY

I wish I could make you happy.

SCOTTY SCOTT

                  O you do!
I'm always happy when I'm here with you.

Strokes her hair.

It's so beautiful and black now is your hair.
Who'd believe it used to be quite fair?

Becky seizes the moment of quiet togetherness.

BECKY

Will you no show me London when you're free.
Can we no go for a stroll, Dad, you and me?

SCOTTY SCOTT

Never! Never! Even in Mrs Bryden's care
you've never ventured out?

BECKY

           No! No!

SCOTTY SCOTT

                  Beware!

BECKY

I've only been to chapel.

SCOTTY SCOTT

           I dread the day
she might get followed there and led astray.
O my little lassie, let me say once more
never ever gang beyond that bolted door.

For young women like yourself the world out there
in London breathes a pestilential air.
Protect her from the blast that's spelt the doom
of many a fair but early withered bloom,
so that her father in brief moments of repose
may breathe the fragrance of his virgin rose.

Scotty Scott bursts into tears.

BECKY

I'll no nag you to go out on to the street
or see London any more, so dinna greet!

SCOTTY SCOTT

Don't worry, lass. This greeting does me good.
Tonight I did more laughing than I should.

To self.

Laughing reminds me that I should be gone.
Time to put the mask of mirth back on.

To Becky.

Goodbye!

BECKY

Come soon!

SCOTTY SCOTT

Aye, but I dinna ken,
since I don't control my fate, exactly when.

Shouting to Mrs Bryden.

Mrs Bryden! Does anybody ever spot
me coming here?

MRS BRYDEN

No, absolutely not.
The street's deserted.

Enter HRH in the street.

SCOTTY SCOTT
Goodbye, dearest! *But*
are you sure that all the windows are kept shut?

MRS BRYDEN
(*nodding*)
There's a house I heard of just behind St Paul's.
It's more secluded, and it's got high walls.
I'll go and look tomorrow.

BECKY
Daddy, please!
From this window here I see green trees!

SCOTTY SCOTT
Don't stick your head out there for mercy's sake!

Scotty Scott thinks he hears something outside.

Someone's outside!

BECKY
I come up here to take
a breath of air, that's all.

SCOTTY SCOTT
Beware! Beware!
People can see you if you stand up there.

SCOTTY SCOTT
(*to Mrs Bryden*)
You see that window there. Don't light the gas.
People 'll see it.

MRS BRYDEN
There's very few as pass.
You trust me, sir. Naeb'dy could get through.

BECKY
(*to Scotty Scott*)
But what are you afeart of?

SCOTTY SCOTT
Not for me, for *you*!
My little daughter!

HRH
Scotty's daughter. Bloody hell!
Who'd've believed it? Well, well, well.

SCOTTY SCOTT
On Sundays at chapel have you ever seen
anyone following? Any gentleman, I mean.

BECKY
No. Never.

SCOTTY SCOTT
If you ever do, cry out.

MRS BRYDEN
Don't you worry, sir, I'll be the first to shout.

SCOTTY SCOTT
If anyone comes here, don't answer. Don't unlock
the door if you hear somebody knock.

MRS BRYDEN
That door 's staying well and truly locked
even if His Royal Highness knocked.

SCOTTY SCOTT
Especially if *he* knocked! Now, goodbye.

Exit Scotty Scott.

BECKY
I feel remorse.

MRS BRYDEN
You feel remorse, pet, why?

BECKY
He's so frightened for me, full of fears
and as he left his eyes filled up with tears.
Poor Dad, so good. I should've let him know
that every Sunday morning when we go
to chapel we've been followed by . . .
you know who.

MRS BRYDEN
Tell your father, why?
Your father is, to put it delicately, dear,
Your father 's just a wee bit, bless us, queer.
So, you hate this young man that we see?

BECKY
Hate him? Oh no, on the contrary,
Since I saw him first I fear I find
I can never get his face out of my mind.
From that first day when our two gazes met
I see his features and I can't forget.
I feel I'm his. In all my dreams I see him, but
in my dreams he's taller by a foot.
He seems strong and gentle, proud and good.
He'd look great on a horse, I know he would.

MRS BRYDEN
He's charming right enough.

HRH slips money to Mrs Bryden.

BECKY
A man like that must be . . .

MRS BRYDEN
(*holding her hand out to HRH for more money*)
O very accomplished.

BECKY
                    Anyone could see
if they only looked into his eyes,
there's a large heart there.

MRS BRYDEN
                    Enormous size!

On each word she utters she stretches out her hand
to HRH.

BECKY

Brave.

MRS BRYDEN
          Boldness itself.

BECKY
          But good.

MRS BRYDEN
                    And *kind.*
He's extremely well proportioned, mind –
his face, his eyes, his nose . . .

HRH
                    If she lists every item
and I'm going to have to pay her to recite 'em
I'm going to be cleaned out.

BECKY
                    I love to hear
you talking about him.

MRS BRYDEN
                    I know, my dear.

HRH

Fuel to the flames!

MRS BRYDEN
          Most generous of men.

276

HRH
(*searching his pockets*)
O God, she's starting up her list again.

MRS BRYDEN
I've thought, when I've watched him in his pew,
his blood is, maybe, tinged with noble blue.

BECKY
It doesn't bother me, how blue his blood is.
I'd like him a student type who studies
here in London, sensitive and smart,
but somewhere still a country boy at heart.

MRS BRYDEN
He'll be everything you hope for, I've no doubt.

Aside.

These modern girls are strange. Can't work 'em out.
Full of contradictions.

To Becky.

Completely mad
about you, though, is that young lad.

*Mrs Bryden holds out hand to HRH but he doesn't
give her anything. Aside:*

The well 's run dry. No pence. No praise.

BECKY
Till Sunday comes again I count the days.
When I can't see him I feel sick at heart.
When last Sunday's service was about to start
I thought he was approaching me to speak,
my heart was racing and my legs felt weak.
Night and day he's on my mind, and he,
I'm sure, thinks of nothing else but me.
He looks so serious I'm sure he'd scorn

party-going, dancing until dawn,
and I've a feeling that there haven't been
other girls before me that he's seen.
He only thinks of me.

MRS BRYDEN
On my life, that's true!

HRH
(*flinging her a ring*)
You give your life for me, this ring 's for you.

Mrs Bryden withdraws to give HRH his opportunity.

BECKY
Sometimes when I'm dreaming I so wish I could
have him before me here in flesh and blood
and I'd say: I . . . I . . . I . . . I . . .

HRH
(*disclosing himself*)
Don't stutter!
'I love you' 's what those lips were made to utter.
'I adore you.' Say it, go on, don't be shy.

BECKY
(*shouting*)
Mrs Bryden! God, not here. No reply.

HRH
Just us. And that's the whole world. You and I.

BECKY
Where did you come from?

HRH
Does it matter where,
Heaven or Hell, so long as I declare
'I love you'?

BECKY

      I pray no one caught sight of you.
Please go away. What if my father knew?

HRH

How can I go away, how can I leave
when I feel your breath, your bosom heave?
You said you loved me.

BECKY

      You listened?

HRH

                   Every word!
The sweetest music that I've ever heard.

BECKY

You've spoken to me, now, for pity's sake, I pray,
you rest content with that, and go away.

HRH

Go away, when your fate's entwined with mine
and our destinies are like twin stars that shine
together in the selfsame patch of sky?
Go, when we're fated, you and I?

How can I go, when Heaven 's chosen me
to open a virgin's soul and make her see,
see love's our sun that's brilliant and benign?
Isn't your heart as warmed by it as mine?

The sceptres Death bestows and then withdraws,
the glory that men win themselves in wars
to make their names or capture vast terrain
to be kings of, however long they reign,
all these crowned conquerors and kings
are merely earthly transient things.
One thing, and only one thing, can transcend
this earth where everything is doomed to end,

and that one thing that we can call divine
is *love*. Be happy, Becky, you have mine.

All you have to do is turn the key
and happiness enters with your lover, me.

Love's the honey hidden in life's flower,
love 's grace supported in the arms of power.
The eagle soaring with the gentle dove,
prey and predator at peace, that's love, that's love.
It's your little hand in my hand now, like so.

   Trying to embrace her.

Let's make love. Let's make love.

BECKY
(*resisting*)

                      Let me go!

MRS BRYDEN
(*apart*)

He's doing well, the lad.

HRH
(*aside, dropping his assumed accent*)

                    I think I've got her!

   To Becky.

Tell me you love me.

MRS BRYDEN

Artful rotter.

HRH

Say it again.

BECKY

          You've heard me once. You know.

HRH

Then I'm a happy man . . .

280

BECKY
> I'm done for, though.

HRH

Be happy with me.

BECKY
> Be happy, but with who?

Tell me who you are.

MRS BRYDEN
> About time, too!

BECKY

At least I know you're not one of those peers
my poor old father always says he fears.

HRH

God forbid! I'm just a student, nothing higher.
My name's Gerald Murray.

MRS BRYDEN
> Flaming liar!

*Duke of Peen and Sir Percival Dillon approach the
outer door of the house.*

DUKE OF PEEN

This way! This way! Over here.

MRS BRYDEN
> (*listening*)
> I believe

there's somebody outside.

BECKY
> God, my father! Leave!

MRS BRYDEN

Yes, sir, go.

HRH
Tell me before I do,
will you love me tomorrow?

BECKY
Yes. And you?

HRH
I'll love you for ever, my whole life through.

BECKY
Ah, you're telling fibs like those I tell my dad.

HRH
You're the only love I've ever had.
One last kiss on those eyes before I go.

HRH kisses Becky's eyes.

MRS BRYDEN
(*bustling HRH out of the door*)
All this bleeding kissing, I don't know.

Exit HRH.
Becky opens the upper shutter to watch HRH
disappear. Various nobles disguised in hoods gather
near the wall protecting the house.

BECKY
I'd like to carve that loved name on my heart:
Gerald Murray.

DUKE OF PEEN
That's the hunchback's tart.

SIR PERCIVAL DILLON
Let's see.

LORD GOSSETT
Back-street baggage by her looks.
It's a shame you have to troll with molls of crooks.

Becky turns and they see her face.

SIR PERCIVAL DILLON
Now what do you think?

POET LAUREATE
Oh yes. Oh *yes*!

LORD GOSSETT
Yes, she's an angel. Full of gracefulness.

SIR PERCIVAL DILLON
This is the hunchback's bit of stuff.

LORD GORDON
Sly old goat!

POET LAUREATE
I think I was inspired when I wrote:

'Where Beauty is, the Beast 's not far behind
when Cupid starts confounding humankind.
Mischievous Cupid loves mismatching Man
and makes Miranda moon for Caliban.'

DUKE OF PEEN
We didn't come here to listen to you drone
but to do a little mischief of our own.
Just like the japes we all did in the dorm,
only now it's kidnapping and chloroform,
snaffling the hunchback's little sweet.

LORD GORDON
She's just our royal master's sort of meat.

LORD GOSSETT
Exactly the type to catch the Prince's eye.

Re-enter Scotty Scott.

SCOTTY SCOTT
Fear 's brought me back here but I'm not sure why.

LORD GOSSETT

I wonder if it's right the Prince's way
of using anybody's women for his play.
How would he feel if someone did the same
to the Princess?

SCOTTY SCOTT
I know why I came.
Lord Kintyre's curse! It's made me ill at ease.

Hears something.

Who's there?

LORD GOSSETT
(*whispering*)
It's Scotty Scott! O what a wheeze.
We can get our two birds with one stone.
Let's do him in.

DUKE OF PEEN
No, leave him alone.

LORD GORDON
Without the comedian around to mock
the joke would only go off at half-cock.

LORD GOSSETT
But the bounder 's bound to interfere.

POET LAUREATE
Leave him to me. I've got a good idea.

To Lord Gossett.

Quick, Gossett, give your keys to this young blade.
It needs a poet's touch, this escapade,
a poet with the sense of the dramatic.

To Sir Percival Dillon and Lord Gossett.

Go into Gossett's, up into the attic,

lower the roof hoist down here to street level,
while I distract our hunchbacked Glasgow devil.

SCOTTY SCOTT
(*hearing them*)
Someone's whispering.

POET LAUREATE
Scotty, is that you?

SCOTTY SCOTT
Who's that?

POET LAUREATE
It's only me.

SCOTTY SCOTT
It's only who?

POET LAUREATE
The Laureate.

SCOTTY SCOTT
Ah, it's so dark tonight.

POET LAUREATE
The Devil's blackboard.

SCOTTY SCOTT
He must have poems to write.
But what are you here for?

POET LAUREATE
You haven't guessed?
It's something HRH heard you suggest:
kidnapping Lord Gossett's wife, and so we're here
to bring about your wonderful idea.

SCOTTY SCOTT
(*to himself, relieved*)
Thank God for that.

Then to Poet Laureate.

What a brilliant wheeze.
How will you get in?

Roof hoist is lowered down as they watch.

POET LAUREATE
This is going to please
our Prince. Think how chuffed he'll be
when we bring him a bit of fluff for company.

SCOTTY SCOTT
Well, if that's the escapade you plan to do,
kidnap Lord Gossett's wife, count me in too.

POET LAUREATE
We're wearing hoods.

SCOTTY SCOTT
Right, give me a hood.

Poet Laureate gives him a hood and Scotty Scott puts it on.

Now what?

POET LAUREATE
Up on to the hoist.

SCOTTY SCOTT
Righto, good.

VOICE OF SIR PERCIVAL DILLON
(*from Lord Gossett's attic*)
Hold on, Scotty, we're going to haul
you up to us.

The hoist begins to lift Scotty Scott into the air.

SCOTTY SCOTT
Steady! Steady! Or I'll fall.

The hoist comes to a stop with Scotty Scott
suspended. Behind him the Lords enter the house
to kidnap Becky.

SCOTTY SCOTT
(*on hoist*)

Have you got her?

VOICE 1
(*from above*)
Yes, Scotty, got her trussed
like a chicken for his oven of lust!

VOICE 2
(*from above*)
We've got the Lady trussed up in a sack
and need to send her down on your broad back.

SCOTTY SCOTT
Aye, humps come in handy. God designed
my shape with just this escapade in mind.

Pause.

Why have you stopped pulling? Haul! Haul!

Removes hood.

What the hell? What's happened to them all?

BECKY
(*from inside the sack*)
Daddy! Daddy! Daddy! Daddy!

Scotty Scott wriggling on the hoist removes his hood
and realises the awful truth. He gives a great
anguished cry.

SCOTTY SCOTT
FUCK!

He drops from the hoist.

Agh! Agh! The curse! The curse! It's struck!

THE GANG
(*singing in receding distance*)
The Ladies! The Ladies!

Act Three: HRH

A gentlemen's club. The usual Lords and Dukes and
HRH's hangers-on.

LORD GORDON
Let's bring the curtain down on this charade.

SIR PERCIVAL DILLON
No, let it hit him where it hurts and really hard.
Let him realise his jests have cost him dear
and don't let him suspect his sweetheart's here.

LORD GOSSETT
Yes, let him search for her all night and day.
But won't the porters give the show away?

MONTGOMERY
They've all been seen to, and they'll all deny
they saw a female person passing by.

SIR PERCIVAL DILLON
We should lead the hunchback on a wild-goose chase,
frantically searching from place to place,
mewling madly for his moll from mews to mews.
We should concoct a trail of cruel clues:
say some pimp bought her and he'd take all week
to scour the brothels and the *Poses Plastiques*,
fearing his bit of fluff 's been forced to ease
drunk sailors' stiffness for a few bawbees.

LORD GOSSETT
Yes, let's throw him off the scent. Let's see
just how far we can prolong his agony.

POET LAUREATE

I left behind a scribbled note that read:
'I've taken your little sweetheart from your bed
and put her into mine. She won't come back,
We're off abroad.'

LORD GOSSETT
And signed it?

POET LAUREATE
Spring-heeled Jack!

They all laugh.

SIR PERCIVAL DILLON
He must be going frantic.

LORD GOSSETT
That I long to see.

LORD GORDON
The poor devil in despair and agony
clenching his fists and teeth! He'll pay
everything he owes us in one day.

*Enter HRH in dressing gown, laughing with Duke
of Peen.*

HRH
What've you bagged there?

DUKE OF PEEN
Scotty's sweetheart!

HRH
Scotty's what?

DUKE OF PEEN
Yes, believe it or believe it not
his sweetheart. Or his wife.

HRH
(*to self*)
His wife! His 'lass'!
He's a proper paterfamilias!

DUKE OF PEEN
Would you care to look her over?

HRH
Yes, I'll say.
I'm glad of anything that comes my way.

DUKE OF PEEN
(*to Becky still in the sack*)
Did you ever dream, my dear, that fate would bring
a private audience with your future king?
Well, that's exactly what your fate has brought,
a grace not often granted to your sort.

Duke of Peen opens the sack and releases Becky.

May I present His Future Majesty,
the Prince of Wales!

BECKY
(*recognising her 'student'*)
The Prince? It canna be?

HRH
Becky!

BECKY
Gerald Murray, God!

HRH
If my friends knew
or didn't know that they were bringing you
doesn't matter if it means that I can throw
my arms around you once again, like so.

HRH attempts to embrace Becky.

BECKY

The Prince of Wales! I beg you let me go!

HRH

Let you go, the beauty I adore?
The Prince re-swears the love the student swore.
We love each other don't we, you and I?
Does being Prince of Wales disqualify
me as a lover? You didn't seem to mind
when I was a student of the serious kind.
Now because you find I'm nobly born
gives you cause for neither fear nor scorn.
If I'm not a yokel, sorry. If it matters, why?

BECKY

He's making fun of me. I want to die.

HRH

By turning down my offer you turn down
all the pleasures of the Court and of the Town,
parties, games and balls, and after dark
sweet nothings whispered in St James's Park,
all the indiscretion and delight
veiled in the concealment of the night.

In this crumbling house of clay where love's the tenant
the spangles of our passion on the pennant
of life's frail fabric, flying, but threadbare,
are, nonetheless, still glittering in the air,
those spangles of our passion without which
life unravels drably stitch by stitch,
its once fine fabric faded into tatters.
I've given a lot of thought to all these matters
and the sum of wisdom is: Give God his dues.

Aside to watching nobles.

Then bed the beauties and imbibe the booze.

BECKY

He's not like the picture that I had of him.

HRH

What did you want? Someone stammering and prim?
One of those bloodless fools who, when they woo
women, think that all they have to do
to win them over is make doleful eyes
and lay siege to beauty with their soppy sighs.

BECKY

Let me go, I've been deceived.

HRH

              Think who *we*'ll be
when millions in the Empire bow to me!
The Prince of Wales, next in succession,
power and pleasure, all in my possession.
Next in succession, that would mean
if I am to be King, then you'd be Queen.

BECKY

But your wife . . .

HRH

            So naive, you touch my heart.
A mistress and a wife are things apart.

BECKY

A mistress is a shameful thing to be.

HRH

So proud!

BECKY

      My father, he will rescue me.

HRH

Your father! All I need to do is utter
the command to return him to the gutter.

Think of it. I'm destined for the Crown
And what's your father? He's a common clown.
Your father eats out of my royal hand.
Your father does whatever I command.

BECKY
(*sobbing*)

You own him too.

HRH
Don't cry so. Come.

BECKY
No! No!

HRH
Won't you tell me that you love me so?

BECKY
No, that's over.

HRH
Becky, please don't cry.
I don't want to make you sob. I'd rather die.
What sort of cowardly monarch will I be
if women are made to weep because of me?

BECKY
Tell me the truth. That it's all been a hoax.
And now you've finished with your stupid jokes
and you and your friends have had their bit of sport,
send me back to Dad, he'll be distraught.
I want to go back home. Home is near . . . O
why should I tell you, you already know.

HRH
And all this time I did believe you cared.

BECKY
Now you're the Prince of Wales, I'm scared. I'm scared.

294

HRH

Scared? Of me?

Attempts embrace.

BECKY
LET ME GO!

HRH
One kiss to say that I'm forgiven.

BECKY
No!

HRH
Weird little thing.

BECKY
Please let me free.

Becky frees herself and runs into the bedroom, locking the door behind her. HRH pulls a key from his dressing-gown pocket.

HRH
It's just as well I've got my bedroom key.

HRH follows Becky into the bedroom and locks the door.

LORD GORDON
Hello, hello. Tell me what's happening then.

POET LAUREATE
(*laughing*)
The wolf's dragged the bleating lamb into his den.
The little lamb's gone bleating baa-baa-baa
straight into the big bad wolf's boudoir.

SIR PERCIVAL DILLON
Poor old Scotty!

DUKE OF PEEN
Sssh, he's here.

LORD GORDON
This is what we do –
Straight faces, and no smirking. Not a single clue.

POET LAUREATE
He only saw me there.

DUKE OF PEEN
Ah, here he comes.
Curtain 's going up. A roll of drums.

Sings.

The Ladies! The Ladies!
The one who's got it made is
the one who can love 'em then flee.

SCOTTY SCOTT
(*joining in*)
There's said to be royals
who don't have the toils
and troubles the Ladies, the Ladies give me.

Applause.

ALL
Bravo!

SCOTTY SCOTT
Where've they hidden her?

ALL
Bravo!

SCOTTY SCOTT
They're all involved in it.

LORD GOSSETT
What ho!

296

SCOTTY SCOTT

O so we're Lord Cheerful are we for the day?

LORD GOSSETT

And how come that's your business, pray?

SCOTTY SCOTT

Only this, don't try to be amusing or
you'll end up even more a bloody bore.

Scotty Scott ferrets around.

Where've they hidden her?

Approaches the Poet Laureate.

Ah, just the man
to ask if it went well, the kidnap plan.

POET LAUREATE

What plan?

SCOTTY SCOTT

The hoods! The hoist!

POET LAUREATE

I'm afraid
you must have dreamed this weird escapade.
The hoods? The hoist? Frankly I recommend
you drink less fizz in future, my dear friend.

Scotty Scott sights a handkerchief and examines it.

SIR PERCIVAL DILLON

He's got my handkerchief. Looking at the crest
like Sherlock Holmes pursuing an arrest.

To Scotty Scott.

Do you require a magnifying glass
to find my monogram?

SCOTTY SCOTT
(*to the Duke of Peen*)
                    Where've they put my lass?
Gone home to sleep it off, the Prince, no doubt?

DUKE OF PEEN
Indeed.

SCOTTY SCOTT
I'd hoped to find him still about.

SIR PERCIVAL DILLON
Home with Her Royal Highness.

LORD GORDON
(*attempting a distraction*)
                        The poet
just told me this one, do you know it?

POET LAUREATE
It's from the Latin, I'm somewhat partial
to those rather raunchy epigrams of Martial:

'The gluttonous geezer Lord Pratt
grew increasingly fat,
as he doted on dinner
his wife had men in her
who doted much more on her twat.'

LORD GOSSETT
(*singing*)
The Ladies! The Ladies!

SCOTTY SCOTT
                Take care! Take care!

LORD GOSSETT
What?

SCOTTY SCOTT
    I said take care.

LORD GOSSETT
And why?

SCOTTY SCOTT
                              Because he'll do
exactly the same epigram on you.

LORD GOSSETT
You! You!

SCOTTY SCOTT
        The strangest beast in the whole zoo
when it's really mad it cries: You! You!

Enter an Equerry.

DUKE OF PEEN
What is it?

EQUERRY
        Her Royal Highness sends
to be informed what HRH intends.
Will His Highness be returning, or stay late
discussing with you here affairs of state?

DUKE OF PEEN
His Highness has retired.

EQUERRY
                              But the Prince
was seen with Your Lordships only minutes since.

DUKE OF PEEN
He's hunting early.

EQUERRY
                Hunting? One presumes
he'd have given notice to the grooms.

DUKE OF PEEN
He's going fishing then.

TONY HARRISON

EQUERRY
             What one finds odd 's
no one told the staff to pack his rods.

DUKE OF PEEN
Dammit, then I'd better make it clear
the Prince is unavailable.

SCOTTY SCOTT
             She's here!
She's with him!

LORD GORDON
             He's really gone insane.
And who is she?

SCOTTY SCOTT
             She's that wee wain
you stole from me. You! You! You.
And you, Sir Percival, were in it too.
You're all aware of what you brave men did,
kidnapping a frightened little kid.

DUKE OF PEEN
(*laughing*)
Lost your sweetheart? With your good looks you ought to
get a replacement quick.

SCOTTY SCOTT
             I want my daughter.

ALL
Daughter!

SCOTTY SCOTT
             Daughter, yes, daughter. Go on, mock.
Mock me, or are you all struck dumb with shock
that the hunchback's father of a lovely child?
Peers of the realm, wolves in the wild

have offspring of their own, so why not me?
Enough's enough. Now set my daughter free.
Yes, gentlemen, you had your little fun,
Very amusing. Very. Now it's done.
I want my daughter. Get that straight.
I know she 's here.

POET LAUREATE
The man 's in such a state.

SCOTTY SCOTT
Was it these demons, these damned crooks of Court
kidnapped my daughter for 'a spot of sport'?
To such Court lackeys the virtue of a maid
's a mere commodity to use for trade.
When the future monarch, when the royal heir 's
a compulsive flaunter of corrupt affairs,
when the Prince's pleasure is an idle poke
virginity round this lot 's just a joke.
They let the Prince debauch their wives and girls
to end up dubbed as Knights, and Dukes, and Earls.
These chastity-corrupters would all charter
their own children out to get a Garter.
Like farmers with spare acres they sublet
their spouses' pudenda for a coronet,
subject their daughters to ordeals of sex
to get some Order dangled round their necks.
Ask any puffed-up Peer: 'Was your wife whored
so her empurpled pimp got made a Lord?'
They'd see every family female flung
to the royal wolf to climb one social rung.
Is there any one of you who dare deny
the truth of what I say, or prove I lie?
You'd all allow your women to be whored
(if you haven't done it yet!) for the reward
of some pretentious title or another.

To Lord Bryan.

You, your wife!

To Lord Gordon.

Your sister!

To the young Sir Percival Dillon.

And *you*, your mother!

*Lord Tourland goes to the sideboard and pours
himself a glass of champagne and hums a few bars
of 'The Ladies! The Ladies!' as he pours.*

SCOTTY SCOTT
(*turning on him*)
Dammit! Dammit! Dammit! Dammit! Dammit!
I ought to grab your bloody glass and ram it
down your gullet! This so-called 'noble' lot,
who claim descent as far back as year dot,
this ever so exclusive social set
who run to yards of entries in Debrett,
who claim ancestral kinship with the great
historical heroes of this ancient state,
are the same illustrious gang who stole
the daughter of this poor unhappy soul.
You're no nobles. I can hear the jeers and hoots
as mere grooms pumped your mamas like prostitutes.
You're no more grand than me. Your proper dads
were probably your father's stable lads.
You're all bastards!

LORD GOSSETT
You oaf!

SCOTTY SCOTT
How much were you paid
to perpetrate this puerile escapade?

O, yes, he'd buy her. Making such a sale's
easy when the buyer 's Prince of Wales.

His shrunken conscience makes him show no qualms
about purchasing the pleasure of such charms.
He likes them young and beautiful, and she's
as beautiful as anything one sees.

Is a rainbow ribbon or a tinsel decoration
the going rate at Court for compensation?
If His Highness finds my daughter willing
would I get a better social billing?

Will his gratification make me grander –
the usual peerage for a Palace pander?
I tell you, sirs, a pettifogging title
might well be an adequate requital
for such low men as you who'd all play bawds
and lease your ladies if it made you Lords,
not *me*! If he could magically bestow
a straightened back on me I'd still say no.

You scourings of the Court, you scum
whose hearts and consciences have all gone numb,
you courtiers are all cowards who'd debauch a
woman and destroy her with your torture.

Your Lordships hear a cripple's desperate cry.
Give me back my daughter. Or I'll die.

Look at this hand. Nothing noble. Nothing royal,
just your ordinary horny hand of toil.
A navvy's hand, a serf's, for spades not swords,
but enough to knock the blocks off a few Lords.
I've waited here too long. Now let's have done.
Give me back my daughter!

> *Scotty Scott makes for the door of HRH's bedroom,
> but is forcibly restrained.*

Ten to one!

All ganged up against me!

Scotty Scott weeps.

Yes, these are tears.

Scotty Scott turns to the Poet Laureate.

You're a poet among these soulless peers.
Poets are meant to have compassionate hearts,
to understand the frail and take their parts.
You were born among the people just like me,
a fellow commoner for all your finery.
Tell me where she's hidden, what they've done.
She is here, isn't she? You're the only one
among these heartless peers with poet's feeling.

No reaction from Poet Laureate.

Poets!

Scotty Scott goes down on his knees.

Look, Your Lordships, now I'm kneeling
to ask for your forgiveness and to tell
Your Lordships that today I'm far from well.
You know me, Your Lordships, I'm the bloke
who'd be the first to laugh and share the joke
when I'm myself, but not today, I'm racked
the way a feller is when he's hunchbacked.
This, you must admit, strange soberness of mine
comes from the pain that cripples my whole spine.
Poor cripples have their bad days. This is one,
but never forget the days when we had fun –
'The Ladies! The Ladies!' you all sing along
when I give my rendition of our favourite song.
Give me, as small return for all the smiles
I've raised, the times I've laid you in the aisles,
for all my turns and tricks and comic patter,

304

a sympathetic hearing in this matter.
I'm your entertainer. Look at me.
Though I'm quickly running out of repartee.

Give me back my child, who, I assume
you've hidden in the Prince of Wales's room.
My one treasured possession, gentlemen.
I beg you, beg you, give her back again.

She was everything I ever had.
The one thing I took pride in, being her dad.

Silence.

I can't make you out, you high-born lot.
Mostly you're sniggering, but when you're not
you're absolutely silent. All right, snigger
at this pathetic, pitiable figure
giving his own head these vicious thumps,
pulling his hair out in colossal clumps.

Looks at a clump of hair.

Hair it'll only take another night
of life like this to turn completely white.

*His frantic self-injury is interrupted by the entrance
of his daughter Becky, dishevelled and distressed,
from HRH's bedroom.*

BECKY

Daddy! Daddy!

SCOTTY SCOTT
My little lass, it's you.

To Lords and Gentlemen etc.

There, sirs, that's my whole family in your view.
My angel! My house would be a house of woe
without you. Well, Your Lordships, now you know

it was with good reason that I wept and cried
when you see this lovely creature at my side.
Doesn't the world seem such a better place
when you see my daughter's innocent face?
What father wouldn't fight with all his might
not to let this beauty from his sight?

To Becky, who is weeping.

Dinna, dinna greet. Don't be afraid.
The whole thing was a foolish escapade.
But it's over now. So don't be so upset.
It gave you a proper scare though I can bet.
But they're not bad sorts. Now they can see
how much you mean to me, they'll leave us be.

To Peers firmly.

Isn't that so?

To Becky.

After so much bitter weeping
I'm laughing now you're back in my safe-keeping.
But you're still greeting.

BECKY
You'd greet if you knew.
I'm so ashamed.

SCOTTY SCOTT
What?

BECKY
I'll only talk to you.
Not in front of these.

SCOTTY SCOTT
(*the truth dawning and shouting at HRH's door*)
Not *her* as well!

BECKY

Just the two of us.

SCOTTY SCOTT
(*to Peers*)
You lot, go to Hell!
And if, by the remotest chance of fate,
His Highness happens by, tell him to wait.

To HRH's Bodyguard.

Tell him for his own sake, you're his bodyguard.
Tell the Prince of Wales I say he's barred.
Tell him, as his minder, not to show his face.

DUKE OF PEEN
What a world, when fools don't know their place.

LORD GORDON
With fools, as with infants, it sometimes pays
to let them, within reason, have their ways.
We'll be in earshot if we go next door.

Exit all Peers except Lord Gossett, who lingers.

SCOTTY SCOTT

Speak, lass.

Notices Lord Gossett.

Didn't you hear? I said *withdraw*!

LORD GOSSETT
(*exiting*)
Lord, the world's turned upside down
when Peers can be commanded by a clown.

SCOTTY SCOTT
(*to Becky*)

Now you can speak.

BECKY

Daddy, earlier he came
secretly into the house . . . the shame, the shame.

Scotty Scott takes her in his arms.

Some time ago (I should have told you then)
he started following me.

Breaks down.

I'll start again.
He never spoke. At chapel I would see him too
watching me intently from his pew.

SCOTTY SCOTT

The Prince of Wales?

BECKY

He sometimes bumped my chair
so I'd look up and see him standing there.
And then tonight he got inside and . . .

SCOTTY SCOTT

and his princely hand
stamped your brow with foul dishonour's brand.
His breath has poisoned the pure air you breathed.
He plucked the bloom virginity had wreathed
your brow with, lassie, my shelter and my ark,
my ray of daylight in the midst of dark.
Your soul rekindled my soul's dwindling flame.
Your dignity discreetly veiled my shame.
You were my refuge from the world's vile spite.
The angel who filled my humble home with light.
My object of devotion, my wee, wee lass,
sunk in the mire of this poisonous morass.
What more can I do after such a blow?
There's nowhere lower that a man can go.
I, prostituted to the Peerage, who purvey

everything that's ribald and risqué,
to titillate corrupted titled toads
whose breeding grounds are cesspools and commodes.
Among this degradation and debauch
you were purity's inextinguishable torch.
Only that chaste daughter that I had
gave an ounce of comfort to your dad.
Me, I've been resigned to bear my lot
(it all seemed part of being Scotty Scott!)
the abasement of the hunchback, the hurt pride
that bled inside my heart until it died,
those insults, 'Quasimodo', 'Humpty', 'ape',
hurled by so-called wits to mock my shape,
I've grown used to it, and I'd prefer
such shit to shower on me. But not on her.
When you're on the gallows, then the view
of some holy shrine nearby can comfort you.
She was the shrine I've let a vandal wreck.
Now there's just the gibbet. The noose. My neck.
Just one day to blow all that apart!
Lord Kintyre's curse. That's when I felt it start.
And I lay my curse on this corrupted Court
that crushes, like a rushing juggernaut,
woman and child, and breaks all laws
made for our guidance by a Higher Cause,
and wipes one crime out with yet another crime
and splatters everywhere with blood and slime
and flings its filth on your pure, faultless brow,
so innocent, unsullied until now.

To HRH's door.

So, wherever you are skulking, Prince of Wales,
may God who weighs all justice in His scales
make you stumble where your grave already gapes
open to swallow you.

BECKY
(to self)
I pray that he escapes.
For though the Prince of Wales has used me ill,
somewhere he's my Gerald. And I love him still.

LORD KINTYRE
(between two policemen)
Since corruption seems to lord it over all
and neither God nor man has heard my call
for justice and vengeance on the one I cursed,
I look at Britain's future and I fear the worst
from hopeless times where monarchs like him thrive.

SCOTTY SCOTT
Not while there's justice. While I'm alive
and drawing breath in Britain I swear an oath
that someone will take vengeance for us both.

Act Four: Becky

SCOTTY SCOTT

How can you?

BECKY

    But I do!

SCOTTY SCOTT

       After all this time you've had
to get over this bewitchment. Mad! Mad!

BECKY

I love him.

SCOTTY SCOTT

   Women's hearts! Explain
why you can love this man.

BECKY

    I canna.

SCOTTY SCOTT

          Insane.
Bizarre.

BECKY

   But, Dad, you know what people say,
love works in a very mysterious way.
I know he's done me only harm and ill
but, though I don't know why, I love him still.
Dearest Father, sweetest, sweetest Dad,
I know you'll think me absolutely mad
but I love him so much that I'd do anything,
even die for him, as I would you.

311

SCOTTY SCOTT

I can forgive you, lass.

BECKY

He loves *me*, I know.

SCOTTY SCOTT

Madness!

BECKY

But he swore, he swore that it was so.
A handsome prince with winning words and ways,
he captivates your heart, and when he turns his gaze
on you, and you look back at him, his eyes are . . .

SCOTTY SCOTT

The sheep's eyes of a wanton womaniser.
I don't want it said in future that he took
my happiness away and wasn't brought to book.

BECKY

You'd forgiven him.

SCOTTY SCOTT

Not forgiven. Nor forgot.
I just needed time to hatch my plot.

BECKY

But these last weeks (and please don't take offence)
I've seen you be quite friendly to the Prince.

SCOTTY SCOTT

Pretence!

You'll have your vengeance, pet.

BECKY

No, Daddy, no!

SCOTTY SCOTT

Would you feel anger, lassie, if I show
that he'd betrayed you.

BECKY

He wouldna. Not the Prince!

SCOTTY SCOTT

Would seeing with your own eyes now convince
you that he did? If he didn't love you any more
would you love him?

BECKY

I don't know, but he swore
he loved me yesterday.

SCOTTY SCOTT

Only yesterday!
Very well, watch this, then tell me what you say.

*Scotty Scott and Becky look through a chink into the
pub. They see HRH in the costume of an officer.*

BECKY

There's only an officer . . .

SCOTTY SCOTT

Use your eyes . . .

Becky finally recognises the 'officer' as HRH.

BECKY

Ah! Daddy!

SCOTTY SCOTT

Have you seen through this disguise?
There's more to come I hate to tell you, lass.

Focus on pub interior.

HRH
(*to Diddicoy*)
Two things, and quick. Your sister, and a glass.

SCOTTY SCOTT

That's what he's like. The next king, by God's grace,

risking his neck in such a squalid place.
Wine goes to his head, and all the more
when there's some low pub Hebe there to pour.

HRH
(*singing*)
The Ladies! The Ladies! etc.

*Enter Magdalena, the Diddicoy's sister, with wine
and glass for HRH.*

HRH
(*to Diddicoy who is polishing his belt*)
We soldiers always say brass gets a better shine
done out of doors. That's how I do mine.

DIDDICOY
Gotcha!

*Exit Diddicoy to where Scotty Scott and Becky are
watching.*

So what's it to be, squire? Live or die?
We've got him now.

SCOTTY SCOTT
Come back, by and by.

MAGDALENA
(*to HRH attempting to fondle her*)
Noooo!

HRH
(*imitating her accent*)
Nooooo! Nooooo's progress. Just a while ago
you pushed me away, and now it's Noooo!
A big step forward. Come here. Let's just chat.

Magdalena sits with HRH.

HRH

It's a week since I first met you at . . .
it was The Hercules . . . I'd gone with . . . who?
Scotty Scott, and fell in love with you.
You're the only one I love.

MAGDALENA

    Me, and the other twenty!
You seem like a bloke that's played around with plenty.

HRH

Yes, I'm a monster. I confess it's true.
I've been the downfall of, well, quite a few.

MAGDALENA

Listen to him brag. A monster among men.

HRH

Look, you invited me to this foul den
where the food 's abysmal and your 'best' Bordeaux
seems to have been slopped out of a po,
served by an ogre whose gorilla scowl
could make the finest vintages taste foul.
How does your brother dare to put his snout
next to your lovely lips' delicious pout?
But yours is the bed that I'll be sleeping in.

MAGDALENA

Digging his own grave!

 HRH fondles her.

    Gerroff!

HRH

    What a din!

MAGDALENA
(*resisting*)

Gerroff! Gerroff! Gerroff! Behave! Let go!
Didn't you hear me when I told you No?

HRH

Eat, drink, make love, behaviour on which we,
that's me and King Solomon, both agree.

MAGDALENA

King Solomon? By the looks of you
you've spent more time in taprooms than church pew.

HRH pursues Magdalena.

HRH

Magdalena!

MAGDALENA

Tomorrow!

HRH
(*picking up chair*)
Tomorrow, just you dare
use that word again, I'll smash this chair.
Beauties don't use that word. I've had it banned.

MAGDALENA
(*sitting down with HRH*)

A truce?

HRH
(*taking her hand*)
God, what a lovely hand!
Though I'm no flagellating Desert Father
I swear, O Magdalena, that I'd rather
be slapped by this hand than feel others stroke
and caress me.

MAGDALENA
That's just your little joke.

HRH

No! No!

MAGDALENA

I'm ugly.

HRH

No you're not!
You should be kinder to the charms you've got.
When love gets hold of us, we men of war
have such hot hearts they'd make Siberia thaw.

MAGDALENA

I bet you read that in a book.

HRH

(*aside*)
She's right!

To *Magdalena*.

Come on! Give us a kiss.

MAGDALENA

Gerrrofff, you're tight.

HRH

Just drunk with love.

MAGDALENA

You're a devilish one,
Captain Carefree, Major Making Fun.

HRH

I'm not joking. Marry me!

MAGDALENA

Then cross your heart.

HRH *crosses his heart.*

HRH

What a dizzy and delicious little tart!

TONY HARRISON

SCOTTY SCOTT
(to Becky as they watch from outside)
Now what do you think? Should he pay the price?

BECKY
How could he? O, the liar! O my heart's like ice.
There's not an ounce of soul in that whole frame.
She's a slut, and yet he's used the same
endearments as he used on me . . .

SCOTTY SCOTT
Sssshh! The day
when he's forced to pay 's not far away.
Revenge?

BECKY
Do what you want.

SCOTTY SCOTT
At last!

BECKY
I'm scared.
What terrifying plan have you prepared?

SCOTTY SCOTT
It's all worked out. And don't try to restrain
your father now. It'd finish off his brain.

Go back home. You'll find clothes there. They're men's.
Take money. Lots. And head back to the glens.
Go home to Scotland and I'll join you there.
There's a wooden chest with all you need to wear,
under your mammy's picture. These last few days
I've been preparing us quick getaways.
Do as I say. Above all don't show your face
in London. Something dreadful's taking place.

BECKY
Come with me, Daddy.

318

SCOTTY SCOTT
Not yet, lass. Not yet.

BECKY
I'm feart.

SCOTTY SCOTT
Dinna be feart, my pet.
Just do all I've told you. Till we meet again.

Exit Becky. Enter the Diddicoy.

SCOTTY SCOTT
You asked for twenty. Here's half now. That's ten.
You're sure he's stopping?

DIDDICOY
Yer, it's going to pour.

SCOTTY SCOTT
Well, he won't sleep in the Palace any more.

DIDDICOY
Take it easy. We're lucky with the weather.
My sister and the storm will work together.

SCOTTY SCOTT
I'll be back at midnight.

DIDDICOY
Don't bother coming back.
I'll chuck him in the Thames inside a sack.

SCOTTY SCOTT
I'd like to throw him in myself.

DIDDICOY
Fine! I'll deliver
the corpse bagged up and ready for the river.

SCOTTY SCOTT
(*counting out the ten guineas*)
Till midnight! Then you'll get the rest I owe.

THE DIDDICOY
This feller, what's he called?

SCOTTY SCOTT
                     You should know
both what he's called and who's your hirer. I'm
called *Punishment,* and he's called *Crime.*

Exit Scotty Scott.

DIDDICOY
(*checking the heavens*)
Storm's brewing. Clouds blacking London out.
Good. Soon there won't be even dogs about.

Back to interior.

MAGDALENA
Gerrrofffof me!

HRH
O, you tease. You tease!

MAGDALENA
(*singing a chorus of 'The Ladies! The Ladies!'*)
But when stout lads present
(you know what is meant)
the Ladies, the Ladies they always say no.

HRH
God, your shoulders! God, your arms! So white!
A body like a goddess, yet you fight.
Tell me, Magdalena, why did God Almighty
make you such a mulish Aphrodite?

MAGDALENA
Enough, my brother's coming.

HRH
                     Just my luck!

Thunder, enter the Diddicoy.

MAGDALENA

That's thunder.

DIDDICOY

It's going to rain like fuck.

HRH

Let it! Let it! More reason to reside
in your lodging and let the storm subside.

MAGDALENA

Hark at him. Talks like the royal set –
'reside' . . . 'reside'. Won't your family fret?

HRH

Family? There's no family. So no fears.
I belong to no one.

DIDDICOY
(*to self*)
Music to my ears.

Rain pelting. Night getting blacker and blacker.

HRH
(*to Diddicoy*)
You, my friend, can go and lay your head
in the cellar. Or in Hell. It's time for bed.

DIDDICOY

Thanks.

MAGDALENA
(*urgently to HRH*)
Go home!

HRH
(*laughing*)
Look how it pours.
It's not fit to put a poet out of doors.

DIDDICOY
(*showing Magdalena the money*)
Make him stay! Look, ten guineas, and the rest
at midnight. After.

To HRH.

Sir, may I suggest
you take my humble room for your repose.

HRH
Fry in July, and freeze December. One of those?

DIDDICOY
Come and look. Would Your Lordship care
to view it?

HRH
Why not?

MAGDALENA
(*looking out of window*)
God, it's black out there.

*Diddicoy and HRH climb up to the attic to view the
room.*

DIDDICOY
There y'are, sir, comfy bed.

HRH
Has it been
made limbless in the service of the Queen?

Seeing broken window panes.

And I see you like fresh air, and show
hospitality to all the winds that blow.

Goodnight!

DIDDICOY
Sleep tight!

Exit the Diddicoy.

HRH
I'm feeling weary. Damn!
I'll have a nap. The girl knows where I am.

HRH removes his boots, lies down. Drowsily.

The Ladies! The Ladies! And Magdalena
a lioness just waiting for her trainer!

HRH falls asleep.
The Diddicoy and Magdalena in the downstairs
room. She's sewing a sack. He's finishing off the bottle
of wine left by HRH. They are both thinking about
the imminent murder.

MAGDALENA
The captain's very charming.

DIDDICOY
Oh, yes, I agree.
He charmed me twenty guineas for my fee.

MAGDALENA
Twenty? Is that all that you could get?
He's worth much more.

DIDDICOY
You're getting soft, my pet.
Go upstairs. Check he's asleep. And fetch
his sword downstairs.

Magdalena goes up into the loft.
Enter, outside in the storm, Becky, dressed in the
riding clothes of a man, boots with spurs etc.
Magdalena looks at the sleeping HRH.

MAGDALENA
He's asleep, poor wretch.
It's really such a shame. Poor lad! Poor lad!

Magdalena comes down from the attic with HRH's sword.

BECKY
(*outside*)
This is so frightening. I must be mad.

He's spending the night here. God don't let
whatever's going to happen happen yet.
I'm sorry, Daddy, sorry. I'm afraid
I've come back here. I've disobeyed.
Before I used to live quite unaware
of the great, wide world and all its care.
Now, from a secluded life, I'm hurled
into the darkest corner of the world,
my happiness, well-being, my virginity,
demolished into dust and bleak debris.
Do all love's fervent, bright flambeaux
only leave behind cold ash and woe?
It's like a funeral. Hard to believe
that soot and ash are all such blazes leave.

Thunder.

Such noise, such thunderclaps! It makes me wonder
If it doesn't come from my heart, this violent thunder.
What am I doing in this hellish night?
My own shadow used to make me jump with fright.
But all the desperation and despair
that makes wronged women daring makes me dare.

Sees light in house.

What's going on? This place makes my heart chilled.
I hope to God that no one's getting killed.

Inside hovel.

DIDDICOY

What weather!

MAGDALENA
Rain and thunder.

DIDDICOY
Wedlock in the sky,
the husband's shouting makes his missus cry.

BECKY
(*outside*)
If my father only knew I'm doing this.

Inside hovel.

MAGDALENA

Brother!

BECKY
(*listening at crevice*)
They're talking.

DIDDICOY
Yeh, what is it, sis?

MAGDALENA
Know what I'm thinking?

DIDDICOY
No.

MAGDALENA
Try guessing, then.
Don't let's kill him. He's a Greek god among men,
sleeping like a baby, the handsome lad upstairs.
And he really fancies me. Or so he swears.
Don't let's kill him.

BECKY
(*outside listening*)
God!

DIDDICOY
                Sew that sack, and quick.
Once my razor's done his little trick,
your Greek god goes in it. With this stone.
And splash into the Thames. So get it sewn.

MAGDALENA
But . . .

DIDDICOY
        Not your business! If I listened to your din
none of the fellers 'd ever get done in.
So sew the flaming sack.

BECKY
        (*outside*)
                It's like I gaze
straight into Hell's most horrifying blaze.

MAGDALENA
All right, but let's talk.

DIDDICOY
        Why not?

MAGDALENA
                        Do you detest
the captain?

DIDDICOY
        No, the military are best.
We share the same profession, he and I.

MAGDALENA
And you're prepared to let that young man die,
an officer with gentleman's finesse
for that ugly devil with a back bent like an S?

DIDDICOY

Look, I get ten guineas to dispose
of him from the hunchback. Then once he knows
the corpse in the sack is in the river
I get another ten, so we'll deliver.

MAGDALENA

But wouldn't it be the same thing if you jump
the hideous little feller with the hump
and kill him for the money?

BECKY
(*outside*)
Daddy!

MAGDALENA
(*insisting*)
Yes, it would!

DIDDICOY

I don't go shedding anybody's blood.
I'm sorry but it goes against my trade
to kill a client, specially one what's paid.

MAGDALENA

So put a log inside the sack instead.
It's dark enough to pass for someone dead.

DIDDICOY

Nah, a log 'd be no bloody good.
Who'd take it for a stiff, a bit of wood?
It's far too rigid, and it feels too rough.
It isn't lifelike. Doesn't bend enough.

BECKY
(*outside*)
This rain's so cold. I'm going to freeze.

MAGDALENA

Pity him.

DIDDICOY

Get lost!

MAGDALENA

Brother, brother, please!

DIDDICOY

Ssshh! He's got to die, so shut it, see.

MAGDALENA

I'll wake him up and say he's gotta flee.

BECKY
(*outside*)

Good for you!

DIDDICOY

And what about my pay?

MAGDALENA

Too bad.

DIDDICOY

Magdalena, let me have my way,
and do the thing that I've been paid to do.

MAGDALENA
(*blocking the staircase*)

I want to save him. I won't let you through.

They struggle.

DIDDICOY

Look, it's nearly midnight, and the hunchback's due.
If somebody, anybody, comes before
asking for shelter, knocking at the door,
I'll kill him instead, and put him in the sack
and you can have your Greek god feller back.

MAGDALENA

O very generous, brother, ta!
Where the hell d'ya think these travellers are?

DIDDICOY

Sorry, it's the best that I can do.

MAGDALENA

So late.

BECKY

(*outside*)

Is something drawing me towards that fate?
If I crossed the threshold I could save
the beast I'm still in love with from the grave.
I'm too young to die. My heart keeps saying: *knock!*

MAGDALENA

In such a storm and nearly twelve o'clock.
Nobody's coming.

DIDDICOY

If they don't, he's dead.

BECKY

(*outside*)

I should call the watch. They're all in bed.
But if this pair blabs, things could be bad –
plotting to kill the Prince – for my poor Dad.
I don't want to die. I've better things to do.
Daddy, I want to live to comfort you.
I'm only sixteen! That's too young to feel
my neck slit open by the cut-throat's steel.

A clock begins to strike 11.45 p.m.

DIDDICOY

That's it, a quarter to. No one 'll show
with only fifteen minutes left to go.
I've got to get a move on. Time's a-flying.

MAGDALENA

(*weeping*)

Wait, Just a bit.

BECKY
(*outside*)
She's crying. Crying!
And I'm doing nothing, when I could
save the Prince by shedding my own blood.
And since he doesn't love me any more
what am I still scared of dying for?
So horrible, to be stabbed. To gasp. To bleed.

DIDDICOY
No more waiting. I've got to do the deed.

BECKY
(*outside*)
What's dying like? If only you could know
what it feels like when they strike the blow.
If only it were painless. But I'm afraid
of seeing it flash towards me, the sharp blade.

*Magdalena still tries to prevent the Diddicoy from
going upstairs to kill HRH.*

DIDDICOY
No one's coming now. I've just got time
to do him in before the midnight chime.

BECKY
(*outside*)
I'm frozen.

Decides.

Right! To die as cold as this.

Becky knocks on the door of the hovel.

MAGDALENA
Someone's knocking!

DIDDICOY
No, it's loose slates, sis.

MAGDALENA

Someone's knocking!

DIDDICOY

That's strange.

MAGDALENA
(*calling out*)

Who's there?

To Diddicoy.

A lad!

BECKY
(*outside*)

Is there a night's shelter to be had?

DIDDICOY

You're going to rest far longer than a night!

MAGDALENA

You've come to the best place here, all right.
This is the best place that you could have chosen.

BECKY

Let me in. I'm really frozen. Frozen!

DIDDICOY

Wait! Wait! Don't let him in just yet.
I need to give my friend a little whet.

Diddicoy sharpens his razor.

BECKY

He's sharpening his razor. I can hear it scrape.
There's no going back. There's no escape.

MAGDALENA

Poor young man. He's knocking on his tomb.

BECKY

Am I going to die? O God to whom
I'm journeying, I beg you to forgive
the Prince my dying will allow to live.

Forgive the Prince of Wales and bless his reign.
And forgive these criminals by whom I'm slain.
Forgive the hired murderer who slays a
child of sixteen with a sharpened razor.
The slaughtered sacrificial lamb 'll lay her
wrecked life down for her betrayer.

God bless the Prince of Wales, long may he reign.
May his prosperity wax and never wane.
If he's happier forgetting, let
him never think of me and totally forget.
To give him life I sacrifice my own.
Let him wield power wisely on the throne.

The razor's sharp by now.

MAGDALENA
(*to Diddicoy*)
Hurry, he won't stay.

Diddicoy tests the blade.

DIDDICOY

Good!

To Magdalena.

Don't open till I say.

BECKY

I can hear them.

MAGDALENA
Just give me the nod.

332

*After a pause the Diddicoy nods. Magdalena opens
the door and Becky enters.*

BECKY

Kill me, but don't hurt me. God, O God.

MAGDALENA
(*shouting*)

Do it! Do it!

BECKY

The sister's just as bad.
God forgive them. And you forgive me, Dad.

The razor flashes down.

Act Five: Scotty

The same riverside hovel as for Act Four. Enter Scotty Scott.

SCOTTY SCOTT
Revenge at last! The blow that's just been struck 's
been worth this anxious month on tenterhooks.
I've worn my mask as ever and kept in
the agony behind the comic's grin.

Goes up to the door of hovel/tavern.

To know that vengeance has been duly dealt
with concrete proof that can be touched and felt.
The very door, and the moment's almost due
for the royal corpse to be 'escorted' through.

Thunder.

What a night! Perfect for such dark doings though –
a storm in Heaven, murder here below.

I feel gigantic! Like those gods who hurled
thunderbolts of wrath down on the world.
I've killed the future king, one who commands
the Empire that extends to distant lands,
who'd lord it over Sikh and Hottentot,
stopped dead in his tracks by Scotty Scott.

Once I've pulled away this princely prop
where will the shock waves and the tremor stop?
It'll make all Europe and the Empire shake
at the coming of some cataclysmic quake.

Once a Windsor's dumped into the Thames
all dynasties look to their diadems.
Rulers reading the sensational reports
want extra sentries mounted round their courts.
Every ruler on his rocking throne
will look at this death here and fear his own.
This act could fan the coals and goad
those with a grievance down revenge's road,
fuel disaffection to a fever pitch
against all royals and the idle rich.
The rebellion starts here with Scotty Scott.
One day they'll raise his statue on this spot.

Questioning the Earth, our Lord Creator
cries, 'What vast volcano bursts its crater?
What force is so mighty? Who? Or what?'
And the Earth gives answer, 'Scotty Scott!'
Shudder at the name of Scotty Scott, a
force to make the British Empire totter!

Dying thunder. Midnight chimes.

Midnight!

Scotty Scott knocks at the door.

DIDDICOY
(*from inside*)
Who's there?

SCOTTY SCOTT
Me!

DIDDICOY
Wait!

SCOTTY SCOTT
Hurry!

DIDDICOY

Wait, I said.

*Pause. Then a half-door opens and Diddicoy pushes
a sack out through it.*

DIDDICOY

He's heavy. Give me a hand and take his head.
He's in the sack, your man.

SCOTTY SCOTT

Joy makes me cry.

Give me a light.

DIDDICOY

No! No!

SCOTTY SCOTT

But why?

DIDDICOY

There's Peelers who patrol round here at night,
and you've made noise enough. No light. No light.
The money!

Scotty Scott gives the Diddicoy ten more guineas.

SCOTTY SCOTT

Here! Such happiness in hate.

DIDDICOY

Let's dump him in the river now. It's late.

SCOTTY SCOTT

I can manage.

THE DIDDICOY

Two makes it quicker, though.

SCOTTY SCOTT

The lightest load 's the corpse of a loathed foe.

THE DIDDICOY

Do as you like then, squire, but take care.
Don't throw the sack from here. It's better there.
It's deeper. And be quick. I'll sling my hook.

Exit the Diddicoy back into the hovel.

SCOTTY SCOTT

How I long to look. How I long to look.
He's in there. In the sack. It's true. It's true.
There's his 'blue' blood seeping through.

Here's the comic, and there's the future king.
Tell me now which one's the underling.
The elitest of Establishment elite
who I can trample now beneath my feet.
The bloody great Panjandrum but
prostrated underneath my booted foot.
One who'd hold an Empire underneath his sway
is Emperor of one wet sack today.
The Prince of Wales, so powerful, so proud,
the Thames his sepulchre, a sack his shroud.
And who brought this about? I'm that man of action
to whom this death brings endless satisfaction.
When *The Times* devotes its front page to the deed
the people won't believe the news they read.
I'll go down in history, renowned
for removing from the world one almost crowned,
who would have had the world beneath his sway,
this would-be king it took a fool to slay.
I'll go down in history, a name
to be scared of in the Hall of Fame.
This almost mighty monarch owes his mighty fall
to a common midget from the music hall,
the buffoon who bounded from the humble boards
to be the latest terror in Tussaud's.
His power would have reached Earth's distant corners

337

with his sycophantic Court of servile fawners,
with his wealth, his gold, his jewels and his gems,
dumped like an abortion in the Thames.

Tomorrow there'll be posters everywhere
and proclamations made in every square
offering rewards regardless of the cost
for news of the Prince of Wales who's lost.
All that princely, pleasure-bent panache
gone like a puff of smoke.

Flash of lightning.

                           Or lightning flash!
Marvellous! O my poor ill-treated lass,
the punishment I promised 's come to pass.
I needed his blood. Badly. A bit of gold
in the right hands. Hey presto! And behold!

Savagely at the sack.

Bloody villain! Can you hear me in your sack?
You took my daughter and you sent her back
dishonoured, and she, my lassie, 's worth
all the royal crowns there are on earth.
Are you listening? The world's turned upside down.
It's me who's commanding now, the common clown.
Because of all the jokes that I still cracked
you never saw beneath the comic act,
blind to the anger burning underneath,
you thought a father's wrath had blunted teeth.
In this unbalanced contest you began
between a future king and common man,
between the weak and strong, the victory's gone
to one no punter would put money on.
I joined the courtiers' queue and stood in line
to lick your royal boots, now you lick mine.

Kicks the sack.

Are you listening? It's me, Your Highness, me,
the Glagow comic, the deformity
your snapping fingers often brought to heel.
You're lying at my feet. How does it feel?
Once the spirit of revenge invades our breasts
it's sleeplessly alert and never rests.
The pygmy's now a giant, the servile flea 's
muscled and menacing like Hercules.
When the slave draws vengeance from its sheath
the kitten roars and shows its tiger's teeth.
And the comic with his sycophantic cracks
becomes the executioner with bloodied axe.

I'm glad you're dead, but wish you could have heard
everything I've said, and this, my parting word:
'I loathe you, Prince of Wales.' Your days as rover,
rake and roué are, regretfully, now over.
Depending on the tide, Your Highness might resort
either to the Tower or to Hampton Court.

Come on, Prince of Wales, into the drink.
One pleasure 's left. To watch your body sink.

> *Scotty Scott lifts the sack, and is about to push it into
> the Thames, when he hears the voice of HRH singing
> a chorus of 'The Ladies! The Ladies!'.*

SCOTTY SCOTT

That voice! That voice! That voice! This eerie night
's just playing tricks on me. Let me get light.

THE VOICE OF HRH

The Ladies! The Ladies!

SCOTTY SCOTT

Hell and damnation! He's got away!
Somebody's gone and robbed me of my prey.
Betrayed! Cheated!

Shouts at tavern/hovel.

Bloody Diddicoy!

Looks at window to see if he can climb in.

Too high!
So what have they used to trick me by?
Some poor soul. I'm scared. It's a corpse all right.
Not a lamp lit anywhere. I need the sky
to send another flash.

Lightning flash and he sees Becky in the sack.

No! No! How? Why?

My wee lassie! Becky! God, it's wet, my hand.
It's blood . . . But whose? My lassie's. I don't understand.
It's an hallucination. No! No!
No! I sent you to Scotland. I saw you go.

God, I beg you, let this nightmare pass.

Lightning flash.

It's her! It's her! My poor wee lass!

BECKY
(*coming to*)

Where am I?

SCOTTY SCOTT
Lassie, all I've ever had
on earth, don't you know my voice? It's Dad.
What have they done to you, those fiends from hell?
Where are you wounded, lassie? I can't tell.
I'm scared to touch you.

BECKY
All I know

's I saw the razor flash.

340

SCOTTY SCOTT
> Who struck the blow?

BECKY

Everything's my fault. I told a lie.
I loved him too much. Now I'll die.

SCOTTY SCOTT

Fate's got me underfoot, my daughter caught
under my vengeance's relentless Juggernaut.
How did they come to do it, lass? Explain.

BECKY

Don't make me, Daddy. I'm in too much pain.

SCOTTY SCOTT

But I'm losing you, and don't know why.

BECKY

Dad, I'm choking!

SCOTTY SCOTT
> Please don't die. Don't die.

Help, somebody! Anybody! Anybody there?
Is my daughter going to die and no one care?
There's the ferry bell there on the wall.
Lassie, let me go a second, while I call
for help. There's a bell there I could ring.
You dinna want me to. How hard you cling.

Help! Help! God, it's like a graveyard here.
Don't die, lassie. Don't die, my dear, my dear.
I'll be totally deserted if you go.
My darling daughter. Don't die. Don't.

BECKY
(*in pain*)
> Oh! Oh!

SCOTTY SCOTT

Is my arm the problem? I'll move it. There.
Is that better? O keep on drawing air
until help comes. Don't die. Don't die.

BECKY

Daddy, I'm so sorry. Ah! Goodbye!

Becky dies. Scotty Scott rings the ferry bell madly.

SCOTTY SCOTT

Help! Help!
                    Oh God, what can you mean
demanding my daughter now? She's just sixteen.
O lass, don't leave your daddy on his own,
never to hear again your tender tone.

*People begin to assemble with torches and lanterns.
As they enter HRH's Bodyguard ushers HRH away
from the scene.*

Heaven was pitiless when it gave me you.
Why weren't you taken long before I knew
the beauty of your spirit? It's so cruel
being allowed to know I had a jewel.
Why didn't you die sooner, like the day
the other children hurt you in their play?
O lassie! Lass!

WOMAN
(*listening*)
He breaks your heart in two.

SCOTTY SCOTT
(*aware of the gathering people*)
You lot took your time.

To a man dressed like a cabbie.

                    You, you great clod, you!
Have you got a carriage?

CARTER
> Yes, but there's no need for that.

SCOTTY SCOTT
Put my head under the wheels and crush it flat.

Scotty goes back to Becky.

Oh lassie!

SPECTATOR
> She's been murdered, the young kid.
Her father's really gone and flipped his lid.
We should separate them.

They try.

SCOTTY SCOTT
> No, leave me alone.
I want to be with her, close to her, my own.

To Woman, who is weeping.

You're weeping. You've got a tender heart.
Don't let those people force us two apart.
Down on your knees, you wretch. You should have died
when she died, by your daughter's side.

Sobs.

WOMAN
You'll have to be a good bit calmer, sir,
or they'll come again and pull you off of her.

SCOTTY SCOTT
No! No! Look there. Look, I believe
she's breathing. I just felt her bosom heave.
Go fetch help, and let my daughter lie
in her father's arms. No, she won't die.
God wouldn't want it. God must surely know
she's all I care for on this earth below.

When you're misshapen people shun
your company, but not this little one.
She loves me. When I'm scorned, she cries.
She supports me. She can sympathise.
She was my comfort always. She is now.
Give me a handkerchief to wipe her brow.

He wipes Becky's brow.

To be so beautiful, and yet so dead.
Look at her mouth, her lips, so rosy red.

When she was two years old, her toddler's hair
not black like it is now, was light and fair.
When she was a baby this is how
I'd hold her to my heart like I do now.

She'd open her angelic eyes and see
not a hump-backed monster but her daddy, me.
She smiled at me. She loved me as I am.
I'd kiss her small sweet hands, poor little lamb.
She isn't dead. Oh no, she's still alive.
She may have fainted but she'll soon revive.
She looked like this before, and then
opened her eyes. She will, she will again.

Now you see I'm reasonable and calm.
You see I'm doing no one any harm.
I'm hurting nobody, so let me be.
My daughter's in my arms and safe with me.

Looking at Becky in his arms.

Not a wrinkle on her brow. Not a trace
of all that agony on her sweet face.
Her hands were cold. She'd been out in the storm.
I put my hands round hers and made them warm.
Feel them!

SECOND WOMAN
Here's a doctor, sir!

SCOTTY SCOTT
I won't stop you, doctor. Look at her.
She's fainted, hasn't she?

The Doctor examines Becky briefly then rises.

DOCTOR
It's no good.
She choked to death, she choked on her own blood.

SCOTTY SCOTT
I brought this dreadful happening to pass.
It was me, her dad, who murdered my wee lass.

Police enter to arrest him. To audience.

Laugh! This is the best laugh of the night.
Laugh at how I've murdered my own wee mite.